SPIRITUAL ECOLOGY
A QUIET REVOLUTION
Leslie E. Sponsel

"This is a subject that should have been documented long ago—this wise and careful book fills an important gap, and does it with real power."

Bill McKibben, author *Eaarth*

"This book is a tour de force. No one has attempted to bring together such a wide range of people and movements under the rubric of Spiritual Ecology. The result is deeply engaging for scholars and activists alike. Sponsel has given us a gem."

Mary Evelyn Tucker,
Forum on Religion and Ecology, Yale University

"Sponsel, a noted scholar of ecological anthropology, traces a broad, ecumenical 'religion of nature' from deep roots in the past to modern advanced thinkers. He argues persuasively that we would not have an environmental crisis today if we treated the earth with respect and reverence. The book offers a fascinating tour through the spiritual landscape, and its extensive notes give readers a rich guide to further reading and reflection."

Donald Worster, author of
A Passion for Nature: The Life of John Muir

"*Spiritual Ecology* is essential reading today, when most of the world seems swept up by the economic dimensions of the environment. Providing a welcome antidote to the current materialistic approach, Leslie Sponsel's keen reminder of the spiritual component of nature is both timely and a reminder that the most effective reasons for conservation come from the heart, not from the wallet."

Jeffrey A. McNeely, Senior Science Advisor,
International Union for Conservation of Nature

"Leslie Sponsel's new book is an excellent guide to spiritual ecology. It is much more: it is an evocation of spiritual ecology—its forms, its dynamic development, and its promise for the contemporary world. Dr. Sponsel, a leading authority on this field, provides a historical overview of the development of ecological and environmental visions in religion from earliest times to the present. He surveys major religions, and, in particular detail, modern writers who have developed new philosophical understandings of religion-environment relationships. This book serves both as a wonderful introduction to the field and an inspiring essay on the basic tenets, values, and goals of spiritual ecology."

Eugene N. Anderson, Professor Emeritus of Anthropology,
University of California Riverside

"I am delighted with this inspiring panoramic introduction to the remarkable people who have personally contributed to the on-going "quiet revolution" that will help solve our contemporary problems of conflict, poverty, and environmental degradation. This source book could only have been produced by an anthropologist with firsthand experience with life in the tribal world and in the ancient great civilization cultural traditions of South and Southeast Asia. This is an absolute treasure trove of cross-cultural ideas and sources for beliefs and practices that respond constructively to global environmental problems and related social justice issues. I immediately went to the library and the Internet to learn even more about particular organizations and people. As an anthropologist who has been concerned with indigenous people and the environment for many years, I am especially pleased with how sensitively Sponsel treats the "ecologically noble savage" issue, and the well-deserved importance he gives to animist beliefs generally."

John H. Bodley, Washington State University

"At a moment in history when political and technological solutions to the environmental crisis have been shown to have their limits, Leslie Sponsel has compiled a wonderful collection of essays on a spiritual approach to ecology. Fundamentally re-envisioning the relationship between the human and nature, *Spiritual Ecology* draws on the wisdom and practical insights of global spiritual traditions from antiquity to the present. This is a foundational text that includes inspirational classics as well as critical essays that explore how a spiritual ecology can deeply inform our debates about our relationship to our planet."

Duncan Williams, School of Religion,
University of Southern California

"Humans possess an inherent inclination to find meaning and purpose through their relation to the world beyond themselves, to what we call nature. This marvelous and informative book explores this need from its roots in tribal cultures through its expression and distortion in the modern era. It is only recently that people have come to believe human progress and civilization mean transforming and transcending our evolutionary roots in the natural world. This book importantly explores and leads the way toward a new movement, 'spiritual ecology,' bringing us back to our spiritual roots in nature."

Stephen R. Kellert,
Yale University School of Forestry and Environmental Studies

"As Sponsel so ably demonstrates, there has always been a dimension of environmentalist thought that is founded on the understanding, explicit or implicit, that nature is sacred. As activists and policy makers seek ways of averting environmental disaster, the time is overdue for this mode of thought to enter the mainstream. This much needed book provides the kind of understanding that might help it to do so."

Kay Milton, Professor Emerita of Anthropology,
Queen's University Belfast, Ireland

"In a world where religious beliefs are too often seen as the source of deadly tension and violent conflict, Leslie Sponsel's *Spiritual Ecology* offers a helpful and healing contrary view. Aptly subtitled, *A Quiet Revolution*, this provocative collection of essays serves as a key resource and guide to the global sources of inspiration, thought, and action that collectively constitute a life-sustaining path for humanity."

Barbara Rose Johnston, Senior Research Fellow,
Center for Political Ecology

"Awareness that the natural world is our essential ground of being, to be revered as sacred, goes back to the dawn of the human journey. Today this awareness returns in the growing recognition that we cannot fully face or adequately respond to what our species is doing to the biosphere without a spiritual apprehension of our non-separateness from it. That is the quiet revolution to which Leslie Sponsel's *Spiritual Ecology* brings a fresh and fascinating overview. To the unfolding history it provides, this lean and lovely book takes the archetypal form of Tree, letting us follow—from roots to branches, leaves and fruit—the organic emergence of our native wisdom."

SPIRITUAL ECOLOGY

SPIRITUAL ECOLOGY

A QUIET REVOLUTION

Leslie E. Sponsel

 PRAEGER

AN IMPRINT OF ABC-CLIO, LLC
Santa Barbara, California • Denver, Colorado • Oxford, England

Library of Congress Cataloging-in-Publication Data
Sponsel, Leslie E. (Leslie Elmer), 1943–
  Spiritual ecology : a quiet revolution / Leslie E. Sponsel.
    p. cm.
  Includes bibliographical references and index.
  ISBN 978–0–313–36409–9 (hardcopy : alk. paper) — ISBN 978–0–313–36410–5 (ebook)
1. Human ecology—Religious aspects. 2. Indigenous peoples—Ecology. 3. Philosophy of nature. 4. Environmental ethics. I. Title.
GF80.S668   2012
304.2—dc23   2012014961

ISBN: 978–0–313–36409–9
EISBN: 978–0–313–36410–5

16 15 14 13 12   1 2 3 4 5

This book is also available on the World Wide Web as an eBook.
Visit www.abc-clio.com for details.

Praeger
An Imprint of ABC-CLIO, LLC

ABC-CLIO, LLC
130 Cremona Drive, P.O. Box 1911
Santa Barbara, California 93116-1911

This book is printed on acid-free paper ∞

Manufactured in the United States of America

For Dr. Poranee Natadecha-Sponsel,
my wife,
colleague,
inspiration,
and joy.

CONTENTS

FOREWORD

What causes environmental degradation? What might mitigate or reverse it? These questions have preoccupied many thinkers, especially since the middle of the nineteenth century, as the negative environmental effects of modern agricultural/industrial civilization intensified and became more obvious.

Some have contended that religion bears a large share of responsibility for the negative trends. Based on his experiences on a long walk to the Gulf of Mexico in 1867, for example, the great Scottish American John Muir, who went on to found the influential, environmentalist Sierra Club, distanced himself from the Christianity of his youth. Muir's experience with nature on that trip, including a debilitating encounter with malaria, led him to conclude that anthropocentrism promoted a view that all creatures were created just for humankind, and that this religion-based view was inconsistent with many natural facts.[1] Some fifty years later, the American ecologist Aldo Leopold famously penned "The Land Ethic," arguing: "A thing is right when it tends to preserve the integrity, stability, and beauty of the biotic community. It is wrong when it tends otherwise."[2] But Leopold thought the predominant religions of his day in America, especially Christianity, were a barrier to such an ethic. Like Muir, he thought religion promoted a view that the nature is merely "a commodity belonging to us" rather than "community to which we belong" and should "love and respect."[3] A couple decades after Leopold wrote his treatise, in 1967, the historian Lynn White, Jr. piled on, claiming that Christianity was "the most anthropocentric religion ever known," arguing that it promoted many environmentally destructive ideas and practices.[4] These sorts of critiques led others to wonder whether other religions were more environmentally friendly. While some answered that some of the religions originating in Asia were nature-sympathetic, others presented evidence that such religions were no better than Western ones at promoting environmentally sustainable societies.[5]

The debate was on, and it fostered three typical responses by religious people and the scholars who study them (who are sometimes devotees of the religions they study).

Some acknowledged that their religions are really not focused on the well-being of environmental systems or nonhuman beings. Rather than being defensive about this, however, these individuals defended their traditions, contending in various ways that the proper priority of religion is the *spiritual* well-being of human beings.

Those sharing deep concerns about pollution and the erosion of Earth's biodiversity, on the other hand, tended to move in one of two other directions.

Some found the criticism of the world's predominant religions compelling and turned away from them. (They considered the first type of response, for example, to be evidence that religion hinders environmental concern and action.) They sought, instead, other philosophical and emotional bases for their environmental concerns. Sometimes they found such bases outside of the world's best-known religious traditions, such as in contemporary Paganism or in Animistic spiritualities (where nonhuman beings are considered kin and in special relationship with human beings). On other occasions, they found such bases in new, nature-based religious forms, or in scientific narratives of cosmological and biological evolution, which were considered meaningful and rationally compelling.

Still others sought to explicate environmentally friendly themes in one or more of the world's predominant religions; if these themes were found lacking or anemic, they endeavored to graft such themes on to these traditions, for example, by fusing understandings of ecological interdependence onto them.

Les Sponsel's *Spiritual Ecology* is about the later two, environmentally concerned, sort of responses. An emeritus professor of ecological anthropology from the University of Hawai'i, Sponsel has long observed the trends he explicates in this book. He has, moreover, personally studied indigenous cultures in the Venezuelan Amazon and Buddhist ecology in Thailand while reading the studies of others about them. He is thus well placed to survey and analyze the spiritual dimensions of human relationships with nature, within the world's diverse religious traditions. But to his credit, he does not stop there. Sponsel recognizes that there is a proportion of the human population that is not religious in any conventional sense (such as by believing in nonmaterial divine beings), but that nevertheless many such individuals have deep environmental commitments that they view as "spiritual" in nature. So he not only provides examples of efforts to turn what we easily recognize as "religion" in more environmentally friendly directions; he also provides examples of how environmentalists, poets, filmmakers, tree planters, atheists, and even "burning man" festival-goers express and promote spiritual connections to nature, and ethical responsibilities to the world's diverse living beings.

Sponsel is inspired by and finds hopeful the exemplars of spiritual ecology he introduces in these pages, and many will find his review of these developments hopeful and inspiring. As a scholar who cares deeply about both people and nature, Sponsel has chosen to focus on the positive and the possibilities, hoping that by doing so he will draw more people into the spiritual movements he finds so positive. This is a laudable objective. I would caution the reader who is new to this subject matter, however, that the ideas and trends Sponsel identifies are still fledgling. Those engaged in spiritual ecology have yet to precipitate dramatic changes in the ways in which the growing number of human consumers (now over seven billion) are impacting the biosphere and its living systems. There are obstacles in most of the cultural systems Sponsel discusses to the positive trends he focuses on and hopes to see gain strength. In short, whether it is possible to *decisively and influentially* transform religious and religion-resembling cultural systems in ways that promote environmental sustainability remains to be seen.[6] The answer will depend on what proportion of humankind gravitates toward these sorts of spiritualities, transmogrifying their traditions into new, dramatically "green" forms, or developing new spiritualities that provide meaning in and respect for nature.

What is clear from the present vantage point is that what Sponsel has labeled "spiritual ecology" (which in many ways resembles what I have called "dark green religion") has gained adherents in a variety of cultural and religious contexts around the world. I think some of the most common denominators to such spiritualities are feelings of belonging and connection to nature, as well as feelings of kinship with nonhuman organisms. That such spirituality is a global and cross-cultural phenomenon suggests that, at least thinking medium and long term, Sponsel's hope may not be an otherworldly fantasy but a real-world possibility. Indeed, although the "biophilia hypothesis" is unproven (it asserts that there is a least a weak affinity among human beings for biologically intact ecosystems because evolution favors such feelings and perceptions), this hypothesis is lent credence by the evidence that nature spirituality has no impermeable regional or cultural bounds.[7] Indeed, feelings of belonging to nature, and aesthetics and spiritualities appreciating the beauties of nature and promoting respect for environmental systems, are a part of the human emotional repertoire.

This affective/emotional capacity suggests that, when combined with a clear understanding of ecological interdependence and mutual dependence, nature-based and focused spiritualities might yet help us to learn our planetary manners.

In the 1940s Aldo Leopold wrote: "No important change in ethics was ever accomplished without an internal change in our intellectual emphasis, loyalties, affections, and convictions. The proof that conservation has not yet touched these foundations of conduct lies in the fact that philosophy and religion have not yet heard of it."[8] As Sponsel demonstrates in this book, however, and in part because of luminaries like Leopold, religion and philosophy (and more disciplines besides) *have* now heard of the spiritual and ethical imperative to protect and restore nature. The question now is how extensive, and effective, will be the response. This book provides a good starting place for considering the possibilities.

Bron Taylor
University of Florida

PROLOGUE

Revolution? Yes indeed, that is precisely what is happening all over the world, a fundamental transformation of humanity and its relationships to nature. It is a nonviolent revolution, but certainly a radical movement in the sense of involving accelerating and profound changes; however, it is relatively quiet and as yet little recognized.[1] This revolution is inner as well as outer; that is, both individuals and societies are being transformed at their very roots. This is a revolution in the sense of an accumulating series of changes that are profoundly transformative with far-reaching consequences, but not in the sense of anything rapid or unified with a single leader. Nevertheless, there is substantial overlap, with many continuities and similarities among the different pioneers from many centuries ago to the present. The main question is whether or not all of this is enough—and will occur soon enough—to circumvent a global ecological catastrophe when human environmental impact reaches a critical threshold or tipping point. Only time will tell. Ultimately, although easier said than done, it is simply a matter of the choice between ecocide or ecosanity! This revolution is called *spiritual ecology* in this book.[2]

Here spiritual ecology refers to the diverse, complex, and dynamic arena of intellectual and practical activities at the interface between religions and spiritualities on the one hand, and, on the other, ecologies, environments, and environmentalisms. Note that each of these domains is plural, reflecting the vastness, variety, variability, complexity, and dynamism of this subject. The designation spiritual ecology is considered preferable to other labels for several reasons. It parallels other approaches to human-environment interaction like historical ecology and political ecology. It is less cumbersome and more direct than designations like *religion and nature* or *religion and ecology*. It is more inclusive than those terms since spirituality is a component of religion, but individuals who do not choose to affiliate with any religious organization and even atheists may still be spiritual. It can encompass a breadth and diversity of religions and spiritualities beyond the few so-called world religions. It provokes thought, discussion, and debate.[3]

Elsewhere in the literature other labels may be used instead of spiritual ecology. They reflect a variant of spiritual ecology and usually a narrower pursuit, like earth spirituality, earth mysticism, ecomysticism, ecopsychology, ecospirituality, ecotheology, green religion, green spirituality, nature mysticism, nature religion, nature spirituality, religion and ecology, religion and nature, religious environmentalism, and religious naturalism. A search of Google.com for these terms reveals a total of several hundred million sites on the these topics. Moreover, they are not limited to cyberspace by any means; instead, most reflect individuals and organizations actively involved on the ground in some aspect of spiritual ecology. For instance, the Alliance for Religions and Conservation has hundreds of projects working with about a dozen world religions in numerous countries to conserve biological diversity. Another example is the booklet *Earth and Faith: A Book of Reflection for Action* published in 2000 by the Interfaith Partnership for the Environment of the United Nations Environment Programme (UNEP).[4]

A multitude of people are involved in spiritual ecology in a great diversity of ways at all levels from the local to the global and in numerous contexts from religious to secular organizations.[5] The immense magnitude and momentum as well as the great interest and promise of spiritual ecology can be appreciated by exploring the website of the Forum on Religion and Ecology at Yale University. Another major reference source is *The Encyclopedia of Religion and Nature*.[6] Certainly religion and spirituality can be most interesting subjects, as are nature, environment, ecology, and environmentalism. Moreover, exploring the interface of these subjects can be even more interesting, and that is the focus of the present book.

Spiritual ecology, however, is far more than simply extraordinarily interesting. It offers great potential and sorely needed hope for restoring a much higher degree of ecosanity in the way many humans relate to nature individually and collectively. Numerous individuals from diverse backgrounds and persuasions are convinced that the ecocrisis will only be resolved, or at least markedly reduced, if there is a very fundamental rethinking, refeeling, and revisioning of the place of humans in nature. They think that religion and spirituality can generate a profound transformation in individuals and societies whereas secular approaches have proven insufficient to resolve the environmental crisis.

Since the first Earth Day on April 22, 1970, there has been a marked increase in environmental information, awareness, sensitivity, responsibility, and action.[7] Whole scientific and academic fields have developed with a focus on environmental questions, problems, and issues—such as environmental economics, environment education, environmental ethics, environmental history, environment law, environmental literature, environmental philosophy, and environmental studies.[8] These and many other approaches are certainly necessary. Indeed, they are contributing significantly to reducing some environmental problems. Yet the ecocrisis not only persists; it is progressively becoming even worse. In 1970, phenomena such as acid rain; the ozone hole; global climate change; deformed frogs; and declining populations of bees, bats, and snakes were not looming large as symptoms of the ecocrisis. New environmental problems are being discovered annually if not more frequently, and, no doubt, more are on the horizon waiting to be identified.[9] Most leaders in government, business, and industry have proven to be so egocentric, greedy, incompetent, irresponsible, and/or myopic as to hold no promise for helping to resolve ecocrises. Like many political leaders, most media and even some environmental organizations have made Faustian compacts with corporations and accordingly ignore many environmental matters.

A quite different approach to the ecocrisis is sorely required, a radical one that far more effectively addresses the ultimate causes of the ecocrisis and effectively generates very fundamental transformations in how humans relate to nature individually and collectively to finally turn things around for the better. Spiritual ecology may be just that approach, but only after coming decades will the extent of its impact be revealed. Yet since the 1990s, spiritual ecology has grown rapidly and already it is having demonstrable positive effects. One case in point is the Interfaith Power and Light Project which, leading by example since 1998, has mobilized 14,000 of religious organizations in 39 of the United States to respond religiously and in other ways to global climate change by promoting renewable energy as well as energy efficiency and conservation.[10] This is only one illustration among a multitude of instances of the potential of organized religions to motivate and guide adherents toward more environmentally sustainable, responsible, and greener behaviors and institutions.[11]

Many scientific, technological, governmental, legal, and other secular fixes for some environmental problems have been successful, yet the ecocrisis as a whole persists and even worsens. Advocates of spiritual ecology consider the ecocrisis to result from human alienation from nature combined with the disenchantment, objectification, and commodification of

nature. Increasingly nature is considered as simply a warehouse of resources to be extracted in order to not only meet basic human needs, but
also to try to satisfy the apparently unlimited greed for profit of rampant
predatory capitalism coupled with the associated modern fixation of many
people and societies on materialism and consumerism. Ultimately such
rapacious selfishness is no less than ecocidal for the biosphere and accordingly also suicidal for the human species. This existential threat is the reason this book is normative as well as descriptive, analytical, and
interpretative.[12]

Turning to the advantages of spiritual ecology, it shifts the focus to
spiritual development in relation to nature, instead of so-called economic
development, which often is at the expense of the health of ecosystems,
human beings, society, and future generations. Nature is a grand cathedral
of beings, rather than an unlimited warehouse of mere objects for exploitation for profit. Substance abuse, suicide, and other problems of many
rich individuals expose the futility of the pursuit of material wealth alone.
The spiritual ecology movement coincides with the growing dissatisfac-
tion with modern industrial society, capitalism, materialism, and consumerism—including their inability to provide a far deeper meaning and
purpose in life that many seek through religion and/or spirituality. An
ongoing survey by the Higher Education Research Institute at the
University of California Los Angeles (UCLA) reveals that, while many
religious organizations may be experiencing a decline in membership,
there is substantial interest in spirituality. The survey also concludes that
there is broad awareness of the sacredness of life and nature. It is important to recognize as well that even atheists and agnostics can be spiritual
people.[13]

Interfaith and ecumenical collaboration is another attribute and attraction of spiritual ecology; it is an arena where individuals and institutions of
many of the diverse religions of the world and the sects within them find
common ground for constructive dialogue and collaborative action. One
example of this is the National Religious Partnership for the
Environment in the United States embraced by major Christian and
Jewish organizations, a collaboration that facilitates change. Yet another
important and hopeful aspect of the spiritual ecology revolution is the
convergence of religion and science. Within Western civilization for many
centuries religion and science have often been mutually antagonistic.
However, in the context of the environmental crisis they also find

common ground for complementary discussions and actions, such as in the
Forum on Religion and Ecology and in the International Society for the
Study of Religion, Nature, and Culture. Scholarly work within these professional institutions is interdisciplinary, multidisciplinary, and transdisci-
plinary reflecting a third type of collaboration among broad and diverse
interests that have often been in conflict: natural sciences, social sciences,
and humanities. These three types of collaboration—among and within
religions, between religion and science, and among the natural sciences,
social sciences, and humanities—are unprecedented historically. These
three developments are extremely positive and hopeful.[14]

Ultimately, the bottom line in spiritual ecology is the recognition of the
considerable relevance of religions and spiritualities in dealing constructively with the ecocrisis. Proponents view this crisis as far more than
merely a social, economic, political, governmental, legal, scientific, and/
or technological matter, but ultimately as a much deeper cultural, moral,
ethical, and spiritual crisis as well.[15] Such considerations have led otherwise secular environmental and conservation organizations, like the highly
respected Worldwatch Institute, to address the relevance of world religions for environmentalism.[16]

Humans are religious or spiritual beings in various degrees and ways, as
well as biological, mental, linguistic, social, cultural, economic, political,
and aesthetic beings. Religion is a cross-cultural universal; no known culture totally lacks religion, although some individuals within any society
may not be religious or spiritual, or only nominally so. Also, some individuals are spiritual, but not religious in the sense of belonging to an organization devoted to a particular religion.

Indisputably, religion is quite often the primary source of an individual's worldview, values, attitudes, motivations, and lifestyle.
Furthermore, religion addresses elemental, perennial, and pivotal spiritual
and ecological questions such as: What is nature? What is human nature?
What is the place of humans in nature? What should be the place of
humans in nature? While the natural and social sciences as well as humanities (such as the arts, history, and philosophy) also address such questions,
religion can be far more influential, given that the last question is a moral
and ethical one, and given that religion can be an extremely powerful
motivating and guiding force deploying major resources for individuals
and societies.[17] To resolve the ecocrisis, or at least to substantially reduce
it and the associated risks and dangers, penetrating rethinking about these

and other questions is required. This rethinking needs to generate a profound change in the way that individuals, organizations, and societies relate to nature, something that has been called "the Great Turning"[18] Such presuppositions underlay to varying degrees most of the considerable variety of approaches within spiritual ecology.

Whereas for some people spiritual ecology may be merely an interesting academic pursuit, for others it is a sacred subject touching on their very deepest concerns, emotions, commitments, and aspirations. Indeed, although usually they do not advertise it, many environmentalists and conservationists are ultimately to some degree spiritual ecologists as well, having been profoundly moved by some kind of epiphany or awesome experiences in nature.[19] To name just a few well-known examples, such persons include Henry David Thoreau, John Muir, W. S. Merwin, Joanna Macy, and Wangari Maathai. The life and work of only a few of the over a hundred personages relevant to spiritual ecology can be explored in the present book.[20] Undoubtedly, critical readers will wonder about the inclusion of some individuals and the exclusion of others. The sample is necessarily selective simply because of the very limited space in a single volume of reasonable length and price. Individuals were chosen because they are especially relevant, and, in addition, because some have been ignored or neglected in related publications.[21]

The spiritual aspect of spiritual ecology may be pursued by an individual alone or in a group of persons in nature, or in relation to a religious organization. It may involve mysticism, rituals, ceremonies, and sacred places and landscapes. The locus of the spirituality may reside in the individual human being and/or in supernatural beings and/or forces in nature, depending on one's belief system. The spiritual domain is the least studied, documented, and understood aspect of spiritual ecology so far, although ultimately it is often the most important one serving as a catalyst for environmental activism.[22]

There are some serious obstacles and limitations facing spiritual ecology. First, there is the status quo and the powerful establishment, which are, to say the least, seriously challenged if not threatened by spiritual ecology. This encompasses hegemonic economic and political interests, individuals and organizations myopically pursuing scientism, Marxists who dismiss or ignore the significance of religion and spirituality, economic enterprises that greedily worship the maximization of monetary profit, and so on. Second, there is the discrepancy between ideals and behaviors among adherents to various religions as well as the need for going beyond rhetoric to take more practical action. Third, there may be factions and tensions within any given religion or religious school or sect.[23] Fourth, far more outreach to the grass roots or communities—such as the example previously mentioned of Interfaith Power and Light—is sorely needed.

Spiritual ecology has surprisingly deep roots extending far back into antiquity, not just for centuries, but even for millennia. Yet only in recent decades has it begun to be recognized by whatever label. Today spiritual ecology is somewhat comparable to a person's awe at first sighting a magnificent and mysterious ancient baobab tree (*Adansonia digitata*). A thousand years or more old, the baobab is grounded with its massive trunk while reaching toward the heavens with its sturdy branches and wealth of seasonal foliage, flowering, and fruiting. As the baobab is often recognized in the savannas of Africa as the Tree of Life, likewise so can be spiritual ecology today.[24] By now spiritual ecology is characterized by its substantial momentum, indeed, exponential growth, extending in a multitude of diverse directions in many levels, sectors, and aspects of societies throughout the world.

The primary aim of this book is to outline an intellectual history of the quiet revolution that is identified here as spiritual ecology while recognizing that there are numerous discontinuities as well as continuities in this history. Moreover, this book attempts to afford balanced treatment to practical as well as intellectual aspects, the practical ones including nature spirituality as well as environmental activism. Indeed, while some individuals may elect to focus exclusively on either the intellectual, spiritual, or activist components of spiritual ecology, many are involved in two or all three of these components in various ways and degrees.

A secondary aim of this book is to provide a resource guide for spiritual ecology, encompassing a representative sample drawn not only from the wealth of print publications, but also of selected films, websites, organizations, and other materials. Accordingly, this book reveals a revolution that is well under way, facilitates the further exploration of the subject for readers who are especially intrigued by particular aspects or the whole, and may even generate further participation in one or more components of spiritual ecology.[25] Here an eclectic, inclusive, and relativistic approach is pursued. The goal is to understand and appreciate different religions and spiritualities as they relate to environments, ecologies, and environmentalisms, and not to judge which one or ones are more valid, useful, or better, but only to learn from the enduring wisdom of humanity as revealed in its religions and spiritualities.

The above and other points will be elaborated and documented throughout this book using a natural framework: one of the most fundamental life forms on the terrestrial surface of planet Earth, the tree.[26] Certain kinds of trees are considered sacred in many religions and cultures of the world, such as in Buddhism the bodhi tree (*Ficus religiosa*) under which the Buddha is said to have reached enlightenment.[27] The first chapter explains the importance of a tree as background for the metaphorical organization of the remaining chapters under the generic parts of a tree. The remaining chapters are grouped under these parts: I. Roots; II. Trunk; III. Branches; IV. Leaves; and V. Flowers, Seeds, and Fruits. Part VI. Hazards addresses the obstacles to spiritual ecology, including its critics and responses to them, as well as secularization. The Epilogue briefly concludes the book with some generalizations. Each chapter profiles key issues and projects as well as personages. Furthermore, each essay goes beyond the main focus on a historical or contemporary pioneer in the development of spiritual ecology to embrace material demonstrating the relevance of the past to the present and even to the future. Each chapter is designed to be a self-contained essay that can stand alone.

Finally, although I am solely responsible for any deficiencies in this book, my greatest debt to several influences should be acknowledged explicitly. My parents, Else and Elmer Sponsel, during my childhood at their tree-lined home in suburban Indianapolis as well as on lakes and rivers in forests during holidays in Indiana and vacations in Colorado, Michigan, Minnesota, and Wisconsin, embodied a deep respect and reverence for nature in its many seasonal manifestations. Thanks to Don and Roberta Lenkeit, I spent a wonderful summer teaching at Mount Royal Junior College in the city of Calgary in Alberta, Canada, and on the weekends enjoyed experiencing the awesome Rocky Mountains nearby.[28] I am grateful for extraordinary experiences in nature in not only the aforementioned places, but also in the Amazon, Ethiopia, Hawai'i, New Mexico, and Thailand.

My wife and research colleague, Dr. Poranee Natadecha-Sponsel of Chaminade University, introduced me to the sacred sites and landscapes of Thailand as well as to Buddhism and its ecological and environmental relevance. Professor Nukul Ruttanadakul, a Buddhist ecologist at Prince of Songkhla University in Pattani, Thailand, generously collaborated in our early field research and greatly informed and inspired us. In addition, I am most grateful for the kind and generous hospitality and assistance during visits in Thailand of Mathana and Pinyo Sanjindavong as well as Sriwalla and Bhandit Sukchot.

In 1981 until my retirement in August 2010, I developed and directed the Ecological Anthropology Program at the University of Hawai'i, and in 2003, an optional Spiritual Ecology Concentration was added. Both the program and the concentration within it were available to undergraduate as well as graduate students.[29] One of the courses, 444 Spiritual Ecology, cross-listed between the departments of Anthropology and Religion, was the primary venue for the development of this book. In addition, Dr. Rebecca Goodman, Director of the Osher Lifelong Learning Institute at the University of Hawai'i where I continue to teach has provided opportunities for exploring several specialized topics within spiritual ecology. Generations of students in my classes have shared informative and critical feedback through their discussions and essays on spiritual ecology. In particular, among my former graduate students, David Adams, Morgan Brent, and Ryan Luskin have been inspirations in their creative activities in spiritual ecology. My work on this subject continues through the development of the Research Institute for Spiritual Ecology (RISE) and its website.[30]

I am greatly indebted to Mary Evelyn Tucker and John Grim of the Forum on Religion and Ecology as well as to Bron Taylor, founder of the International Society for the Study of Religion, Nature and Culture, for their scholarship, leadership, inspiration, and encouragement.[31] The books of Roger S. Gottlieb and David Kinsley were and continue to be indispensable background sources. These extraordinary scholars— Gottlieb, Grim, Taylor, and Tucker—have laid much of the indispensable intellectual foundation for the recent development of spiritual ecology.[32]

I am most grateful to colleagues Eugene Anderson, Bron Taylor, and Mary Evelyn Tucker for recommendations for the final revision of the manuscript of this book. Likewise, I am most grateful to the staff of ABC-CLIO/Praeger, especially Anthony Chiffolo and Vicki Moran; to the staff of PreMediaGlobal, especially Sethu Baskaran Natarajan; and to the independent copy editor, Elsa van Bergen.

Last but not least, although they have not been involved in spiritual ecology per se, I must acknowledge and express deepest gratitude to my two intellectual gurus during the formative years of graduate studies in anthropology, professors David Bidney of Indiana University and Kenneth A.R. Kennedy of Cornell University, truly extraordinary exemplars of the highest quality of scholarship, collegiality, and integrity.

In conclusion, much of what this book is all about is encapsulated in a quote from a related work by Carl von Essen: "Mystical experience of nature can be of particular relevance to our troubled age, bringing deeper into our consciousness and emotions the logic that nature sustains humanity as humanity must, in turn, sustain nature. Rationality alone, however, cannot be our guide in the task of restoring our environment. A spiritual connection to nature must inspire the emotional commitment that is the yin, complementing the yang of intellectual understanding."[33] Welcome to the spiritual ecology revolution!

CHAPTER 1. WHAT'S IN A TREE?[1]

Trees are extraordinary revelations of the spirit in nature. And, given the multitude of ways that trees and their products benefit and enrich human culture, they are an especially appropriate symbol of the interdependence of spirit and nature.

Steven C. Rockefeller and John Elder[2]

Lord Krishna in the Bhagavad Gita of Hinduism said: "Look at these great blessed souls, who live only for the welfare of others. . . . The birth of trees is truly the most blessed in the world, for they contribute to the well-being of all other creatures. Just as no one needy returns disappointed from generous persons, so too one who approaches trees for shelter. They meet the needs of others with their leaves, flowers, fruits, shade, roots, bark, wood, fragrance, sap, ashes, and charcoal. Offering life, wealth, intellect and speech to benefit others is the height of service of embodied beings for fellow creatures." Such views are reflected in the centrality of trees in the life of the forest-dwelling Gonds of central India. They believe that during the day the trees work hard in providing food, shelter, and shade for people, while during the night the spirits in the trees emerge.[3]

Similarly, as Nathaniel Altman observes: "A tree becomes sacred through recognition of the power that it expresses. This power may be manifested as the food, shelter, fuel, materials used to build boats, or medicine that the tree provides. How a tree is used will vary according to geography, species of tree, and the particular needs (and ingenuity) of the human culture involved. Sacred trees have also provided beauty, hope, comfort, and inspiration, nurturing and healing the mental, emotional, and spiritual levels of our being. They are symbols of life, abundance, creativity, generosity, permanence, energy, and strength."[4]

In Thailand, from Bangkok to the remotest rural settlements and fields, one encounters occasional tree trunks with colorful cloth wrapped around them. Often located at their base is a small spirit house with offerings of food, water, candles, and incense. Locals believe that some spirit resides in the tree. Someone who harms a sacred tree might suffer bad luck,

1

sickness, or even death if the spirit seeks revenge. Consequently sacred trees are usually respected and protected.

Sacred trees may function to simultaneously humanize nature and naturalize humans in Thailand and elsewhere. Often the tree as part of nature is humanized by becoming the residence of the spirit of a deceased person, while humans are naturalized by recognizing that after death their spirit may reside in nature. The unity of humanity, nature, and the supernatural is a basic philosophical tenet shared by the religions of Animism, Buddhism, and Hinduism, among others. It is fundamental to spiritual ecology in general.

Sacred trees are extraordinary in their age, size, shape, or some other attribute. In one village in Thailand a giant ironwood tree, or Malacca teak (*Afzelia bakeri*), was considered sacred. The secretions of the tree looked like blood in color and consistency. Villagers mentioned that twice lightning hit and burned other trees in the area but did not strike this one because of its extraordinary power. Some residents witnessed an unusual light near the tree in the early evening as well.[5]

A particular association with one or more religions often accounts for a certain species of tree being considered sacred. The banyan (*Ficus bengalensis*) and bodhi (*F. religiosa*) have been associated with Buddhism from its beginning. The Buddha achieved enlightenment under a bodhi and to this day this species is a symbol of that event.[6] In Hinduism the bodhi is considered to be the home of the gods Brahma, Krishna, Shiva, and Vishnu. These associations account for the species designation of the bodhi. The banyan tree is sacred for Hindus as well. Furthermore, the bodhi and banyan are introduced species in various countries such as Thailand where they occur beyond their natural geographical range.[7] Thus, the broader biogeographical distribution of these species can only be explained by taking into account their religious association.[8]

Diverse cultures worldwide recognize sacred trees. For instance, the Celts, Druids, and many other societies in ancient Europe venerated single trees, groves, and forests, especially those of oak (*Quercus* spp.). Oak and spruce (*Picea* spp.) were of special significance in old Germanic rituals, the source of the tradition of the Christmas tree. Yew trees (*Taxus* spp.) were especially significant in ancient Britain with church yards constructed around or near them. To this day there are hundreds of shrines throughout Europe associated with particular trees.[9]

In the United States, the Mormon religion was born near the town of Palmayra in New York State. There it is still possible to visit the Sacred Grove where Mormons believe that their prophet Joseph Smith first experienced divine revelations. In the United States and elsewhere some families plant trees at the birth of a child or as a living memorial when a relative dies. A tree that survived the bombing of the Federal Building in Oklahoma City and another called the Survivor Tree at the site of the 911 Memorial in New York City both have become a symbol of renewal, thus something of a sacred tree. Likewise, a tree that survived the bombing of Hiroshima in Japan during World War II is considered sacred.

Beyond its religious significance, a tree, whether or not it is considered sacred, can have economic and ecological values. For example, T. M. Das of the University of Calcutta estimates that a tree living for 50 years generates \$31,250 worth of oxygen, \$62,000 of air pollution control, \$31,250 of soil erosion control and soil fertilizer, \$37,500 of water, and \$31,250 of shelter for animals.[10] The services provided by this single 50-year-old tree total \$193,250. Its value as lumber would be a mere fraction of this. Furthermore, a tree cut for timber is only used once, unlike its continuing ecosystem services as a living resource. This illuminates the difference between sustained harvesting of natural interest and the natural capital of a tree or forest.[11]

If a single tree is viewed as part of a hierarchy of progressively larger ecological systems, then it can be significant for environmental and biodiversity conservation. Biodiversity encompasses not only the number of species in a given area, but also the diversity of their interconnections and interactions. A large tree can host a multitude of other species such as lianas (vines), ephiphytes, mosses, and fungi. There may be dozens to hundreds of species of resident and transient animals, such as insects, birds, bats, frogs, lizards, monkeys, snails, snakes, and squirrels. Millions of microorganisms may also inhabit a single tree.[12] Interacting with these species are others functioning as competitors, mutualists, parasites, predators, and other types of symbioses. For instance, each animal species may host a distinctive combination of other species of internal and external parasites. In addition, bats, bees, birds, insects, monkeys, and other animals may pollinate flowers of the tree and those of the same species in the surrounding environment. Some animals eat fruit from the tree and disperse the seeds elsewhere, thereby stimulating growth of other individuals of that species and even reforestation. Indeed, some seeds are dependent for germination on the chemicals in the digestive tract of certain animal species. In these and other ways diverse animal species link individual trees of the same species into much wider networks of reproduction and production.[13]

The fact that most of the species associated in some way with a single tree are quite small might appear to detract from their value for biodiversity conservation. However, the overwhelming majority of species that compose biodiversity are also quite small in body size; indeed the vast proportion is invertebrates.[14] In the main, it is the smaller organisms that power ecosystem processes such as energy flow and nutrient cycling.

A large tree like a banyan or redwood can also create microclimates and microenvironments for plants, mosses, fungi, and other organisms that grow on its leaves, branches, trunk, and roots as well as on and in the adjacent ground. Leaf fall and other litter from the tree provide nutrients for animals and plants on the ground through, for example, chemical decomposition and decomposer species. A giant tree may also act like a water pump with its deeper taproots pulling water toward the surface, a phenomenon referred to as hydraulic lift.[15] Some of this water may become available for surrounding plants. The roots of a tall tree may also transfer nutrients to the surface. Acting like a sponge, the tree captures and slowly releases some rainwater that might otherwise increase runoff and soil erosion. In sum, trees are a very important component of the composition, structure, function, and dynamics of many ecosystems.

Collectively through space, and cumulatively over time, the conservation effect of sacred trees must be quite significant. For instance, there are more than 63,000 villages and 37,000 temples throughout Thailand. Many of these are associated with single trees, groves, or forests that are considered sacred. Temple groves and forests may range up to one hectare or greater in size.[16] In addition, the cumulative impact over time of trees, groves, and forests that are considered sacred must be very substantial since a belief in them may extend over centuries. In Thailand, for example, Buddhism dates from at least 700 years ago, Hinduism 800 years, and Animism millennia. Each of these religions includes beliefs in sacred aspects of nature. It can be hypothesized that sacred trees, like other sacred sites and places in Thailand and elsewhere, may function, in effect, as a widespread, varied, and ancient "system" of protected areas that are community based and religiously sanctioned. This is not generally recognized by governmental and nongovernmental agencies promoting environmental and biodiversity conservation from the top down with Western concepts of protected areas such as wildlife sanctuaries and national parks.[17]

From the perspective of the systems approach in ecology, a single tree can contribute significantly to environmental and biodiversity conservation. When a large tree is considered sacred, and accordingly afforded special protection from harm, then it may help to conserve a multitude of other species and their symbioses as well as particular microclimates, microenvironments, and soil and water resources. These manifold ecological functions of a single tree are multiplied many times over in groves and forests that are even more important for conservation. If a single 50-year-old tree is worth something like $193,250 in the value of the total environmental services that it generates, then just imagine what an entire forest is worth!

If there were wider appreciation of the numerous and diverse meanings and significances of trees, then many people might appreciate even more groves and forests, and consequently be more concerned about their sustainable use, management, and conservation. Perhaps this is part of the ecological wisdom behind the fact that in the Buddhist country of Bhutan it is illegal to cut down any living tree. Whether or not a tree, grove, or forest that is considered sacred is intended for the purpose of conservation, or fits any Western concept of conservation, it may still, in effect, function for conservation purposes or protecting biodiversity.

In conclusion, a tree is far more than just a tree, given its numerous, diverse, and complex interrelationships as part of a nested series of increasingly larger ecological systems. It is far more than merely an economic resource, given its religious, spiritual, and symbolic associations, and far more in many other respects as well. As Henryk Skolimowski writes, "If we reconstructed human spirituality painstakingly, we would end up with a mangnificent tree whose branches go in so many directions, yet all trying to touch the heavens."[18] While this quote neglects aspects of the disunity and negative side of religions, in general it reflects the journey ahead in our exploration of spiritual ecology. For some readers this journey may be a kind of pilgrimage. This chapter elucidates the main reason that this book through the designation of its parts has been organized around the generic components of a tree.

PART I. ROOTS

The roots of spiritual ecology are numerous and deep, perhaps extending back at least some 30,000 years in the case of the Upper Paleolithic cave paintings in France and Spain. Some experts have interpreted this prehistoric art as Animism, a belief in multiple spiritual beings and forces in nature. Animism is manifest to this day by many indigenous and other people around the world. Indigenous societies are usually relatively sustainable ecologically, and their religious worldview and values are often a major factor in their environmental relationships. Animism is also manifest in contemporary Pantheism and Paganism among some other nature religions. In Asia and beyond, the Buddha is surely one of the giants of spiritual ecology, his life and teachings intimately associated with nature, especially trees. In the West, Saint Francis of Assisi is most famous for his ecospirituality; legend has it he even preached to birds as part of the community of divine creation. These and many other matters at the very foundation of spiritual ecology are sampled here. Like the roots of a tree, they nourish the structure that has grown to flourish as spiritual ecology today. They facilitate the vital rethinking, revisioning, and refeeling of the place of humans in nature that is so very necessary for restoring some modicum of ecosanity.

Chapter 2. Enchanted Nature, Animism[1]

Animists are people who recognize that the world is full of persons, only some of whom are human, and that life is always lived in relationship with others. Animism is lived out in various ways that are all about learning to act respectfully (carefully and constructively) toward and among other persons.

Graham Harvey[2]

The word *Animism* derives from the Latin *anima* which refers to spirit, soul, or life force. The term was applied by the famous British social anthropologist Sir Edward Burnett Tylor (1871) in his classic treatise *Primitive Cultures*. There he constructed the minimal definition of religion as a belief in spiritual beings. Furthermore, Tylor theorized that Animism was the earliest stage in the evolution of religion and is the ultimate foundation for all religions.[3] Today in anthropology Animism is used as the generic term for a multitude of diverse religions focused on the belief that nature is inspirited by extraordinary beings and forces. In this book the word Animism is capitalized as is the custom for other religions.

Scholar and Animist Graham Harvey writes that "consciousness is embedded in the nature of all things and seems intimately linked to matter at every level."[4] In general, Animists think that spiritual powers permeate and animate nature, inhabiting animals, plants, rocks and other objects in the environment. Usually these forces are envisioned as souls or spirits. Whether or not they are personified, often they are conceived as male or female. They have the power to influence humans for good or bad. Humans may influence them to some extent with certain rituals and offerings, especially when performed by specialists like shamans and priests who can communicate with the supernatural. In the process, Animism challenges conceptual dualities like object/subject, thing/person, inanimate/animate, animal/human, nature/culture, natural/supernatural, body/mind, and life/death.[5]

With its considerable spatial and temporal range, Animism arguably qualifies as the great, major, or world religion, instead of Buddhism,

Christianity, Hinduism, Islam, or Judaism. Animism is by far the oldest religion of humanity. Its antiquity seems to go back at least as far as the period of the Neanderthals some 60,000 to 80,000 years ago. In the Zagros Mountains of northern Iraq, in the cave of Shanidar, archaeologists discovered some of the earliest evidence of intentional burials, which may reflect a belief in the afterlife. These graves appear to contain offerings of flowers, the latter revealed by pollen remains. The same species of flowers still grow in the region to this day, and eight of them are known to possess medicinal properties. They might have been intentionally placed on the grave, although recently it has been hypothesized that they might have been introduced by a rodent.[6] In any case, Animism contrasts markedly with other major *religions that are far more recent in comparison, originating within only the last* few thousand years.

Animism is the religion common to most indigenous traditional hunting-gathering, fishing, farming, and herding societies throughout the world.[7] In addition, it comprises a substratum in the religion of many people who would identify themselves primarily with Buddhism, Christianity, Hinduism, Islam, Judaism, or another major religion. Moreover, not only does Animism survive and thrive in the religious beliefs of a multitude of diverse cultures, especially indigenous ones, but it also has been revitalized in areas where it was long suppressed, like Europe and North America where it may be referred to as Paganism or Neo-paganism.[8] In Estonia, for example, there are remnants of a widespread phenomenon in Europe: wooded meadows that were traditionally used as sites for Pagan ritual. Incidentally, wooded meadows are also unusually high in biodiversity, a coincidence often associated with sacred places in nature.[9] Moreover, as Harvey observes, for Animists, " ... particular places are persons in their own rights. Places are not only environments and ecologies, but persons, individuals, agents, active and relational beings, participants in the wider ecology of life."[10]

Animism is, by far, the most widespread of all of the religions of the world. It was the religion of the foraging or hunting-gathering societies that lived on much of the land of this planet until the evolution of agriculture, beginning roughly about 10,000 years ago in the Old World and a few thousands years later in the New World. Animism endures as the only religion for many such societies.[11] For example, Australian Aborigines traditionally believe that their kinship is directly connected to ancestral spirits in the biotic species and landforms of their habitat, a phenomenon referred to as totemism.[12] Uluru (Ayres Rock) is one of the most famous sacred places in nature in Australia. Traditional Hawaiians recognized supernatural power (mana) in sharks, forest plants, rocks, volcanoes, tides, streams, wind, rainbows, and numerous other "natural" phenomena.[13] In Animism such beliefs together with their associated taboos, rituals, and practices may help manage and conserve the natural environment.[14]

Animism can also comprise a substratum of popular religion in many societies, even though individuals may identify with one or more of the so-called great religions. For instance, Asians often incorporate aspects of Animism in their religion along with Buddhism, Confucianism, Daoism, Hinduism, or Islam. Accordingly, Shintoism in Japan is a variant of Animism that coexists and sometimes mixes with Buddhism.[15] In Thailand people who are primarily Buddhists may still believe in spirits that dwell in a place like a sacred tree. Furthermore, in Thailand a small house or shrine for the local spirit is located in the yards of most homes and other buildings as well as many farm fields and orchards. The spirit house provides shelter for the spirit being that was disturbed by the construction of the human building and other new land uses. Offerings like water, fruit, candles, incense, and/or flowers are supposed to be put in the spirit house on a daily or regular basis. Millions of spirit houses exist throughout the country.[16]

Rice is another illustration of how spirits permeate life and nature for Animists. It is one of the most important food and cash crops in the world today. However, in its Asian homelands rice is not merely a material entity for nourishment nor can it be adequately understood only in this way. It is also associated with the spiritual domain, and especially with the rice goddess. An elaborate complex of ritualistic, symbolic, and artistic expressions are connected with rice in Asia and elsewhere.[17]

Some variant of Animism persists in about half of the 7,000 cultures in the world today. Indeed, manifestation of Animism occurs in contemporary Europe, North America, and elsewhere in the form of Paganism or Neo-paganism which has many different expressions and is intimately related to nature as well.[18]

In addition to its great antiquity as well as to its continuing ubiquity and vitality, Animism is important because it is the original nature religion.[19] The ecological resonance and reverberations of Animism are probably part of the reason for its persistence. For example, the interrelationships and interdependencies within environmental systems are elemental principles of Animism as they are for other variants of spiritual ecology as well as for the Western science of ecology. Some environmentalists even consider themselves to be Neo-animists or Eco-pagans. On the other hand, there are entirely naturalistic forms of Animism based on personal relationships that people have with non-human organisms or on scientific understandings of their consciousness and emotions.[20]

Apparently Animism may be an elemental manifestation of human nature. If so it most likely will persist in some form well into the future. Its ecological and environmental relevance is obvious. It has the potential to contribute significantly to helping restore some modicum of ecosanity in the contemporary world. From the perspective of Animism, Harvey marshals a radical critique of modernism and its hegemony, which he considers to be not only aberrant but even pathological. He rejects modernism's disenchantment of nature. Also, Harvey rejects modernist dismissals that Animism is primitive, simplistic, and irrational. Harvey writes: "If every 'thing' we humans encounter might in fact be a living person, the implications and ramifications are immense. It is this that generates the particular etiquettes, protocols and dialogues that are at the heart of the lived realities that are animism."[21] Accordingly, Animism merits far more recognition and appreciation than it has received in the past as the world religion and also for its very substantial ecological relevance. It generates a relationship with other persons, using the term *persons* in the broadest sense, which is genuinely respectful, reverential, and responsible.

CHAPTER 3. THE ORIGINAL SPIRITUAL ECOLOGISTS, INDIGENOUS PEOPLES

For Indigenous peoples, land cannot be owned, bought, or sold. She does not belong to us, we belong to her. We are born out of this land; we spend our lives on this land as her guests; and after death we go back to that same land. . . . Although Indigenous peoples around the world vary widely in their customs, traditions, rituals, languages, and so on, land is considered by all as the center of their universe, a parent, a giver of life, the core of our cultures, rituals, and traditions.

Nomalungelo I. Goduka[1]

A most remarkable case of the practical application of an indigenous spiritual ecology is the Kahoʻolawe Island Reserve. The small island of Kahoʻolawe is located 6 miles southwest of Maui in the Hawaiian Islands. It was inhabited for over a thousand years. Native Hawaiians called the island *Kanaloa* after the god of the ocean. Since ancient times it has been a sacred place (*wahi pana*) for spiritual regeneration (*puʻuhonua*). From the beginning of World War II until 1990, the U.S. military took control of the island to use for bombing practice from ships and airplanes. The Protect Kahoʻolawe *ʻOhana* was formed by a group of Native Hawaiians to protest the bombing of their sacred island and call for its return. At last in 1993 this transpired with the passage of a law by the U.S. Congress recognizing the cultural significance of the island and directing the Navy to remove unexploded ordnance and restore the environment. In the same year the State Legislature of Hawaiʻi established the Kahoʻolawe Island Reserve restricting the island and a 2-mile zone around it for exclusive use by Native Hawaiians for their subsistence, cultural, and spiritual purposes as well as for environmental restoration, historic preservation, and education. Ancestral temples, shrines, and other religious and cultural places have been rededicated through appropriate ceremonies. Gradually the environment and cultural sites on the island are being restored and revitalized.[2]

Many of the some 300 million Indigenous persons worldwide adhere to Animism, a belief in multiple spiritual beings and forces in nature. The religion of Animism is an integral component permeating their daily life, culture, and ecology.[3] The basic holistic principles of a viable and vibrant spiritual ecology are especially pronounced in most traditional indigenous societies. Such principles variously emphasize that humans, nature, and the supernatural comprise a functional, spiritual, and moral unity through their interconnectedness and interdependence. The awesome and mystical powers of an enchanted nature attract appropriate respect, reverence, and reciprocity. Humans are embedded in a kinship network encompassing nonhuman beings in nature including their spirituality. Indigenes affirm and celebrate this through a wealth of symbols, myths, and rituals. Thus, traditionally for most Indigenous societies, religion promotes and maintains the dynamic equilibrium within and between their social and ecological systems.[4] When disequilibrium is detected, it is usually treated spiritually as much if not more than in some material manner.The mediator between Indigenous people and their biophysical and spiritual environments is the shaman, a part-time religious specialist.[5]

In the Amazon most traditional Indigenous people think in a monistic rather than dualistic manner; their biological, cultural, and spiritual ecologies are complementary in many ways.[6] Usually they have a holistic view of their relation to the natural and the supernatural worlds, even if they distinguish between ordinary and extraordinary phenomena. Most consider the human body to be the residence of one or more spirits. Many more spirits are believed to inhabit mountains, forests, waters, and rocks in the local landscape which is often viewed as sacred geography. Accordingly, the forests and waters of the Amazon are a source of spiritual as well as physical sustenance.[7]

In the Venezuelan Amazon when a Yanomami man leaves his village or camp to go hunting in the forest he believes not only that he experiences the ordinary plants and animals, but also that the extraordinary might transpire. He thinks that the spirit guardians of the animals may allow him to kill certain prey for food, or even facilitate this by placing them in his path. As long as he engages in appropriate respect, reciprocity, and rituals, then he and his relatives will enjoy the nourishment of meat. However, if he or someone else disrupts the spiritual world of the forest, then there may be negative repercussions; the hunter or a member of his family or community may become sick or even die. Then the local shaman attempts to restore balance and harmony to nature and society.[8]

The shaman monitors the conditions of the interwoven ecological, human, and spiritual communities and tries to make adjustments through communicating with helper spirits to mediate, in the Amazon often with the assistance of tobacco or hallucinogenic plant substances like *ayahuasca*.[9] Indigenous Amazonians try to promote the survival and well-being of their community through an elaborate system of taboos, rituals, symbols, and associated oral traditions.[10]

There is a tendency among traditional Indigenous societies in the Amazon to avoid or prohibit killing animals like the harpy eagle, jaguar, anaconda, river otter, and dolphin. In effect, even if only inadvertently, this recognizes the ecological role of these keystone species as top carnivores crucial in the regulation of prey populations. Various combinations of carnivore and herbivore species are avoided or taboo among Indigenous cultures. This may have a conservation effect, even if unintentional, by creating a mosaic of game reserves that free a somewhat different combination of species in different areas from predation pressure. Furthermore, among some societies, faunal taboos may channel hunting away from the less accessible and more vulnerable herbivore species, like tapir or deer, to those that provide a better cost/benefit ratio together with a more sustained yield, such as large rodents like the paca or capybara.[11] Special places in the forest and in water bodies may be considered sacred, or the haunts of dangerous spirits, and avoided accordingly, thus in effect creating game sanctuaries.[12]

The Desana in the Colombian portion of the northwest Amazon, are also intimately tuned into their forest and river ecosystems, not only through their subsistence activities, but also through their social organization, cosmology, myths, symbols, and rituals. Their shaman even serves as a manager of natural resource harvesting by regulating a complex system of faunal and sexual prohibitions. In these and other ways, the Desana population maintains a dynamic balance with its environment below the carrying capacity. Consequently, they do not irreversibly deplete the natural resources and degrade the ecosystems in their habitat. They are circumscribed by other groups and therefore cannot expand geographically, unless resorting to warfare and conquest.[13]

Living in another tropical rainforest region, the Sakkudai of the Mentawai Islands of Siberut in Indonesia are somewhat similar to the Desana. Reimar Schefold notes: "The traditional ecological balance on the island did not, in any case, exist in spite of the people. It existed with them. The Mentawaians long ago evolved ritual prescriptions and pro-scriptions that, expressing their ideology of harmony, prevented any ruth-less exploitation of the environment."[14] Their respect for spirits in nature is reflected in strict taboos that prevent over-hunting. The hunters avoid sex before the hunt as well as certain foods. The Sakkudai regard any intervention in the environment to be sinister and disruptive of ecological equilibrium. Certain rituals are performed to restore and maintain the equilibrium of the system. Elsewhere similar beliefs and practices are found in many indigenous societies.[15]

The Maya live in the northern sections of the lowlands of the Yucatan peninsula, the central highlands of the state of Chiapas in southern Mexico, and portions of the Central American countries of Belize, Guatemala, Honduras, and El Salvador. Maya range from lowland into the highland wet and dry forests with tremendous variation in their ecol-ogies, cultures, languages, and histories. Nevertheless, they have in common core religious principles in the sacred text called *Popol Vuh*, which was written down after initial contact with the Spanish. The natural and supernatural realms are intimately interconnected and interdepen-dent. For example, a supreme deity first created animals and plants, and then the animals helped create humans from corn, which is still considered to be a sacred plant. Accordingly, the relationship between humans, ani-mals, and plants should be one of respect, caring, and cooperation. Many Maya show profound reverence and compassion for animals and plants in their habitat through their daily activities as well as in their sacred sto-ries, rituals, chants, and prayers. For instance, when trees are cut to clear an area for a swidden garden, the farmer appeals to the guardian spirit of the forest. Spirituality permeates the beings and things in their forest. Clearly nature is far more than merely a resource or commodity.[16]

The Maya and other Indigenes who find sanctuary in rain forests and other relatively remote areas are the descendants of some of the original spiritual ecologists. Many maintained a relative balance and harmony within their society and between their society and the ecosystems in their habitat. Their habitat as a whole was not degraded or endangered after centuries or even millennia of habitation and use. However, there are some Mayan areas where over-population and over-exploitation may have led to deforestation and other problems long before European influen-ces.[17] In addition, some portions of Mayan forests are anthropogenic with unusual concentrations of useful trees.

The background behind many of the foregoing principles regarding the relationship between religion and ecology is the pioneering work of Roy Rappaport. His dissertation research with the Maring of Papua New Guinea formed the basis of his subsequent book *Pigs for the Ancestors: Ritual in the Ecology of a New Guinea People*. This widely read classic ethnography stresses the collection of empirical and quantitative data as well as the application of systems theory to examine the functional role of ritual in regulating the relationship between the dynamic fluctuations in a human population and its natural resources. Rappaport's subsequent studies—his collection of essays *Ecology, Meaning, and Religion*, and his monumental treatise *Ritual and Religion in the Making of Humanity*—are largely theoretical. The latter book reflects his deep concern for ritual forms that could help humanity respond to the enormous challenges in the management of society and environment. Furthermore, it is a religious book as well as a comprehensive study of religion.[18]

Because native religion is often the most crucial factor promoting social as well as ecological integration, balance, and harmony, missionization from alien religions can be highly disruptive spiritually and ecologically as well as socially, culturally, and psychologically. Paradoxically, and dangerously, generally adaptive indigenous systems are being degraded and even destroyed by maladaptive ones, first with European colonialism, then after national independence with internal colonialism, and in more recent decades with globalization. Throughout the world the basic patterns and processes undermining and even destroying indigenous societies and their environment are remarkably similar, if not always identical under diverse circumstances economically, politically, and otherwise. Indigenous culture and spiritual ecology are usually antithetical to the generally anthropocentric and utilitarian environmental ethics of colonial and industrial societies which tend to segregate, objectify, and commodify nature as if it were no more than a warehouse of material resources to exploit for consumption, commerce, and profit.[19] This cancer of colonialism and its recent variants are degrading if not destroying many sacred places of Indigenes throughout the world.[20]

Indigenous societies that are likely to survive colonial contact have several crucial attributes:

geographical and economic marginality;

balance between separation and integration (not assimilation);

attachment to ancestral lands, self-sufficiency, and self-determination allowed by a democratic state respecting multiethnicity;

a stable or increasing population;

memory of precontact and contact history in combination with a conscious counter-cultural strategy opposing colonials;

common identity with meaningful and resilient traditions including their own religion; and

political organization and mobilization as well as networking with other Indigenous organizations and relevant environmental and human rights non-governmental organizations.[21]

The Kogi of Colombia fit these criteria for cultural survival to a large extent. They are descendants of the Tairona society that survived the invasion of the Spanish in 1514. The Kogi have remained in the Sierra Nevada de Santa Marta in Colombia because of their tenacious determination to maintain their own cultural autonomy as well as the geographic protection of the rugged terrain of the mountains. Their habitat varies ecologically with increasing altitude from tropical rain forest to savanna to alpine meadows and glaciers, reflecting in some ways a microcosm of the climatic zones of the world. The Kogi believe that they live at the heart of sacred Mother Earth. They practice environmental stewardship through a series of material and ritual cycles of exchange between the sea coast and the mountain top. These exchanges are supposed to maintain the vitality and fertility of their diverse ecosystems. Much of it is guided by their priests who also select which elements from the outside world are accepted or rejected. The Kogi are alarmed by how outsiders, whom they call younger brother, are degrading Mother Earth. For example, they observe the melting of glaciers high in their mountains as a result of global climate change. They try to cope with these threats through their cosmology and rituals as well as by warning outsiders of their deleterious environmental impacts.[22]

Many Indigenous spiritual and practical beliefs and actions comprise no less of a system of land and natural resource use, management, conservation, and development than their Western counterparts, if Western myopic, elitist, racist, and ethnocentric thinking is rejected.[23] Furthermore, most traditional Indigenous societies are usually sustainable and green in their beliefs, values, and practices. They have been tested, developed, and refined over many centuries or even millennia; thus they are grounded pragmatically as well as sanctioned religiously.[24]

Most Indigenous ways of knowing, being, and communicating challenge the modernist assumptions about their own supposed universal monopoly on knowing, understanding, truth, and reality that sustains the power of their colonial regimes as master narratives and fuels a synergy of genocide, ethnocide, and ecocide in Indigenous territories and elsewhere.[25] In the final analysis, spiritual ecology involves philosophical, religious, moral, and ethical paradigms that view nature as sacred, although this does not necessarily mean that the associated societies are always in harmony with their environment, given the discrepancies that too often exist between ideals and actions. Accordingly, the primary working assumption of spiritual ecology is that the natural and the supernatural are not discrete and incompatible domains, but instead interwoven into the very fabric of human existence and experience, even though they might be distinguished analytically by researchers.[26] An analogy may help: compare spirit to wind. With the naked eye humans can not actually see the wind, but certainly they can observe its physical effects, such as in the motion of leaves in a tree.[27] Contemplating this analogy can facilitate more open-minded and deeper thinking about the potential of spiritual ecology as a legitimate arena of practical action on behalf of the biosphere including humanity.

Indigenous individuals reside in many different countries and ecosystems, many practicing some variant of Animism as the descendents of the original spiritual ecologists.[28] Among contemporary Native Americans who may be spiritual ecologists in some way and degree are Paula Gunn Allen, Jeanette Armstrong, Gregory Cajete, Phillipe Deere, Vine Deloria, Nicholas Black Elk, Jack Forbes, Leslie Gray, Donald A. Grinde, Joy Harjo, Debra Harry, Linda Hogan, Winona LaDuke, Oren Lyons, Simon J. Ortiz, Audrey Shenandoah, Leslie Marmon Silko, David Sohappy, and Jace Weaver. As in the case of Kahoʻolawe, many Indigenous individuals and organizations are engaged in some kind of environmental activism, including ecological restoration, and this is often motivated ultimately by their spiritual ecology. The time is long overdue for the world to listen to the wisdom of Indigenous people and to begin to do many things quite differently from the pathology of the dehumanizing and desacralizing obsessions of Western capitalist materialism, consumerism, and greed that even endangers the home planet as a whole.[29]

Environmental, economic, social, cultural, and spiritual health are all interrelated and interdependent. The Indigenous societies remaining in the refuge of the rain forests of Latin America and elsewhere provide adaptive repertoires for others to consider in designing and developing more ecocentric, sustainable, and green economies, societies, cultures, and spiritualities, if they are to have any healthy future. Many Indigenous societies can serve as heuristic models for others to rethink, refeel, and revision their place in nature. Rappaport astutely observes: "Nature is seen by humans through a screen of beliefs, knowledge, and purposes, and it is in terms of their images of nature, rather than of the actual structure of nature, that they act. Yet, it is upon nature itself that they do act, and it is nature itself that acts upon them, nurturing or destroying them."[30]

CHAPTER 4. ECOLOGICALLY NOBLE OR IGNOBLE?[1]

It's hard to believe, but there seems to be an attempt to try to discredit the now familiar image of the American Indian as an ecological model, thus eliminating in a single blow one of the fundamental inspirations for the modern environmental movement and a festering source of recurring guilt that is lodged deep in the American psyche.

Kirpatrick Sale[2]

Since the Greek and Roman philosophers of antiquity, and mostly with the age of European geographic exploration, the "savage" has represented the "primitive" condition of humans in a state of nature prior to domestication of plants and animals. The earliest stage of cultural evolution in prehistory and their supposed analogues, historic hunter-gatherers, have been constructed in two diametrically opposed ways, basically as either positive or negative.[3]

The French Enlightenment philosopher, Jean-Jacques Rousseau (1712–1778), is usually associated with the idea of the "noble savage," but not necessarily accurately.[4] In any case, he theorized about the original natural state of humankind as a vehicle for critiquing civilization as unnatural and dehumanizing with, among other faults, inequality.[5] There are elements of romantic primitivism in his writings. There is also nature religion. He was a pioneer in spiritual ecology, not only enjoying walks and botanizing in the countryside, but in the process having mystical experiences with the "great pageant of nature" sensing a "unity of all things."[6] William French notes that "Rousseau was a watershed figure in the eighteenth century whose writings did much to popularize a growing sense of reverence for nature."[7]

For Rousseau the "noble savage" may have been the original spiritual ecologist. Although he did not believe that any return to some golden age was feasible or desirable, it was the original state of nature where humankind realized its elemental potential for simplicity, integrity, and virtue, a point echoed in such contemporary movements as deep ecology and its critique of modernity.[8] To this day positive ideas about "savages" or "primitives" are often a component in spiritual ecology discourse, although usually different designations such as Aborigines, First Peoples, Indigenes, or Native Americans are employed. Elements of the so-called "ecologically noble savages" with their earth spirituality, ecomysticism, or nature religion are discernible in contemporary Animism, Paganism, New Age spiritualities, and similar phenomena.[9]

To this day, the "noble savage" is envisioned as living in harmony socially and ecologically. In romantic primitivism the "savage" is thought to be superior to civilization in terms of freedom, innocence, simplicity, generosity, goodness, purity, and peacefulness. Furthermore, "savages" are conceived as living in an egalitarian community with property held in common rather than privately. It is theorized that such an ideal or utopian condition of humanity thrived in a natural paradise during a golden age, and supposedly the remnants of this can be found in some extant traditional indigenous societies.

By the eighteenth century, Europeans who were engaged in this cult of exoticism launched a critical analysis challenging their own society and its morality and politics by glorifying the "savage" in contrast to degenerate civilization. Some primitivists even rejected civilization, at least in their discourse, although rarely in actual practice. In theory the "noble savage" offered a better alternative to European society, the former variously identified as archetypal communists, philosophers, ecologists, environmentalists, conservationists, pacifists, healers, and spiritualists.

For primitivists many traditional Indigenous societies are not simply a more desirable condition for humanity; they are much closer to nature, most dwelling in balance and harmony in supposed wilderness.[10] A close correlate is that such societies practice various kinds of nature religion or ecospirituality. Civilized societies and religions are critiqued as unnatural and environmentally destructive. Environmental organizations from the Sierra Club to Earth First! have often stereotyped Native Americans and other Indigenes as stewards or guardians of nature, a tendency occasionally referred to as green primitivism or ecoprimitivism. For instance, a prominent U.S. politician and environmentalist, Stewart Udall, in his book on the history of the environmental conservation movement writes: "The most common trait of all primitive peoples is a reverence for the life-giving earth, and the Native Americans shared this elemental ethic: the land was alive to his loving touch, and he, its son, was brother to all creatures. His feelings were made visible in medicine bundles and dance rhythms for rain, and all of his religious rites and land attitudes savored the inseparable world of nature and God, the Master of Life. During the long Indian tenure the land remained undefiled save for scars no deeper than the scratches of cornfield clearings or the farming canals of the Hohokams on the Arizona desert."[11]

The "noble savage" was usually popularized through the arts (poetry, novels, drama, opera, art, music) but occasionally surfaced in philosophy and eventually during the development of the social sciences. French painter Paul Gaugin escaped to Tahiti to live and portray an idyllic life. Among the better known examples in literature are Daniel Defoe's *Robinson Crusoe* (1719), Jonathan Swift's *Gulliver's Travelers* (1726), James Fenimore Cooper's *Last of the Mohicans* (1826), Henry Wadsworth Longfellow's *Song of Hiawatha* (1855), William H. Hudson's *Green Mansions* (1904), and Ursula K. Le Guin's *The Word For World Is Forest* (1972). The popularity of movies, such as *Bambi* (1942), *The Jungle Book* (1967), *Emerald Forest* (1985), *Dances with Wolves* (1989), *Beauty and the Beast* (1991), *Fern Gully: The Last Rainforest* (1992), *The Lion King* (1994), *Pocahontas* (1995), and *Avatar* (2009), indicate that ideas about the "ecologically noble savage" and idyllic nature or wilderness remain attractive to the public.[12]

Some outstanding ethnographic examples of the "noble savage" are Ishi of the Yahi, Kayapo, Kogi, Koyukon, Kuna, Mbuti, Semai, Tahitians, and Tasaday. In the first textbook on spiritual ecology, David Kinsley describes the Ainu, Australian Aborigines, Mistassini Cree, and Koyukon, all hunter-gatherers, as basically "ecologically noble savages" by virtue of their nature religions which tend to promote sustainable and green subsistence economies and cultures.[13]

The opposite of this romantic view, the "ignoble savage," is commonly associated with English philosopher Thomas Hobbes (1588–1679). He imagined "savage" life as poor, nasty, brutish, and short. His negative view considers "primitive" life to be permeated by disharmony, conflict, and violence, both socially and ecologically. Ritualized violence, such as blood sacrifice and cannibalism, is another common correlate. Such a narrative is reflected to this day in anthropology, most notably in the ethnography of Napoleon A. Chagnon.[14] In the realm of classical music, this perspective appears to be reflected in Igor Stravinsky's *Rite of Spring* (1913). In literature Joseph Conrad's (1902) *Heart of Darkness* and William Golding's (1954) *Lord of the Flies* exemplify Hobbesian views as do the movie sequels to the latter (1963, 1990). More recently, there is the movie *Apocalypto*

(2006) about a brutal blood-thirsty prehistoric civilization, apparently designed to insult Mayan people. These and many other cases demonstrate that Hobbesian ideas persist in popular media.

Anthropologist Colin Turnbull depicts the Mbuti as the epitome of the "noble savage" in the way their culture and religion are embedded in nature. They are supposed to have lived for millennia as an integral part of the forest in all of its beauty, goodness, and mystery. Their profound dependence, understanding, respect, and affection regarding the forest are reflected in the words of one Mbuti quoted by Turnbull: "The forest is a father and mother to us ... and like a father or mother it gives us everything we need—food, clothing, shelter, warmth ... and affection."[15] Turnbull writes: "They were a people who had found in the forest something that made their life more than just worth living, something that made it, with all its hardships and problems and tragedies, a wonderful thing full of joy and happiness and free from care."[16]

In recent decades such positive views have been criticized under the rubric of the "myth of the ecologically noble savage" by conservation biologist Kent H. Redford and others. Redford was one of the first in recent times to challenge the idea that Indigenous societies are necessarily in balance and harmony with nature. He asserts that Indigenes are not inevitably conservationists, even though they may be very knowledgeable about the ecology of their habitat. He opines that traditional Indigenous societies have long had substantial impacts on their environment, even in precontact times, and that this increases with Westernization as well. Redford reasons that Indigenes have the same capacities, needs, and desires as Westerners, and that they lack any cultural barriers or controls to temper their use of natural resources. Any previous sustainability is simply coincidental because of low population density, abundant land, limited technology, and little involvement if any in a market economy, circumstances that are becoming increasingly rare. Redford concludes that Indigenous societies do not provide viable models for the sustainable use of natural resources and environmental conservation.[17]

On various grounds Redford's assertions are problematic. It is well documented that the environmental impact of many traditional subsistence societies was comparable to natural processes and did not lead to natural resource depletion and environmental degradation to an irreversible degree.[18] Often such societies have an archaeological and/or historical record extending back centuries, or even millennia, proving their long-term sustainability. Western environmental impact is far greater than that of traditional Indigenous societies.[19] Redford grossly underestimates just how powerful an influence worldview, values, and attitudes can have on land and resource use, part of the arena of spiritual ecology.[20] Although more recently Redford tempered his position considerably, some of the same thinking remains in various sectors of academia, science, society, and government.

A more recent example of an attempt to totally invalidate the idea of the "ecologically noble savage" is Shepard Krech's book *The Ecological Indian: Myth and History*.[21] There he compiles striking negative examples from prehistoric and historic times, ranging from Pleistocene megafaunal extinctions to wasteful drives of huge buffalo herds over cliffs by Plains Indians to the depletion of beaver populations by native trappers for the fur trade with Europeans colonists. However, in his survey he fails to acknowledge the fact that far more numerous examples exist in which Indigenous societies have achieved some modicum of economic sustainability and ecological balance.[22]

Another extreme example of an academic attacking this idea is the book by Robert Whelan titled *Wild in Woods: The Myth of the Noble-Savage*.[23] He presents a series of negative examples to try to demonstrate that no "ecologically noble savage" societies exist. There are the usual suspects, such as that Paleoindians were responsible for the extinction of Pleistocene megafauna in the Americas. The Kayapo of the Brazilian Amazon allowed logging and mining in their territory in return for royalties. The Tasaday of the Philippines are a hoax. The Piro and the Yuqui of the Amazon do not have any conservation ethic.[24] The Semang of the Malaysian rainforests are polluters.[25] These are presented as proven facts of science. However, they are all problematic. The overkill hypothesis is unproven. There is no scientific consensus as to whether or not the Tasaday were authentic.[26] The Kayapo, Piro, and Yuqui, like so many other negative examples, are not entirely traditional, but have been subjected to Western influences to which they have had to adjust.[27] Scrutiny of the Semang reveals that most of their pollution comes from Western sources. Beyond these difficulties with Whelan's evidence is the problem that he totally ignores any positive cases. A few negative cases do not prove that no positive cases exist.[28] He fails to resolve the paradox of how Indigenous peoples could interact intimately on a daily basis with their habitat and not notice and modify their behavior in reaction to any decline in key natural resources. He fails to consider how a society could survive for centuries or even millennia in the same region if it depletes its resources and degrades its habitat. Nevertheless, there are cases in prehistory long prior to any Western contact of serious resource depletion and environmental degradation, but they are not the majority.[29]

As so often happens with ardent critics of the "ecologically noble savage," there is an ideological motivation. Whelan is obviously a political conservative defending the status quo including Christianity, missionization, colonialism, market economy, capitalism, industrialism, and consumerism.[30] For instance, Whelan writes: "However, the most characteristically modern note of the *furore* which surrounded the events of 1992 [Columbian Quincentenary] was the emphasis on the environment. Columbus had not only exploited the Indians, it was alleged, but he had been responsible for introducing into America an exploitative, European, Judeo-Christian-based attitude towards nature that led to the rape of the environment. This European ethic had crushed the Native American ethic of living in harmony with nature to the lasting detriment of both America and the planet."[31] Whelan also asserts: "It seems that native peoples may not always have lived by a conservation ethic in the past, and that their modern descendents can still be just as destructive as the white man."[32] This ignores the tremendous differences between Native Americans and the invading European colonists in their demography, technology, economy, culture, and religion, and the tremendous differences in their ecological consequences. This is not to say that no proponents of the "ecologically noble savage" concept have any political agenda of their own. Science and scholarship are not necessarily apolitical and amoral. (In a subsequent book Whelan takes on spiritual ecology directly.)[33]

An environmentalist propounding and defending the "ecologically noble savage" vision is Kirkpatrick Sale.[34] He argues that the consequence of Christopher Columbus's "discovery" of the "New" World was genocide, ethnocide, and ecocide.[35] Sale believes that many Indigenous societies were ecologically sustainable prior to Western contact. He responds to attacks on Indigenous peoples, such as those of Krech, by noting that his "argument eventually comes down to saying that the Indians do not have any moral standing as ecologists because European conquerors destroyed their cultures and forced them into the capitalist system." Furthermore, Sale writes: "For all their catastrophic and turbulent history, the one thing that did endure in so many of the various Indian cultures was their earth-based spirituality and the ecological wisdom it spawned. The attempt to destroy that is a shoddy and soulless business indeed, the worst among many egregious examples of the American professoriate serving the systems that are so efficiently destroying the earth."[36] As Johnson cogently remarks, "Defining, defending, and denying the Earth ethic of Native Americans has become an academic blood sport."[37] But this issue is not merely academic. Such arguments can seriously undermine Indigenous interests such as land and resource rights, something that has transpired repeatedly in the history of the Western colonialism in the Americas and beyond. The Western exploitation of "frontiers" is variously rationalized as progress in developing unpopulated or underpopulated as well as unused, underused, or misused land and resources.[38]

At the same time, there are very complicated and difficult issues here. For instance, in 1999 some members of the Makah on the northwest coast of the state of Washington decided to exercise their treaty rights and revitalize their culture by resuming whaling after the gray whale was removed from the endangered species list in 1994. This ignited a controversy that attracted international as well as national attention with deeply felt concerns about sustainability, environmentalism, conservation, and animal rights, versus those about ecocolonialism, Indigenous sovereignty, treaty rights, and human rights. Many Makah firmly believe that whaling is historically pivotal to their economy, society, culture, and religion, and thus a matter of cultural survival, well-being, and identity. In such a situation of competing worldviews, values, and attitudes, it is hard to negotiate any win-win solution. The interests of the Indigenes and environmentalists appeared to be antithetical rather than mutually reinforcing. However, the dispute was even more confusing because there was disagreement among the Makah and among the environmentalists.[39]

To document their cases, sometimes the proponents and opponents of the idea of the "ecologically noble savage" pursue research in historical ecology.[40] However, this may be augmented significantly by examining diachronically successive cultures occupying the same region over extended periods of time—the work of comparative historical ecology.[41] For example, compare the historical ecology of the Hawaiian Islands before and since Captain Cook's landing in 1778. The Hawaiians pursued some forms of resource management and conservation, but they also had a significant impact on their environment. They converted most of the

lowland forests into farm fields, terraced valley slopes, constructed fish-
ponds on reef flats, and harvested forests for birds, timber, firewood, and
medicinal and other plants. However, subsequent colonizers had far
greater environmental impact through harvesting sandalwood and other
timber; the development of monocrop plantations of sugarcane and pineapple; the tourist industry with hotels, golf courses, and other facilities;
and the militarization of large areas. The Hawaiian colonists introduced
some 40 or 50 exotic species of plants and animals, and they may have
contributed to the extinction of some 60 native species (mainly birds) over
a period of some 1,500 years or more prior to Western contact. In sharp
contrast, subsequent European, American, and other colonizers introduced nearly 16,000 exotic species while more than 200 endemic species
of plants and animals have become extinct, averaging at least one species
per year. In short, in contrast to Native Hawaiians, subsequent colonizers
caused at least 260 times as many introductions and more than three times
as many extinctions, all in just one-seventh of the time. The difference in
environmental impact is attributable to many factors, but surely religion is
one and likely the major one.[42] As Cunningham notes, "It was this ability
to perceive natural phenomena as sentient beings that was at the heart of
traditional Hawaiian spirituality."[43] The prevailing Christian interpretation of the Bible was a major factor influencing the environmental impact
of Westerners, missionization starting as early as 1820.[44]

It should be mentioned that the vision of the "ecologically noble savage" is considered by some to be a heuristic model for a desirable future,
if humanity is to survive within the carrying capacity of the planet and
without alienation among fellow humans and from nature. This is envisioned, for instance, in science fiction. Kim Stanley Robinson writes:

> All manner of alternative futures are now being imagined, and
> many of them invoke the wilderness, and moments of our distant
> past, envisioning futures that from the viewpoint of the industrial
> model look 'primitive.' It's not that they advocate a simple return to
> nature, or a rejection of technology, which given our current situa-
> tion would be nothing more than another kind of ecological impos-
> sibility. Rather, they attempt to imagine sophisticated new
> technologies combined with habits saved or reinvented from our
> deep past, with the notion that prehistoric cultures were critical in
> making us what we are, and knew things about our relationship to

the world that we should not forget.[45] Beyond science fiction, others are actually pursuing such a future in practice as well as theory in their individual or communal lifestyles, some identified as green anarchists, green primitivists, green tribalists, and so on. Many are philosophers who critique industrial society—and even civilization—and/or resist the present system and focus on creating alternative green lifestyles, communities, and societies in diverse ways.[46]

Whether it is the relationship of "savages" to one another or with nature, Westerners tend to adhere to either a positive or negative perception; "savages" exemplify either a life of harmony socially and ecologically to a greater degree than any other culture, or they are antithetical to sociality and nature. There is a tendency as well to consider Indigenous traditions to be invariant and uncontested. However, the real world is far more complicated and varied than such antithetical dualistic thinking. Such either-or, all-or-none, and always-or-never postures are unrealistic. Both polar opposites, the "noble savage" and the "ignoble savage," are simplistic, reductionist, and essentializing stereotypes. The strongest proponents of either pole ignore the tremendous variations among and within today's some 7,000 distinct cultures, including the diversity of their environment impacts. It is far more scientific and scholarly to consider this enormous cultural diversity through the examination of particular cultures on their own merits, rather than to over-generalize in either idealistic or derogatory excess. The noble and the ignoble representations of the "primitive" each need to be scrutinized for the possibility of a hidden agenda and its ramifications through scholarly deconstruction and demystification. Nevertheless, many Indigenous cultures can provide profound knowledge, wisdom, and insights for realizing a far better place for humans in nature in practical and spiritual ways. (See Table 4.1, which places Indigenous societies that are sustainable in the perspective of trends in cultural evolution. Trends from indigenous to industrial societies move from left to right for each of the 12 phenomena.)

Table 4.1. Trends in Cultural Evolution

1. Population—nomadic to sedentary settlement pattern with increasing population density, nucleation (settlements to cities), and pollution
2. Food—wild to domesticated foods with shift from foraging to farming, and polycropping to monocropping
3. Energy—somatic (human and animal) to extrasomatic (water, wind, wood, fossil fuel, nuclear) sources of energy for work
4. Land—extensive (horticultural) to intensive (agricultural) landuse; land tenure—community/public to private/corporate ownership
5. Economy—subsistence (satisfying basic physiological needs) to market of surplus production to materialist consumerism; local self-sufficient to regionally and then globally interdependent economy (globalization)
6. Waste—from organic products that are readily biodegradable to, more recently, those like metals and plastics. which disintegrate very slowly and are toxic
7. Scale—small and decentralized to large and centralized societies (states), the latter with increasing import of natural resources from ecosystems in distant regions
8. Differentiation—egalitarian to hierarchical (stratified) societies, the latter with increasing inequality in access to resources, goods, and services and institutionalized warfare with militarization of institutions and regions
9. Alienation—daily to occasional contact with and feedback (monitoring human impact) from the natural environment; eventually with alienation from nature and other humans, and increasingly decisions made by agents far removed from the locations they affect
10. Worldview—ecocentric to anthropocentric and egocentric worldviews, attitudes, and values; also sacred/moral to secular/amoral and utilitarian orientation to nature; may include shift from biophilia (love of nature) to biophobia (fear of nature)
11. Balance—some degree of dynamic ecological equilibrium with recognition of limits to increasing disequilibrium with false assumption that there are no limits (i.e., ecological transition)
12. Impact—environmental modification to conversion (natural to cultural landscapes) and fragmentation (remnant patches of nature); also toxification with industrialization; local to global impact on biodiversity and ecosystems[47]

CHAPTER 5. NATURAL WISDOM AND ACTION, THE BUDDHA[1]

With its philosophical insight into the interconnectedness and thoroughgoing interdependence of all conditioned things, with its thesis that happiness is to be found through the restraint of desire in a life of contentment rather than through the proliferation of desire, with its goal of enlightenment through renunciation and contemplation and its ethic of non-injury and boundless loving-kindness for all beings, Buddhism provides all the essential elements for a relationship to the natural world characterized by respect, care, and compassion.

Bhikkhu Bodi[2]

From birth to death the life of the Buddha was intimately associated with nature, especially trees. The Buddha, originally named Siddhattha Gotama, was born around 2,500 years ago under a Sal tree (*Shorea robusta*) in a grove called Lumbini Park near Kapilavatsu (now Madeira) in the border zone between present day India and Nepal. Around the age of 29 he started a vision quest for six years with various spiritual masters while experimenting with asceticism, usually in groves or forests. At last in Bodhgaya he reached enlightenment under a large bodhi or pipal tree (*Ficus religiosa*) and became the Buddha or "one who has awakened." Thereafter the Buddha meditated for weeks beneath several different species of trees: Nigrodha or Indian fig (*Ficus indica*), Mucalinda (*Barringtonia acutangula*), and Rajayatana or kingstead (*Buchanania latifolia*). Next he went to the royal Deer Park of Isipatana in Sarnath (now Dhamek), just north of Benares (now Varanasi) on the side of the Ganges River in northeastern India.[3] He knew that five spiritual seekers (*bhikkhu*) with whom he had previously associated dwelled there. There he gave his first discourse or sermon called the Setting in Motion the Wheel of the Dharma (*Dharmacakra-pravartana* Sutta). In it the Buddha explained the pivotal core principles of all Buddhism, the Four Noble Truths and the Noble Eightfold Path (Tables 5.1 and 5.2). During the remaining 45 years of his life the Buddha wandered over much of northern and eastern India as a spiritual teacher or master. He died at

31

Table 5.1. The Four Noble Truths

All existence is suffering (*dukkha*).
Suffering is caused by ignorance and desire.
Suffering can end.
The way to end suffering is the Noble Eightfold Path.

the age of 80 reclining between two Sal trees in a grove outside the small town of Kusinagari and in the company of many of his followers. For about four centuries after the Buddha died he was symbolized by the Dharma wheel, a footprint, and natural elements such as the lotus flower, Bodhi tree or leaf, deer, elephant, and lion, rather than any human image.[4]

During his life the Buddha often dwelled, meditated, and preached in natural sites such as groves of trees, forests, mountains, and caves, and his followers have emulated this habit. Accordingly, a famous modern Thai scholar and forest monk, Buddhadasa Bhikkhu, observed that the Pali word for temple and monastery means park and forest as well.[5] Furthermore, Buddhadasa writes: "Everything arising out of Dhamma, everything born from Dhamma, is what we mean by 'nature.'[6] This is what is absolute and has the highest power in itself. Nature has at least four aspects: nature itself; the law of nature; the duty that human beings must carry out toward nature; and the result that comes with performing this duty according to the law of nature."[7]

The Jatakas, a collection of 547 parables, confirm the connection between the Buddha and nature as well. They are accounts of the previous incarnations of the Buddha, most in the form of an animal that sacrifices its own life to save others. The Jatakas illustrate the core Buddhist virtues of wisdom, nonviolence, compassion, loving-kindness, and generosity. They also imply that animals have a moral sense—that is, the capacity to

Table 5.2. The Noble Eightfold Path

Right understanding
Right resolve
Right speech
Right action
Right livelihood
Right effort
Right mindfulness
Right meditation

make ethical decisions and behave accordingly. They demonstrate the interconnectedness and interdependence among beings as well, a principle shared with Western biological ecology.[8]

Some of the Buddha's thought may reflect the fact that the environment in which he lived was changing already because of growing population and economic pressures.[9] Purushottama Bilimoria asserts that the Buddha's preference for forests as a setting for his meditation and teaching may reflect in part the environmental situation: "Gotama was likely reacting to rapid commercial urbanization and the rise of the merchant and artisan classes in his region, and a concomitant agrarian economy responsible for the deforestation of the Ganges region and consequent vanishing of animal life from its natural habitat."[10] Surely if nature was relevant to the Buddha, then it is also relevant to Buddhism.[11]

The Four Noble Truths and the Noble Eightfold Path are at the heart of the understanding and practice of the Dharma, the teachings of the Buddha. The Four Noble Truths address the universality, causes, and reduction of suffering (*dukkha*). Ultimately, a Buddhist aims at ending her or his own suffering by seeking enlightenment (*nibbana*) in the present life and thereby avoiding the suffering inherent in the endless cycle of rebirths (*samsara*).[12]

If in the Dharma, the teachings of the Buddha, *beings* refers to nonhumans as well as humans, then ecological and environmental concerns are inherent in Buddhism. This is apparent, for instance, in the Metta Sutta:

> May all be well and secure,
> May all beings be happy!
> Whatever living creatures there be,
> Without exception, weak or strong,
> Long, huge or middle-sized,
> Or short, minute or bulky,
> Whether visible or invisible,
> And those living far or near,
> The born and those seeking birth,
> May all beings be happy![13]

Especially in the Mahayana tradition of Buddhism in East Asia individuals may become Bodhisattvas by suspending personal pursuit of enlightenment in order to help relieve the suffering of other beings and promote their Buddha-nature, one's inherent potential to become a Buddha. Furthermore, in Mahayana all beings and all things potentially possess Buddha-nature including trees and even rocks.[14]

The way to reduce suffering and pursue enlightenment is to strive to comply with the Noble Eightfold Path. Furthermore, each of its eight principles is relevant to nature to the degree that it is correlated with extending nonviolence (*ahimsa*), compassion (*karuna*), and loving-kindness (*metta*) to all beings.[15] This is illustrated throughout the Jataka legends.

As part of the Noble Eightfold Path, for example, right livelihood includes occupations and lifestyles that do not harm any beings. However, it is impossible to live without causing some harm; even vegetarians harm plants when they are used as food. But a Buddhist should strive as much as feasible to minimize any harm. Here the basic distinction between need and greed is pivotal. By pursuing the Middle Way an individual tries to satisfy as modestly as possible the four fundamental needs that the Buddha recognized: food, medicine, clothing, and shelter. As a result an individual can minimize his or her ecological footprint or environmental impact, including the inevitable waste and pollution from resource consumption. This is reminiscent of the concept and practice of voluntary simplicity.[16]

If the first negative precept of nonviolence (*ahimsa*) and the first positive precept of compassion (*karuna*) and loving-kindness (*metta*) apply to all beings, then the environmental implications are obvious and undeniable.[17] Furthermore, some elements of Buddhism and ecology are similar if not identical, although this is most likely sheer coincidence. In any case,

both Buddhism and ecology hold a monistic rather than dualistic worldview;

do not dichotomize either organism and environment or human and nature;

consider all life, including humans, as subject to natural laws;

apply systems thinking regarding the unity, interrelatedness, and interdependence of the components of nature; and

advocate respect and even reverence for nature.

These complementary parallels between Buddhism and ecology can be mutually reinforcing in both theory and practice for Buddhists.[18]

The *sangha*, the monastic community of monks and nuns, is ideally a sustainable, green, just, and peaceful society. The *sangha* is a small-scale and egalitarian community grounded in nonviolence, moderation, co-operation, and reciprocity in satisfying basic physical needs. Members pursue spiritual development instead of materialism and consumerism.[19] Consequently, with their vow of poverty and voluntary simplicity, among other attributes, monks and nuns hold a mirror up to society on a daily basis. They are highly respected and revered members of society in Asian countries and have extraordinary sociocultural status, prestige, and power. Monks and nuns have significant potential to contribute to more sustainable environmental worldviews, attitudes, values, and practices of lay Buddhists by drawing on the ecological wisdom in the Buddha's life and the Dharma as well as through the example they set.[20]

Many of the more than 200 regulations for monks in the monastic code (*vinaya*) are ecologically relevant.[21] The purpose of several of the rules is to prevent monks from knowingly harming any living being—human, animal, or even plant. *Bhutagama*, the Pali term for a living plant, identifies the home of a being. It is a serious offense for a monk to purposefully cut, burn, or kill any living plant. Harming any animal is also proscribed. Monks should strain or at least check the water that they consume for drinking and other purposes to avoid knowingly harming any visible organisms in it. Monks cannot pollute water in any manner. Thus, in these and many other ways monks are supposed to respect and protect all kinds of other beings.

Many temple complexes are sacred ecosystems with groves of bodhi, banyan, and other trees and their associated fauna. Lay Buddhists as well as members of the *Sangha* are not supposed to disturb plants, animals, and other natural phenomena in and around a temple complex. For instance, Suan Mokkh, a monastery founded in 1932 by Buddhadasa Bhikkhu near Surat Thani in southern Thailand, encompasses 120 acres of forest. In effect it is an island refuge of biodiversity. It is surrounded by rice paddies and rubber tree plantations.[22] Yet even much smaller sacred sites can add up to be ecologically significant, if together they are viewed collectively through space and cumulatively over time, and if it is recognized that most of biodiversity is invertebrates, which are most significant in ecosystem processes like energy flow and nutrient cycling.[23]

Following the Buddha's example, many monks and nuns have devoted much of their time to solitary life and meditation in forests, caves, and along mountains. These secluded and peaceful sites in nature facilitate meditation and enlightenment. This is yet another demonstration of the mutual relevance of Buddhism and nature.[24]

Some forest and village monks have become environmental activists, at least in recent times. They view deforestation as sacrilegious and a threat to the forest monk tradition because the forest is their sanctuary. In addition, out of compassion for the suffering that humans and other beings experience as a result of deforestation, many monks have implemented environmental education programs, sustainable economic development projects, and rituals to protect remaining forests and other aspects of the environment in Buddhist and other countries. One specific tactic is to encourage people to plant trees as an act of merit that also benefits the environment.[25] Another is tree ordination whereby a monk ceremoniously wraps saffron colored cloth around a tree to signal its sacredness. To kill a monk is the worst crime in Buddhism. In effect the tree becomes a surrogate monk and is usually protected.[26]

From ancient times to the present many Buddhists have embarked on pilgrimages to sacred sites associated with the life of the Buddha and other Buddhist personages as well as to temples, shrines, and other sacred places, often located in forests and/or on mountains.[27] One of the most famous is Mount Kailas and at its foot Lake Manasarovar in Tibet. They are sacred to Buddhists, Hindus, Jains, and adherents of the Tibetan Bon religion.[28] Sacred places associated with Buddhism usually require certain prescriptions and proscriptions, such as not harming any beings; thus they function, in effect, as sanctuaries for nature.

Socially engaged Buddhism emulates the example and teachings of the Buddha through the active application of compassion, loving-kindness, and other principles for the benefit of other beings.[29] Among the foremost leaders of socially engaged Buddhism is Sulak Sivaraksa, the prominent Thai author, intellectual, publisher, social critic, and political activist. He is the founder of the International Network of Engaged Buddhists and several other nongovernmental organizations that include a component of environmentalism. He was a recipient in 1995 of the Right Livelihood Award known as the alternative Nobel Peace Prize. One of his books develops further E. F. Schumacher's groundbreaking ideas by applying Buddhist thinking to developing sustainable economics in the face of globalization.[30]

Several other Asian initiatives in Buddhist environmentalism deserve mention. The Buddhist Perception of Nature Project was launched in

1985 and resulted in several important publications including the identification and reproduction of environmentally relevant texts from the Dharma.[31] In 1986 the Venerable Lungrig Namgyai Rinpoche issued "The Buddhist Declaration of Nature" at the World Wildlife Fund 25th Anniversary conference in Assisi, Italy.[32] In 1993 the International Conference on Ecological Responsibility: A Dialogue with Buddhism held in New Delhi, India, agreed on the declaration "Towards Ecological Responsibility: An Appeal for Commitment."[33] Recently a country-wide network of Buddhist clergy was established; it is called the Association of Buddhists for the Environment (ABE) in Cambodia. His Holiness the 17th Karmapa Ogyen Trinley Dorje instituted "Enlightened Activity" and the Thrangu Environmental Club in India. In Thailand the abbots of many local temples have developed remarkable environmental initiatives, such as "The 99,999 Trees Project" that encourages people to plant trees for merit. It started at Wat Nawakaram near Khon Kaen in northeastern Thailand, but the idea has spread into many other parts of the country.[34] At Wat Lan Kuad near the border with Cambodia monks even built a temple complex with over 1.5 million recycled beer bottles.[35]

Buddhism spread beyond Asia into Europe, North America, and elsewhere by at least the mid-nineteenth century.[36] Henry David Thoreau (1817–1862), one of the icons of Western environmental literature, studied Asian philosophy and religion. In 1844, he published in the Transcendentalist periodical *The Dial* the first Buddhist scripture in English, translating from French a portion of the Lotus Sutta.[37] Since then Buddhism has influenced the West in a multitude of diverse ways. For some five decades His Holiness the 14th Dalai Lama of Tibet has been the most influential Asian Buddhist through his worldwide travels and many books. His 1999 book, *Ethics for the New Millennium*, was on the *New York Times* Bestseller List. This and his other books often include some discussion relevant to environmentalism. In his 1989 speech accepting the Nobel Peace Prize he proposed that Tibet become an international peace zone and ecological reserve. In 1990 he was the keynote speaker at the interfaith symposium on "Spirit and Nature: Why the Environment is a Religious Issue" at Middlebury College in Vermont.[38]

The importance of Buddhism in environmentalism in general in the West is evidenced by a list of some of the personages it has influenced and this can be confirmed by an examination of their publications:

Robert Aitken (Zen scholar), Alan Hunt Badiner (journalist), Martine
and Stephen Batchelor (scholars), Fritjof Capra (quantum physics),
Mark Coleman (wilderness meditation), Bill Devall (deep ecologist),
Rita Gross (ecofeminist), Ruben L. F. Habito (Zen scholar), Ernst
Haeckel (biologist coined word ecology), Joan Halifax (anthropologist
and Buddhist spiritual healer), Daniel H. Henning (deep ecologist), Ken
Jones (engaged Buddhist and Green Party activist), Philip Kapleau (Zen
vegetarianism), Stephanie Kaza (environmental ethics), Petra Kelly
(German Green Party), Rick Klugston (Director of the Center for
Respect for Life and the Environment), John Diado Loori (Zen environ-
mentalist), Joanna Macy (Buddhist systems thinker and teacher), Peter
Matthiessen (novelist), Thomas Merton (Trappist monk and writer),
William S. Merwin (ecopoet), Arne Naess (founder of deep ecology),
Helena Norberg-Hodge (Ladakh Project), Steven C. Rockefeller (leader
in Earth Charter), E. F. Schumacher (Buddhist economics), John Seed
(Council of All Beings), Albert Schweitzer (reverence for life), Gary
Snyder (Zen poet and deep ecologist), Michael Soule (founder of conser-
vation biology), David Suzuki (biologist), Henry David Thoreau (envi-
ronmental essayist and poet), Christopher Titmuss (insight meditation
teacher), Alan Watts (counterculture mystic), and Duncan Ryuken
Wiliams (scholar).

Some Buddhists have critically examined the growthmania associated
with the rapacious materialism and consumerism in America together
with alternatives for reducing the ecological footprint of individuals and
societies.[39] Peter Timmerman poses the penetrating question: "How can
we survive on a planet of ten billion points of infinite greed?"[40]
Incidentally, an entire country, Buddhist Bhutan, has turned away from
increasing Gross National Product to instead increasing Gross National
Happiness.[41] Ultimately to promote the survival and welfare of humanity
and nature profound transformations are needed toward more sustainable
and greener lifestyles and societies including radical simplicity.[42]

Global climate change is a reality. The only questions are how bad will
it get, how rapidly, and what measures can be taken to reduce and cope
with its human and environmental impacts?[43] Some Buddhist environmentalists have also been actively concerned with this issue, in particular
John Stanley, David R. Loy, and Gyurme Dorje. In 2009, they co-edited
the remarkable book *A Buddhist Response to the Climate Emergency* with
chapters written by prominent Asian and Western Buddhists from all of

the major traditions. In addition, they developed an accompanying website that includes a Buddhist Declaration on Climate Change.[44]

By now there are more than a thousand Buddhist centers in America alone and many operate extensive mailing lists and informative websites. Often they pursue practices like conserving energy and other resources, recycling, and reducing waste and pollution. Voluntary simplicity is a Buddhist as well as an environmental virtue. Vegetarianism is often pursued using local organically grown foods. Such activities can be observed at Bodhi Tree Forest Monastery, Tullera, Australia; Earth Sangha in Washington, D.C.; Eco-Dharma Centre, Catalunya, Spain; EcoSangha in Seattle; Green Gulch Farm in Sausalito, California; Zen Mountain Center near Mountain Center, California; and Zen Mountain Monastery at Mt. Tremper, New York; among many other Buddhist centers.[45]

Discussions regarding the relevance of Buddhism to nature, environment, ecology, and environmentalism have provoked some criticisms; these revolve mainly around two issues: actual behavior in contrast to ideals, and academic interpretations of texts. However, it should be recognized that there are internal contradictions and discrepancies in every religion as well as within other sectors of society such as government, science, medicine, and education. In the case of Buddhism, the deficiency is not in the Dharma itself, but in Buddhists who are, after all, mere humans, and imperfect like any other humans.[46] There are serious environmental problems in Buddhist countries.[47] Accordingly, one of the Buddhist declarations on the environment, "Towards Ecological Responsibility: An Appeal for Commitment," calls for people of all religions to practice the noble ideals that they preach as well as strive to live a simple lifestyle, use natural resources responsibly, and implement greener environmental actions.[48] Part of the solution is for the public to become better informed about any negative environmental consequences of their behavior and the positive alternatives.[49]

The second main criticism stems from the differences between text and context. This refers to the purely academic understanding of Buddhism, especially the scholarly interpretation of ancient texts in contrast to the actual understanding and practice of Buddhism by its adherents today.[50] Behind much of this criticism is the accusation that Westerners are imposing their modern concerns for ecology and environmentalism on Buddhism, and in the process, appropriating and distorting Buddhist

doctrines, traditions, and texts. Supposedly an authentic scholarly interpretation of the texts by the critics demonstrates that Buddhism is irrel-
evant to such contemporary concerns. However, there is considerable
room among Buddhologists (scholars of Buddhism) for differences of
opinion in the interpretations of the exact same texts.[51] Academic textual
interpretations can be puritanical, literalist, essentialist, absolutist, or fundamentalist, and, in extreme cases, reminiscent of paleontologists inter-
preting the fossil record without any reference to living descendants.
Some ardent critics tend to ignore the reality on the ground: Buddhism
as an enduring lived religion in which core principles like the Eightfold
Noble Path have been applied in coping with various practical matters of
daily life and society for over 2,500 years in a multitude of very different
historical, societal, cultural, linguistic, political and national contexts.[52]
The scholarly study of Buddhist texts in isolation may not have much relevance for the actual reality of the daily practice of Buddhism as a lived
religion; in some cases it can be academic in the negative sense of the term
and even misleading.[53] In any case, most ordinary Buddhists are not
familiar with many of the ancient texts in any depth if at all, but that does
not render them less of a Buddhist in their practice of the basic principles.
Indeed, Seth Devere Clippard argues that Buddhist environmental ethics
is better located in contemporary Buddhist practice than in ancient texts.[54]

Already ample evidence has been cited above to rebut some of the spu-
rious posturing of critics, such as the facts of environmental activism by
Asian Buddhists who are intelligent, informed, and independent agents
regardless of any Western influences. It is also crucial to recognize that
there are individuals who are both Buddhist scholars and practicing
Buddhists. The most notable Asian scholar monks are Buddhadasa
Bhikkhu of Thailand, Thich Nhat Hanh from Vietnam, and his
Holiness the 14th Dalai Lama of Tibet, all three of whom understand that
Buddhism has significant ecological and environmental relevance.
Incidentally, each of these personages represents one of the three main
traditions of Buddhism—Theravada, Mahayana, and Vajrayana, respectively.[55] In addition, it is important to realize that the Buddha himself
repeatedly emphasized that individuals should test his teaching against
their own reason and experience, instead of blindly accepting authority,
tradition, or dogma; by implication this presumably includes texts.

From the published statements of some critics it is obvious that they are
apologists for their own religion, usually Christianity. They are reacting

defensively to criticisms of Christianity as environmentally unfriendly and to suggestions that Buddhism might be a better alternative.[56] This is biased and therefore self-defeating scholarship.[57]

One other claim by some critics is that Buddhism is egocentric and escapist, concerned only with individual enlightenment through meditation, and, therefore, ignores practical problems of ordinary human existence such as the environmental crisis. Ironically, this claim disregards the example of the Buddha himself, who through his discourses was concerned with relieving the suffering of others, and who, among other things, opposed the suffering caused by the caste system and animal sacrifice in India. Furthermore, this claim ignores socially engaged Buddhism which is not any modern invention, even though the particular term is. Witness the practical ideal of Boddhisattva, particularly in the Mahayana tradition. Most of those marshalling this criticism largely, if not completely, ignore the numerous publications and activities on socially engaged Buddhism, including Buddhist environmentalism, that have flourished, especially since the 1980s. As one indicator of the enormous amount of activity in Buddhist environmentalism, on July 3, 2011, a search of Google.com revealed 1,660,000 sites for "Buddhism and ecology," 342,000 for "Buddhist environmentalism," 1,700,000 for "Buddhism and nature," 32,300 for "ecoBuddhism," 16,200 for "ecological Buddhism," 6,040 for "Green Buddhism," and 44,300,000 for Buddhism.

There is no doubt, however, that the world of the Buddha some 2,500 years ago was very different than ours today.[58] People in centuries past never conceived of the environmental problems like anthropogenic mass species extinction or global climate change that have increasingly preoccupied many in recent decades. Yet inevitably new challenges, problems, and issues emerge that necessitate creative interpretations and applications of Buddhism by its followers. Surely this must have transpired throughout the 25 centuries of the history of Buddhism, considering the many contexts and situations in which it has spread and flourished.[59] That Buddhism has endured for so long is clear proof of its continuing relevance and adaptability for its adherents.

If reason and morality follow upon adequate knowledge and understanding of the worsening environmental crises from the local to the global levels, then this may lead to wisdom and action in improving the ways that people interact with nature. The distinctive difference of Buddhism is that, instead of grounding environmentalism in the self-interest of the individual (egocentrism), society (sociocentrism), or the human species (anthropocentrism) as most Western approaches advocate, it is based on respect for other beings and things as interconnected and interdependent as well as possessing their own intrinsic value or Buddha-nature (ecocentrism).

The Buddha repeatedly stated that ultimately he taught only about two matters: the cause and the end of suffering. Inevitably suffering will increase in the future because of the pressures of human population growth, the failure to distinguish between needs and wants, and the assumption of industrial society and capitalist economies that unlimited material growth and economic development are possible in spite of a limited resource base. Consequently inequality, competition, conflict, violence, and war will only intensify in the future generating even more suffering. Therefore, Buddhism will likely become even more relevant than ever before, given its central focus on suffering.[60]

There is no better way to conclude this chapter than with the thought-provoking insights of Thich Nhat Hahn: "Scientists tell us that we have enough technology to save our planet. . . . Yet we don't take advantage of this new technology. . . . The technological has to work hand-in-hand with the spiritual. Our spiritual life is the element that can bring about the energies of peace, calm, brotherhood, understanding, and compassion. Without that, our planet doesn't stand a chance."[61]

CHAPTER 6. MEDIEVAL RADICAL, SAINT FRANCIS OF ASSISI[1]

There is no question that Francis was in advance of his age, as he anticipated all that is liberal and sympathetic in modern times: the love of nature, the love of animals, the sense of social compassion, the sense of the spiritual dangers of affluence.

Henryk Skolimowski[2]

"Assisi is perhaps the only place commonly revered by Christians of all expressions and by Buddhists, Muslims, and animists as well" asserts Norbert Brockleman.[3] The reason is the association of Assisi with the legendary Saint Francis, " . . . perhaps the most widely admired figure of the Middle Ages."[4] Located at the foot of Mount Subasio, which since antiquity has included a sacred spring, the medieval town of Assisi in Italy has been recognized as a UNESCO World Heritage Site since the year 2000. It is visited by more than five million tourists annually. This is the birthplace of Francesco Bernardone, dated at 1181 or 1182, who eventually became known worldwide as Saint Francis of Assisi. It is where he lived most of his life until death in 1226.

The church of San Damiano is where Francis is supposed to have experienced his first revelation from God. This led him to renounce his wealthy family and its materialism to pursue instead an ascetic life of humility, celibacy, simplicity, poverty, and charity, one marked in particular by a sincere compassion and loving-kindness toward all beings, nonhuman as well as human. Some of his ideals are reflected in the famous "Canticle of the Creatures" that he composed in 1225. In it nature is allegorical; Francis humanizes God's creation through his reference to affective kinship terms and bonds conveying respect and reverence for all of creation, inanimate things as well as animate beings. It even reflects a version of species equity as opposed to speciesism; that is, the equality of all beings as part of God's creation, instead of a strictly anthropocentric and hierarchical worldview of inherent human superiority. As Susan P. Bratton observes, "Francis treated the nonhuman portions of the cosmos as equals." Moreover, Francis viewed nature in terms of profound kinship within a community based on the biblical idea that God is continually creating the diversity that exists in nature and embracing it through love (Genesis 1:31, 9:12–16).[5]

The Canticle represents what might be called a theistic ecocentric environmental ethic, or more commonly *creation spirituality*.[6] In it Francis recognized and celebrated the interconnectedness and interdependence of all beings and things, something confirmed by the twentieth century in the sciences of evolution, genetics (shared DNA code), and ecology.[7] The Canticle is a forerunner of some elements of deep ecology as well as spiritual ecology. Francis's profound compassion, loving-kindness, and reverence for creation extended to sheep, lambs, bees, worms, snakes, flowers, stones, the four elements, vineyards, and harvests.[8] Biographer Omer Engelbert writes: "Francis cherished the tiniest forms of life. He would pick up worms lying on the road and put them to one side to keep them from being crushed. ... He built nests for doves. ... He gave his new cloak to redeem two lambs being carried off to the butcher."[9] Thus, Francis rescued animals from harm and even mediated between humans and animals when either were endangered as in the famous legend of the wolf of Gubbio. In turn, animals were attracted to Francis, something that profoundly influenced him.[10] His legendary sermon to the birds at Bevagna in 1215 is celebrated in many ways, such as in a passage in the journals of his fellow Franciscans titled *The Flowers of Saint Francis*, in the famous painting by Giotto di Bondone in the Basilica, and even in a piano composition by Franz Liszt called "St. Francis of Assisi Preaching to the Birds."[11]

Francis and his fellow Franciscans prayed and meditated in quiet and often in solitude in forests and caves and on islands and mountains. Nature was their cathedral for the worship of God as much as any human construction.[12] For Francis and his followers, the divine spirit permeated all creation, a variant of Pantheism with some elements of Animism as well.[13] Francis even walked over rocks with reverence in consideration of Christ being referred to as the rock in the Bible.[14] David Kinsley writes:

> It is in the life of Saint Francis of Assisi that we have the most unambiguous example in medieval Christianity of the affirmation and embrace of nature. ... Francis's rapport with nature, his interest in it and love for it, is often described in terms of its relationship to the religious life, aspects of the life of Jesus, or its utility for human

beings. . . . Francis had affection for nonhuman creatures as brothers and sisters, and in this sense he stands apart from almost all other Christians who came before or after him. . . . Francis saw in them beings who had an intrinsic worth. He valued individual animals and would often go out of his way to protect them from harm.[15]

In his seminal essay on "The Roots of the Ecologic Crisis," Lynn White, Jr., an expert historian on Medieval Europe, astutely observes: "The key to an understanding of Francis is his belief in the virtue of humility—not merely for the individual but for man as a species."[16] White went further; he even proposed Francis as the patron saint of ecologists.[17] Then on November 29, 1979, Pope John Paul II in his Papal Bull called "Inter Sanctus" declared Francis to be the "Heavenly Patron Saint of Ecologists" in recognition of his "marvelous gift of fostering nature." Moreover, Susan Power Bratton asserts: "The Franciscan declaration that nature was worthy of human attention, and therefore of scholarly study, forwarded systematic observation of nature and the development of the empiricism which produced modern science. Not coincidentally, a number of the greatest medieval scientists were Franciscans."[18]

Francis's worldview and values were likely stimulated in part by the economic and ecological changes that he witnessed from early in his life. Medieval Europe of the later twelfth and early thirteenth centuries underwent a period of far-reaching transformations with the transition from feudalism to capitalism, ensuing class struggles, increasing urbanization, marked population growth, agricultural expansion, and extensive forest clearance. These conditions, plus the powerful force of Francis's charisma and example, already by 1226 attracted some 20,000 followers to the mendicant order of the Franciscans in Italy, Spain, France, Germany, England, Hungary, Turkey, Morocco, and the Holy Land.[19] Franciscanism was the most powerful social and spiritual movement of its age, it presented a radical alternative way of thinking, seeing, feeling, and being. Furthermore, Franciscans were active in the universities of the thirteenth and fourteenth centuries, and became missionaries in many parts of the world.[20]

Francis referred to himself as the Poverello (poor little man).[21] The relationship between Francis's life committed to poverty and all of Creation as kin is best stated by Norman Wirzba: "Many accounts of Francis speak eloquently of his intimate identification with the wide creation and his intense delight in particular creatures. It is as though by entering into friendship with creation Francis also entered more deeply into the power and grace of God. The prerequisite for this friendship, however, was the holy poverty that stripped Francis of self-interest and self-possession. Throughout his life he admonished his followers to be like Christ in refusing to grasp anything for themselves alone. The creation does not exist for us to possess or manage, but to celebrate."[22] Leonardo Boff remarks: "The more radical poverty is, the closer the human beings come to raw reality, and the more it enables them to have an overall experience, and communion without distance, in respect and reverence for otherness and difference. Universal kinship results from this practice of essential poverty."[23]

The Franciscans have been recognized by some as the first environmental movement, although others would vehemently dispute this.[24] Today many Franciscans are environmental activists, but not the majority. Brother Keith Warner worked with a reforestation cooperative in the Pacific Northwest in planting 600,000 trees and lobbied with the Religious Campaign for Forest Conservation. Franciscan sisters run Michaela Farm for organic food production in Oldenberg, Indiana. Sister Rita Wienken directs the Franciscan Earth Literacy Action Center on 500 acres in Tiffin, Ohio. Boff practices liberation theology in Brazil and in 1997 authored the book *Cry of the Earth, Cry of the Poor*.[25]

Some Catholic laypersons have also been influenced by Francis as well, but again, not the masses most of whom appaear indifferent to environmental concerns. One particularly interesting and moving case is that of journalist Bert Schwartzchild from San Francisco, a sister city of Assisi. During a vacation in the Assisi area he was hiking on Mount Subasio on October 4, 1982. He heard gun shots and was disturbed to discover that birds were being hunted for sport. Schwartzchild decided to camp out that night. He heard a beautiful nightingale song, and then the bird mysteriously approached close to him. This became a deeply moving spiritual experience for him. It stimulated him to launch an international campaign to conserve Mount Subasio and prohibit hunting.[26] This led to the formulation of the Mount Subasio Declaration and eventually the establishment of the Subasio Regional Park, Assisi Nature Council, and Action for Nature. Mount Subasio reaches an altitude of 1,290 meters. It includes three ecological zones: the lowest with olive trees; the middle with ash, beach, maple, and oak forest; and the top with meadows and karst terrain.

The Mount Subasio Declaration of 1985 includes a statement recognizing the profound influence of Saint Francis's " ... extraordinary perception of the communion of all living beings and inanimate things through his profound love of the whole of Creation and for his cosmic vision in which all parts of nature are felt as necessary to the whole and therefore respected in a spirit of brotherhood. ... "[27] Notable among the other environmental activists involved in these developments to protect Mount Subasio were artist Maria Luisa Cohen and head of the Sierra Club David Brower.

Francis was particularly concerned with the poor and sick, the latter including outcast lepers who were most despised and feared by medieval society. Francis even lived among lepers, provided care for them, caressed them, and ate from the same bowl.[28] In this and many other respects, including his treatment of nonhuman beings, he presented a serious challenge to the secular and religious establishments of his day.[29] Nevertheless, in spite of the Franciscan movement no real revolution developed. How different the world might have been—at least the Catholic portion—if it had.

Each year many Catholic churches perform a special ceremony to bless animals in honor of Saint Francis. At this ceremony in the Cathedral of Saint John the Divine in New York City composer Paul Winter's *Missa Gaia Earth Mass* is performed and dedicated to Francis.[30] Participation in the ceremony reflects biophilia, the natural affinity of humans and their affective attraction for animals and nature in general from childhood onward.[31] Certainly Francis's inclusiveness in showing respect, reverence, compassion, and loving kindness for all beings is exemplary. He is widely recognized and appreciated beyond Catholicism as well. For instance, he is among those selected for inclusion in the book *Fifty Key Thinkers on the Environment*.[32] At the same time, it needs to be emphasized that Francis's view of nature and relationship with it was first and foremost as God's creation. He was not an ecologist who is a student of nature nor an environmentalist who is its defender, these domains did not develop until the twentieth century even if they have ancient roots.[33] However, the primacy of God in Francis's mind does not negate his very special relevance for ecology and environmentalism. His special kind of ecology was a vehicle for his spirituality.

For some Catholics, Francis is the original spiritual ecologist. This is reflected in the growing amount of literature and films exploring his relevance for modern environmentalism, much of it by Catholic authors, editors, and/or publishers.[34] Francis prioritized the spiritual over the material, one of the fundamental principles of spiritual ecology. For Medieval Europe he was radical, and he remains so to this day. Indeed, the converse, prioritizing the material over the spiritual, is one of the causes of ecocrises.

Finally, a statement by Boff is most appropriate in concluding this chapter: "Intuitively and without any previous theological training, Francis reclaimed the truth of paganism: this world is not mute, not lifeless, not empty; it speaks and is full of movement, love, purpose, and beckonings from the Divinity. It can be the place for encountering God and God's spirit, through the world itself, its energies, its profusion of sound, color, and movement. The Sacred dwells in it; it is God's extended Body."[35]

PART II. TRUNK

Two icons in the history of nature studies and environmentalism are Henry David Thoreau and John Muir, famously associated with Walden Pond and Yosemite, respectively. They actually lived spiritual ecology in nature. Each in their own way were radical and revolutionary ecosaints. Their distinctive legacies certainly endure. Less well known is the ever provocative and controversial Rudolph Steiner who pioneered in what he referred to as spiritual science in the face of the chasm and antipathy between religion and science in Western civilization growing since the Enlightenment. Among many others who are part of the trunk of spiritual ecology, several merit special mention though limited space does not allow discussing them at length: George Perkins Marsh for his early warning about human resource depletion and environmental degradation; Anna Botsford Comstock who led the development of the field of nature study, Rachel Carson who sounded the alarm about the chemical poisoning of nature, and Aldo Leopold for his Land Ethic. Each of them had awesome experiences in nature. The contributions of the above pioneers are among the components that comprise the magnificent trunk of spiritual ecology.

CHAPTER 7. THE SPIRIT OF WALDEN, HENRY DAVID THOREAU

... the wellspring for the passion that drove public speech and action in behalf of the environment was in large part religious and ethical. Environmentalism, in short, had become one version of nature religion in the lingering shadow of American transcendentalism.

Catherine L. Albanese[1]

A man lives alone in a forest where he is dedicated to experiencing nature in as intimate a manner as possible and with deep reverence. No, in this instance he is not a Buddhist monk or other holy personage in Asia, rather he is Henry David Thoreau (1817–1862) at Walden Pond woods near Concord, Massachusetts from July 4, 1845 to September 6, 1847. Yet already in 1840, Thoreau translated a portion of the Lotus Sutra from French into English, the first Buddhist scripture to be published in English, in this case in the transcendentalist journal called *The Dial*. Thoreau, like his fellow transcendentalist and mentor Ralph Waldo Emerson, was profoundly influenced in his thinking by reading Asian religions and philosophies. As John James Clarke remarks, "It might be going too far to suggest ... that Thoreau embarked on his Walden experiment in the spirit of Indian asceticism, ... nevertheless he was evidently influenced by oriental concepts of self-discipline, detachment, and contemplation, and repeatedly expressed admiration for the emphasis of Hinduism upon meditation and non-attachment."[2] Also, Thoreau tended to emphasize vegetarianism in his diet.[3] While residing at Walden Thoreau usually ate only the foods that he grew in his own garden. He planted no more than he could consume himself.[4]

Emerson's thinking was permeated by Hindu ideas as was that of Alexander von Humboldt and Ernst Haeckel, two early German pioneers in ecology.[5] But unlike them and Thoreau, Emerson was not an outdoor person or field naturalist, although he read extensively about natural history. Thoreau read Humboldt, Charles Darwin, Charles Lyell, and others. In particular, Humboldt represented a cosmic vision of nature as one great whole to be approached through the loving and precise study of its multitude of details in the wild, rather than in dead specimens in a laboratory or museum, viewing the organism and its environment ecologically as part of an interconnected web of life.[6]

Thoreau is most famous for his experiences at Walden recorded in 1854 in his book simply titled *Walden; or, Life in the Woods*. Therein he stated his main goal: "I went to the woods because I wished to live deliberately, to front only the essential facts of life. And see if I could learn what it had to teach and not, when I came to die, discover that I had not lived."[7] Also he reflected: "The earth I tread on is not dead, inert mass; it is a body, has a spirit, is organic, and fluid to the influence of spirit, and to whatever particle of that spirit is in me."[8] Thus, Thoreau resonated with elements of thought and practice in Animism and Pantheism as well as Buddhism and Hinduism. Living at Walden for more than two years became a practical, spiritual, and symbolic exercise for Thoreau.[9]

Transcendentalism is pivotal for understanding Thoreau. The most outstanding proponent of transcendentalism was his friend Emerson, also a philosopher, essayist, and poet from Concord. Emerson wrote in his essay *On Nature* (1849) that "Particular natural facts are symbols of particular spiritual facts. ... Nature is a symbol of spirit."[10] The book of nature, like the Bible, revealed sacred truths. Emerson lectured widely, founded the Natural History Society as well as the transcendental movement, and edited its magazine *The Dial* (184–1844). As the previous quote alludes, transcendentalism is a free-thinking alternative to customary ideas about religion, instead focusing on self and nature as the locus of spirituality. It is opposed to scientism, which worships science as the exclusive path to knowledge, understanding, and truth. Transcendentalism prioritizes spirit over matter while rejecting the purely objective, empirical, and analytical approach to nature. Most fundamentally, it recognizes, explores, and celebrates the unity of nature and spirit. Thus, transcendentalists seek enlightenment through communion with nature, as did Thoreau at Walden. Moreover, transcendentalism is a syncretic mixture of Native American spiritualism, Asian spiritual traditions, Pantheism, European romanticism, and natural philosophy.[11] Clarke writes: "The underlying philosophy of New England transcendentalism ... represented a commitment to ancient and universal ideas concerning the essential unity and ultimately spiritual nature of the cosmos, combined with a belief in the ultimate goodness of man and the supremacy of intuitive over rational thought. Its deeply spiritual outlook was one which sought to go beyond creeds and organized religions in favour of a religious experience deemed to be universal."[12]

The transcendentalists were the most significant literary movement in nineteenth-century America. They were strongly influenced by the German idealists Immanuel Kant and Johann Wolfgang von Goethe, and by the English romanticists Thomas Carlyle, Samuel Taylor Coleridge, and William Wordsworth; both movements reacted against Enlightenment philosophy and science. In turn, American transcendentalists Emerson, Thoreau, Margaret Fuller, and others influenced Walt Whitman, Emily Dickinson, and T. Starr King.

To better understand Thoreau and other New England transcendentalists it is helpful to briefly examine the historical ecology of New England in its Native American, European colonial, and industrial eras. The Indians had adapted to the natural landscape of the region. Natural resources were used for subsistence to meet basic biological and social needs. These were pursued through swidden farming as well as hunting, fishing, and gathering in a rotational system of land use with communal rights. While sustainable, their subsistence economy included the use of fire. They had a cumulative impact on their habitat over the long-term, influencing plant communities and associated fauna. In marked contrast, however, the European colonials transported ideas about economy and nature as well as animals and plants from their homeland. They viewed land and resources as commodities in a market economy. Colonists engaged in intensive farming and the raising of domestic livestock from Europe, practices which together with permanent land use and private property ultimately proved unsustainable. Their forest clearance for agriculture, construction of buildings, ships, and eventually railroads, mining, and other activities contributed to resource depletion and environmental degradation. Industrialization accelerated human impact on nature including the pollution of soil, water, and air. Thoreau was among those witnessing the legacy of agricultural development and the beginning of industrialization. It is no wonder that Thoreau and other individuals became alarmed at the growing impact of society on the environment of New England. The degradation of nature was also desecration from the perspective of many like the transcendentalists. Likewise, Thoreau lamented the colonial impact on Native Americans whom he tended to view as closer to nature.[13]

Thoreau was unusually critical of the society, religion, government, warfare, and science of his time. He rejected materialism, industrialization, and urbanization. Instead, he advocated a return to a rural agrarian lifestyle in communion with nature as much as possible. The church was viewed as an artificial box that cut off the worshipper from nature and encouraged hatred of the forest which he envisioned as a natural temple.

Thoreau considered Walden Pond to be an eye on the world, Heaven, Earth, and one's inner self. He considered the unity of life as encompassing a vast and complex economy of nature. For Thoreau, a sustainable domestic economy should be the foundation for society's treatment of nature; the rest would follow from that. He recognized and pursued the intrinsic value of nature—namely, that nature deserves respect and reverence in its own right. Accordingly, Thoreau walked barefooted, sat for hours on end in solitary contemplation of nature, swam naked in the pond, submerged himself in the swamp, and so on.[14] In his 1862 essay "Walking" Thoreau wrote: "When I would recreate myself I seek the darkest wood, the thickest and most interminable and, to the citizen, most dismal swamp. I enter a swamp as a sacred place, a sanctum sanctorum. There is the strength, the marrow, of Nature."[15]

Thoreau was an individualist, libertarian, dissident, social critic, subversive, abolitionist, and pacifist as well as a nature mystic. Fellow citizens in Concord criticized his Pagan and Pantheistic tendencies as well as his positive views of Hinduism and Buddhism.[16] However, Thoreau asserted: "If a man does not keep pace with his companions, perhaps it is because he hears a different drummer. Let him step to the music which he hears, however measured or far away."[17] But Thoreau was not simply an independently minded nonconformist, he was a remarkably farsighted visionary. Robert L. Dorman remarks: "In the twentieth century, when his fame and influence were the greatest, Thoreau was to be recognized as the archetype of the Romantic loner-naturalist and the patron saint of the environmental movement."[18]

The legacy of Thoreau is apparent in the work of many nature writers, ecologists, environmentalists, and conservationists (especially preservationism), as well as in the specific environmental movements of bioregionalism, back to the land or reinhabitation, and voluntary simplicity. Elements of environmental philosophy, environmental ethics, deep ecology, ecopsychology, and spiritual ecology are also part of his legacy. For example, Thoreau realized a basic principle of ecopsychology, the connection between alienation from nature and human health problems, physical and emotional.[19] Among those that Thoreau clearly influenced are John Muir, Rachael Carson, Aldo Leopold, Edward Abbey, Arne Naess, Gary Snyder, Annie Dillard, Wendell Berry, and E. F. Schumacher, all seminal environmental thinkers and leaders in their own right.[20] For instance, Muir carried writings by Thoreau and Emerson on his travels and clearly revered them as spiritual mentors.[21] At the same time, in spite of Thoreau's famous mantra about wilderness as the preservation of the world, he was a localist; he was attached to his own region almost exclusively. Thoreau did not travel widely beyond adjacent states in New England, this in marked contrast to Muir, Humboldt, Darwin, and other naturalists.[22]

As one illustration of Thoreau's economic and environmental wisdom, he wrote that "a man is rich in proportion to the number of things he can afford to let alone." This also reflects the Taoist admonition of Dao De Jing: "He who knows he has enough is rich."[23] Zoologist Daniel Kozlovsky in his book *An Ecological and Environmental Ethic* even formulated the fundamental rule of ecology: "Live as simply and as naturally and as close to the earth as possible, inhibiting only two aspects of your unlimited self; your capacity to reproduce and your desire for material things."[24] Perhaps Kozlovsky had Thoreau at Walden in mind. Likewise, Thoreau's example is reflected in engineer Jim Merkel's book *Radical Simplicity*.[25] Merkel identifies his spiritual principles for radical simplicity as kindness, compassion, love, responsibility, limits, and fascination.[26]

Thoreau's approach to nature as a naturalist, environmental philosopher, and nature writer and poet was in sharp contrast to that customary in the science of his time and since; it was spiritual, holistic, ecological, ecocentric, and subjective. He emphasized the intrinsic rather than extrinsic value of nature. For instance, Thoreau believed that trees had inherent rights as living entities.[27] Through fieldwork he observed nature alive, rather than as dead specimens in the laboratory or museum. His approach was to engage in communion with nature, instead of becoming alienated from it. Yet many of his observations of nature foreshadowed later scientific discoveries. For example, his essay on "The Succession of Forest Trees" published in 1860 anticipated the development of community ecology and its concept of ecological succession in modern science. Still, science has usually neglected the aesthetic and especially spiritual values of nature, at least overtly.[28]

Thoreau accumulated thousands of pages of journal entries with detailed observations on the natural history and landscape of the Concord area as well as from his limited travels into other states. Yet most of Thoreau's publications are actually posthumous, some surprisingly recent: *Excursions* (1860), *The Maine Woods* (1864), *Cape Cod* (1865), *A Yankee in Canada* (1866), *Natural History Essays* (1980), *Faith in a Seed* (1993), and *Wild Fruits* (1999). In 1906, the publisher Houghton, Mifflin & Company printed the series *The Writings of Henry David Thoreau* in no less than 20 volumes.[29]

Dorman identifies Thoreau as the patron saint of American environmentalism.[30] Surely Thoreau is also an original American spiritual ecologist, exemplary in his thoughts and actions.[31]

CHAPTER 8. WILDERNESS DISCIPLE, JOHN MUIR

*Few are altogether deaf to the preaching of pine trees. Their sermons on
the mountains go to our hearts; and if people in general could be got
into the woods, even for once, to hear the trees speak for themselves,
all difficulties in the way of forest preservation would vanish.*

John Muir[1]

Who is the most famous environmental conservationist of the nineteenth
century and why? Many informed people would probably quickly answer
without hesitation John Muir, although others might name Theodore
Roosevelt or Gifford Pinchot in addition.[2] Muir achieved national recognition by authoring hundreds of newspaper and magazine articles as well
as 14 books advocating the virtues of nature and its preservation, especially
wilderness protection.[3] But there was far more to Muir's environmentalism than his prolific publishing.

Muir was a lifelong pacifist, worldwide vagabond, roving mountaineer,
astute naturalist, recognized botanist, inspiring nature writer, crusading
environmentalist, and, without any doubt, underlying all of that, a profound nature mystic. He lived and communed with nature in Yosemite
almost continuously from 1869 to 1873. Theodore Roosevelt, U.S.
president from 1901 to1909, requested in 1903 that Muir guide him in
Yosemite. Muir convinced him to camp overnight. This three-day camp-
ing experience inspired Roosevelt to launch various conservation policies
with far-reaching consequences. The "naturalist president" set aside no
less than 230 million acres of wild America for posterity.[4]

In guiding the president in Yosemite, and through his environmental
campaigns, and other initiatives as well as his writings, Muir was a prime
mover in the establishment of national parks and forests in the United
States. These included Yosemite, Sequoia, Mount Rainier, Petrified
Forest, and the Grand Canyon. His work also laid the ground for the creation of the U.S. National Park Service in 1916. Today in the United
States there are 59 national parks covering 51,900,000 acres. They attract
millions of visitors each year.[5] Moreover, Muir's preservationist efforts
were emulated gradually in other countries throughout the world. As Bill

McKibben observes, "Muir's prose introduced an ecstatic new grammar and vocabulary of wildness into the American imagination; in some sense, every national park on the planet owes its existence to the spell he cast."[6]

Muir was one of the founders of the Sierra Club in 1892 with its initial purpose of preserving his most sacred space, the Sierra Nevada in California, which he referred to as the "range of light." He served as its first president and primary spokesman for 22 years until his death in 1914 at the age of 76.[7] By now the Sierra Club is one of the oldest and largest environmental organizations in the world, its current membership around 1.4 million.

Some more personal background on Muir helps in understanding these and other aspects of his last legacy. He was born in 1838 in Dunbar, Scotland, a small farming and fishing community. During his childhood he explored the surrounding coast, moors, and hills.[8] In 1859 his family emigrated to homestead in the frontier of central Wisconsin near Portage. There he explored the nearby forest, lake, bog, and other environments. In 1861–1862, he took courses of special interest at the University of Wisconsin, but did not finish a degree. (Later in 1897 he was recognized with an honorary LLD degree at Wisconsin.) Muir's courses included geology, botany, and literature. Thereafter Muir was self-taught by nature in what he called the University of Wilderness.

During his youth Muir suffered temporary blindness in one eye from an accident in a carriage factory where he worked in Indianapolis, Indiana. He vowed to dedicate the remainder of his life to studying God's creation. After he regained his eyesight, from September 1867 to March 1868 Muir traveled and botanized alone by walking about a thousand miles from Indianapolis in Indiana to Cedar Keys in Florida. During this journey he minimized his material burden by carrying only a rubberized bag with a comb, brush, towel, soap, change of underwear, a few books including the New Testament, a journal, map, and plant press.[9] This was something akin to a vision quest. In his journal Muir recorded his change of address as "John Muir, Earth-planet, Universe."[10] Indeed, Muir was a worldwide explorer. After Florida he explored Yosemite from 1868 to 1872. By 1873 he was based in the Bay area of San Francisco, but was still hardly sedentary. He visited Alaska 1879–1899, the Southwest 1905–1914, traveled around the world to Europe, Asia, Australia, and New Zealand 1903–1904, and to South America and Africa 1911–1912.[11]

In some respects Muir's travels were pilgrimages in nature. Thoroughly grounded in Christianity by his father, Muir memorized most of the Bible during his childhood. However, subsequently he concentrated on passages of the Bible that sustained his ecospirituality, instead of those that Lynn White and others have interpreted as encouraging the exploitation and destruction of nature.[12] Yet in time the mountains of Yosemite became Muir's temple.[13] Also, some authors have detected elements of nature mysticism, transcendentalism, Pantheism, Animism, Buddhism, and Daoism in Muir's writings. Muir became a nature mystic, finding the spiritual in nature itself.[14]

While a student at the University of Wisconsin Muir had been inspired by reading the transcendentalists Ralph Waldo Emerson and Henry David Thoreau. Later he carried some of their writings with him on various trips.[15] Emerson himself journeyed to Yosemite where he met Muir in 1871. Later in 1893, after the deaths of Emerson and Thoreau, Muir visited Concord and Walden Pond.[16] While Muir never read extensively into the literature of Asian philosophies and religions, he visited India during his world tour of 1903–1904.[17]

Wilderness has long provided a very special space for many to experience the awesome beauty, power, and mystery of nature.[18] Muir believed that wilderness could heal and liberate people, at least temporarily, from the oppressive burdens of civilization, cities, and materialism. This is not a unique view. John Lionberger in *Renewal in the Wilderness: A Spiritual Guide to Connecting with God in the Natural World* depicts wilderness as an extraordinary transformative place where people can partake, in solitude and silence, in an ancient universal experience that brings them to the present moment, returns them to their very essence, and deeply connects them with the transcendent. He explores wilderness from the perspectives of Buddhism, Christianity, Islam, Judaism and other religions. Surely Muir and other pioneering spiritual ecologists would endorse work such as Lionberger's[19]

Interestingly, the name "Muir" refers to "a wild stretch of land."[20] More than any other space, Muir was personally attracted to wilderness. He saw it as the primary source of humanity's spiritual health. The late twentieth-century concepts of biophilia and topophilia—the love of nature and landscapes, respectively—as well as the developments of deep ecology and ecopsychology during the same period, were anticipated in some ways by Muir. Clearly he was well aware of the ecological interconnections and interdependencies within nature; he had reverence as well as respect for nature; and he viewed nature as having intrinsic value, including things like rain and rocks in addition to plants and animals.[21] He would even climb a tree at night in order to experience the excitement and force of a storm.[22]

Muir perceptively identified the universal need for beauty, purity, and spirituality in nature as part of the public interest in his call for the federal government to preserve remaining areas of wilderness.[23] As Robert L. Dorman observes about Muir: "His spiritual and aesthetic pleas on behalf of wilderness preservation, taken from the journal and published as books and articles of broad appeal, were to make wilderness an *institution* in the sense that it was to acquire an enduring value in the public mind."[24]

Throughout much of his adult life Muir pursued all three basic components of spiritual ecology—intellectual, spiritual, and activist. Catherine L. Albanese remarks about Muir and others: "It became increasingly clear that the wellspring for the passion that drove public speech and action in behalf of the environment was in large part religious and ethical. Environmentalism, in short, had become one version of nature religion in the lingering shadow of American Transcendentalism."[25] This religious or spiritual aspect helps explain the deep emotion and dedication often involved in environmentalism as well as the potential for conflict with competing interests.[26]

Strictly speaking, Muir was a *nature preservationist*, in contrast to his contemporary Gifford Pinchot (1865–1914), who was a resource conservationist. Muir wanted to protect wilderness as untouched areas of nature, and for its own sake as well as for its aesthetic and spiritual significance for humankind. In contrast, Pinchot's "wise-use" approach was the rational and efficient use, management, and development of land and natural resources for present and future generations, reflecting the concepts of multiple use and sustained yield. He was committed to increasing commercial timber production, but myopic in neglecting its larger ecological consequences. Pinchot was trained as a professional forester at the National Forestry School in France. In 1901 Pinchot launched the School of Forestry Studies at Yale University. Then in 1905 he was appointed by President Roosevelt as the first Chief of the newly established U.S. Forest Service. In that capacity Pinchot was instrumental in the development of the first system of National Forest in the U.S., already by 1909 covering as much as 195 million acres.[27]

Pinchot and Muir, each in their own way, were seminal influences in the development of U.S. government policies for environmental conservation during 1890–1920, its formative period and the time of rapidly diminishing frontier and resources as well as unprecedented rates of population growth, industrialization, economic development, and urbanization.[28] But their different perspectives fueled a heated debate between Muir, whom many considered to be a romanticist, elitist, and shortsighted fanatic, in sharp contrast to Pinchot's pragmatic and progressive conservationism. Eventually a debate exploded between the two men over the damming of the Hetch Hetchy Valley adjacent to Yosemite National Park to construct a reservoir to supply water for San Francisco. Muir vehemently opposed the project with all his heart and soul. The two friends became estranged. The controversy dragged out through 1903–1913 as the two men debated in popular magazines like the *Atlantic Monthly*, *Century, Harper's Weekly*, and *Outlook*.[29] However, ultimately Pinchot was successful, and the dam was built. J. E. de Steiguer comments that "perhaps because of this struggle, coupled with his crushing defeat, Muir soon retired from public life and died not long afterward."[30] However, Muir might yet win because more recently there have been calls to remove the dam and allow the valley to recover naturally.[31]

These two environmental pioneers had very different views of nature and the causes of resource depletion and environmental degradation about which George Perkins Marsh, among others, had sounded the alarm.[32] Pinchot, a conservationist, utilitarian, and anthropocentric bureaucrat, reduced such problems simply to the inefficient use of resources and instead championed sustainable use through scientific and technocratic management. In contrast, Muir, an ecocentric idealist, took a much broader perspective in considering such problems to result from increasing land and resource consumption generated by population growth and economic development. He emphasized the preservation of the forest cover of watersheds and their soils following George Perkins Marsh.[33] These two schools of thought, exemplified by Muir and Pinchot, persist to this day.[34]

These opposing schools also illustrate the false dichotomy between environment and economy—that is, that they are supposedly mutually exclusive, and that it is necessary to pursue one at the expense of the other. This neglects the fact that an economy and a society can only be as healthy as their environment, a fact that is increasingly being driven home at great human as well as economic expense by the growing impact of global climate change. Perhaps, instead of an either-or situation, to some degree the opposing positions of Muir and Pinchot may be reconciled by recognizing that some areas should be exploited sustainably, while others should remain wilderness, especially those that are richest in biodiversity. Yet which areas, how much of them, and in what ways will continue to be contested.[35]

The establishment of national parks required "pure nature" and thus, as a consequence, in many cases led to the expulsion and dispossession of indigenous societies from their homelands. This was a reflection of the times. However, this gross injustice often occurs to this day in spite of far more recognition of the relationship between human rights and environment. Wilderness was envisioned as an uninhabited natural Eden, not as a landscape inhabited by and partially created by Native Americans.[36] The debate which flourished in the 1990s over the so-called "myth of the ecologically noble savage" has implications for questions of wilderness conservation. The conflict over whether or not to allow some kind of human use of protected areas, and especially by local indigenous and other communities who have long resided in the place, continues, although some environmental organizations advocate co-management with local communities.[37] While national parks and other protected areas help preserve regions of nature that are sacred to Westerners, the sacred places of Native Americans and other indigenes are often contested, threatened, degraded, or even destroyed.[38] This conflict between Western and indigenous perspectives, the former focused on political economy, the latter on spiritual ecology, mirrors the contrasting perspectives of Pinchot and Muir in some ways. A related issue is the essentialist versus constructionist perspectives on nature: for example, whether wilderness really exists in nature independently of humans, or is simply imaginatively conceptualized by particular human groups for their own political, economic, aesthetic, and other purposes (as a historical, cultural, and political construction).[39]

Muir's life and work, including the debates and conflicts he confronted, illustrate one of the strengths and one of the weaknesses of spiritual ecology. On the one hand, underlying environmentalism there is often a foundation of religious and/or spiritual experience in nature that generates deep passion, motivation, and commitment to work on behalf of the welfare of nature. On the other hand, such ecospirituality may be opposed by purists and absolutists among both conservative theists and radical atheists. Few environmentalists, and especially those who are scientists, will openly admit their grounding in spiritual experiences in nature for fear of being dismissed as irrational, superstitious, and/or delusional, thereby weakening their cause. However, if many more would admit such ecospiritual grounding, then this might add to the momentum and force of spiritual ecology as well as environmentalism and conservation in the long run.

Muir's seminal contributions undoubtedly endure in many ways, as demonstrated by Muir Woods National Monument established in 1908 just outside San Francisco; John Muir College founded in 1966 at the University of California in San Diego; a special conference on Muir at the University of the Pacific every five years since 1980 as well as the John Muir Center established in 1989; the minting of the California State Quarter featuring his image in 2005; and his induction into the California Hall of Fame at the California Museum for History, Women, and the Arts in 2006.[40] Muir's far-reaching influences are apparent in the subsequent work of prominent nature writers and environmentalists like Aldo Leopold, Rachael Carson, Arne Naess, Gary Snyder, David Brower, and a multitude of others.[41] Perhaps most of all Muir's legacy is manifest in the generations of leaders and members of the Sierra Club. Clearly humanity and nature would be far poorer without the legacy of the wilderness spiritual ecology of Muir.[42]

CHAPTER 9. SPIRITUAL SCIENCE, RUDOLF STEINER

*For what lies inside the human being is the whole spiritual cosmos in
condensed form. In our inner organism we have an image of the entire
cosmos.*

Rudolf Steiner[1]

Austrian Rudolf Steiner (1861–1925) has not been adequately recognized
as a pioneer in spiritual ecology. Trained in the rigors of science, math-
ematics, and philosophy, he was a highly original and progressive thinker.
He developed anthroposophy (wisdom of the human being) from elements of European transcendentalism and theosophy in pursuit of synthesizing science and mysticism, something he initially termed *spiritual
science*. In so doing he was able to transcend the confines of a narrow naturalistic, materialistic, mechanistic, and reductionistic worldview.

Before saying more about Steiner, something should be said about transcendentalism and theosophy. Transcendentalists privileged the spiritual
or intuitional over the material or sensory sources of knowledge and
understanding, individual experience over the social, and originality over
conformity. They opposed religious orthodoxy and regimentation, but
recognized the divine in humanity and nature. While not rejecting
Christianity they also explored the religions of Asia. They pursued ration-
alism yet championed emotional experience. Transcendentalists like
Ralph Waldo Emerson and Henry David Thoreau experienced nature in
pastoral and wilderness settings supposedly uncorrupted by civilization.
Nature was a book to be read and interpreted. Basic tenets of theosophy
include pursuing a middle ground to reconcile science and theology, a
middle ground that engaged the ancient wisdom ranging from that of traditional indigenous people to Buddhism, humankind as an integral part of
a process in which cosmic evolution becomes conscious of itself, and
monism (the unity of all beings as more basic than any differences or
distinctiveness).[2]

Returning to Steiner, it is important to understand that he rejected
faith-based spirituality. He defined spiritual science as the rational and
scientific investigation of the spiritual world. He distinguished between

65

religion based on belief and spirituality based on the senses and other forms of perception. He asserted that spirituality augments the physical sciences. He claimed to base his thinking on direct perception and knowledge of spiritual phenomena, supersensory knowledge. Steiner considered indigenous and other traditional beliefs in spiritual beings and forces, sometimes referred to as elemental beings, to be grounded in spiritual reality.

Steiner hoped to revolutionize humanity's relationship to nature, envisioning a spiritual co-evolution of humankind and nature. The natural and spiritual were a unity (monism). He believed that nature became conscious through human beings. He sought to develop a spirituality based on an ecology that recognized the interdependencies in nature. In such thinking Steiner is even more relevant today than before, given the ongoing and worsening ecocrisis.[3]

Steiner was strongly influenced by Johann Wolfgang Goethe and edited the poet's nature writings. In 1912 Steiner established the Anthroposophical Society, which by now has around 50,000 members in 70 branches in 50 countries. It is associated with some 10,000 institutions, among them more than 1,000 Waldorf schools. Another practical application of his holistic philosophy is biodynamic agriculture, a forerunner of elements of organic farming without chemical fertilizers and pesticides, engaging not only natural processes but also the spiritual aspects of nature. Steiner viewed the healthy farm as a self-nourishing and maintaining organism, and advocated organic fertilizers, limited tillage, and free-ranging livestock. Steiner also anticipated some of the problems resulting from the use of chemicals in farming, industrialization, and deforestation among other twentieth-century developments.

By the end of the nineteenth century, Steiner had gained substantial academic respect, but recognizing that the academic establishment would reject many of his ideas he addressed instead the wider public through his numerous lectures (over 6,000), voluminous writings (some 40 books), both now published in 330 volumes, and his diverse creative activities including in natural medicine, architecture, art, drama, and farming. To this day many have recognized the validity and utility of many elements of Steiner's work.[4] For instance, Bron Taylor writes: "Steiner sought esoteric truths in nature and encouraged others to do so as well. Through the philosophy he developed, called *anthroposophy*, the invention of biodynamic farming, and the Waldorf schools he inspired, he contributed substantially to sustainability movements and green politics in Europe and beyond."[5]

At the same time, much criticism and controversy has surrounded Steiner from his time to the present.[6] Yet many of his ideas are echoed by a multitude of diverse individuals in other contexts and terms, although this may be completely independent of Steiner.[7] Undoubtedly some aspects of Steiner's writing are clearly factually inaccurate and even just plain ridiculous in light of modern knowledge. Yet to summarily dismiss in total Steiner's thought would be comparable to the proverbial throwing out the baby with the bath water. One of the most critical prerequisites for spiritual ecology is an open mind—which is also the case for any science and scholarship worthy of the name.

The purpose of anthroposopy is best described on the website of the organization, General Anthroposophy Society:

> Anthroposophy is a source of spiritual knowledge and a practice of inner development. Through it one seeks to penetrate the mystery of our relationship with the spiritual world by searching for answers and insights that come through a schooling of one's inner life. It draws, and strives to build, on the spiritual research of Rudolf Steiner, who maintained that every human being (anthropos) has the inherent wisdom (sophia) to solve the riddles of existence and to transform both self and society. .... He is increasingly recognized as a seminal thinker of the 20th century and one of humanity's great spiritual teachers.[8]

To illustrate Steiner's profound thinking, here are some excerpts:

"In the human being continual material processes go on that are really spiritual processes."

"We are really so closely linked to the world that we cannot take a step into nature without falling under the direct influence exercised on us by our intimate relationship with everything."

"It is certainly not without interest to see that in the case of cultures which have preserved the best parts of humanity's ancient, sacred wisdom there is a deep sympathetic and loving treatment of animals."

"A plant by itself is not a reality."

"Children should feel from the very beginning that they are standing on a living earth. This is of great significance for their whole life."

"Now a farm comes closest to its essence when it can be conceived as a kind of independent individuality, a self-sustaining entity."[9]

Such ideas are reflected in spiritual ecology to this day, whether or not they derive directly from Steiner, some of his contemporaries or antecedents, and/or have been independently discovered.[10]

PART III. BRANCHES

A great number and variety of impressive branches radiate from the giant trunk of spiritual ecology. The relevance for environmentalism of Martin Buber, the famous Jewish philosopher, has not been sufficiently recognized, even though he viewed nature as a fellow subject, instead of a mere object. Lynn White, Jr., ignited a firestorm of controversy in mainly blaming the application of the prevalent interpretation of selected passages in the Bible for the environmental crisis. The various reactions by Christian theologians and others to White's thesis generated the field of ecotheology which remains an important component of spiritual ecology to this day. Transcending ecotheology is the cosmic ecospirituality of Pierre Teilhard de Chardin and Thomas Berry as major branches of spiritual ecology. They among others greatly influenced several extraordinary scholars who variously developed the intellectual scope, aims, and substance of contemporary spiritual ecology since the 1990s; highlighted here are Steven C. Rockefeller, Mary Evelyn Tucker, John Grim, Bron Taylor, and Roger S. Gottlieb. Any scrutiny of the status of spiritual ecology before and since their benchmark contributions demonstrates their profound and far-reaching intellectual impact through organizing and documenting a professional approach to the subject. Furthermore, they continue to make important new contributions. Others who should at least be noted—although space does not allow discussion at length—are Neopagan specialist Graham Harvey; Jain Satish Kumar as prime mover behind the development of Schumacher College and the periodical Resurgence; Seyyed Hossein Nasr, who pioneered the study of Islam and ecology; and explorer of Buddhist environmental ethics and sacred trees Stephanie Kaza.

CHAPTER 10. NATURE AS THOU, MARTIN BUBER

But it can also happen, if will and grace are joined, that as I contem-
plate the tree I am drawn into a relation, and the tree ceases to be an
It. ... Does the tree then have consciousness, similar to our own?
I have no experience of that. But thinking that you have brought this
off in your own case, must you again divide the indivisible? What
I encounter is neither the soul of a tree nor a dryad, but the tree itself.
Martin Buber[1]

Martin Buber (1878–1965) was a Jewish philosopher and theologian born in Vienna, Austria. In 1930, he became an honorary professor at the University of Frankfurt am Main in Germany, but resigned his professorship in protest when Adolph Hitler came to power in 1933. He left Germany in 1938 for Jerusalem in what was then the British Mandate for Palestine. He held a professorship in philosophy at the Hebrew University from 1938 to1951. Buber is generally recognized as one of the most prominent Jewish philosophers of the twentieth century.

A prolific author, Buber is best known for his book *I and Thou*, published in 1923. That book is a synthetic thesis about dialogical existence. He envisioned two modes of consciousness: being and interaction, I-Thou and I-It. *I-Thou* is a subjective relationship and a dialogue emphasizing the intrinsic value of the other as autonomous, equal, and an end in itself. In contrast, *I-It* is an objective relationship and a monologue emphasizing the extrinsic value of the other as a means to one's own ends. An individual is involved in these in relation to other individuals, objects, and reality in general. Ultimately, however, any relationship connects with God. For Buber, the Hasidic ideal involved living in the unconditional presence of God without any separation between daily and religious life.[2]

As a contemporary example, in the old-growth forests of the Pacific Northwest the I-It and the I-Thou relationships are exemplified respectively by a logger and Julie "Butterfly" Hill. She displayed extraordinary dedication in trying to protect a forest area. She occupied a small platform in a giant redwood tree named Luna where she lived 200 feet above the ground for 738 days starting in 1997. She braved winter cold and storms among other hazards and even the possibility of death. Hill and her team were successful in obtaining a 3-acre buffer zone around Luna in perpetuity from Pacific Lumber/Maxxam Corporation. Thereafter Hill launched the Circle of Life Foundation and more recently the Exchange Network. While not Jewish, Hill clearly relates to nature as Thou.[3]

Although not necessarily directly influenced by Buber, an informal Jewish environmentalist group, the Redwood Rabbis, is of interest here as well. Since 1995, its members have campaigned against deforestation and in favor of the protection of the old-growth redwood forests and groves of California. They have pursued letter writing campaigns, public demonstrations, civil disobedience, and inter-religious collaboration as well as religious rituals and ceremonies. In January 1997, for example, they protested the logging of ancient redwoods in the Headwaters Forest ecosystem of Humbolt County, northern California, an area of around 60,000 acres. Some 250 people, including 100 Jewish worshippers, began with the Tu Bi Shevat, the Jewish New Year Ritual of the Trees. A representative from the local chapter of the Sierra Club described the threat to the ancient redwood forests of the Maxxam Corporation from Huston. Then a participant chanted the Kaddish, a mourner's prayer, in memory of the many beings killed or displaced by the logging operations. Next, as an act of civil disobedience, the group planted redwood seedlings along an eroded stream bank inside the property of Maxxam, which had refused permission to plant. They wanted to demonstrate their hope for restoration of the lands and waterways degraded through the clear-cutting by the logging company. Charles Hurwitz, Maxxam CEO and a major stockholder, was a prominent member of the Jewish community of Huston and many officers and board members were also Jewish. Thus, the demonstrators appealed to him to honor the traditional Jewish reverence for trees. However, some leaders and members in Hurwitz's Jewish community in Huston objected to the personalization of the issue of the redwoods and to the politicization of the High Holidays. In any case, The Redwood Rabbis convinced Maxxam and its subsidiary, Pacific Lumber, to establish a forest reserve of 7,470 acres and to apply restrictions on logging in the Headwaters Forest of Northern California, the largest stand of unprotected old-growth redwoods anywhere. Redwoods can grow up to 300 feet tall and live for 2,000 years. Surely these noble ancient beings merit reverence and protection.[4]

There have been other environmental actions on this redwood issue by various Jewish groups. For instance, in 1998, the Coalition on the Environment and Jewish Life (COEJL) asked for stronger protection of the Headwater Forests and all redwoods. The COEJL was established in 1993 and by now has 29 member organizations throughout the United States representing the full range of Jewish traditions.[5]

It is noteworthy that there has long been a special reverence for trees in Israel:

> In ancient times it was a custom to plant a cedar sapling on the birth of a boy, and a cypress sapling on the birth of a girl. The cedar symbolized the strength and stature of man while the cypress signified the fragrance and gentleness of woman. When the children were old enough, it was their task to care for the trees which had been planted in their honour. Today the main celebrations on Tu Bi Shevat is the tree planting ceremony, when pupils from every school assemble and follow their teachers into the country-side to plant young seedlings. ... It makes the children aware of the need for re-forestation and soil conservation to beautify the country.[6]

Viewing and treating nature as Thou instead of It extends far beyond Buber and Judaism as an attitude, by whatever name, at the very foundation of spiritual ecology. It is reflected in diverse manifestations of spiritual ecology, such as John Muir's preservationism to protect wilderness in contrast to Gifford Pinchot's conservationism to use land and resources sustainably. The former emphasizes the intrinsic value of nature and a more ecocentric approach, the latter emphasizes the extrinsic value of nature and a more anthropocentric approach. Nature as Thou is also manifested in various ways in Animism, Paganism, Pantheism, and deep ecology.[7] For instance, the founder of deep ecology, the Norwegian philosopher Arne Naess, asserts that deep ecology involves a transformation from I-It attitudes to I-Thou attitudes in the human-nature relationship, thereby explicitly acknowledging Buber's ideas.[8]

The influence of Buber on Jewish environmentalist thought and actions may not always be apparent, but as one of the most famous Jewish philosophers of the twentieth century he profoundly influenced contemporary thinking about elemental relationships between humans, humans and the divine, and humans and nature. Hava Tirosch-Samuelson writes: "Buber's ideas became ecologically relevant and very influential, because he extended the "I-Thou" relationship to an encounter with nature. ... Buber personified natural phenomenon and recognized not only the need of humans to communicate with natural objects but also the inherent rights of nature. Nature is a waiting Thou, waiting to be addressed by the wholeness of our own being."[9] Accordingly, Rabbi Michael Lerner remarks: "... the upsurge of Spirit is the only plausible way to stop the ecological destruction of our planet. Even people who have no interest in a communal solution to the distortions in our lives will have to face up [to] this ecological reality. Unless we transform our relationship with nature, we will destroy the preconditions for human life on this planet."[10]

Chapter 11. Challenging Christians, Lynn White, Jr.

Both our present science and our present technology are so tinctured with orthodox Christian arrogance toward nature that no solution for our ecologic crisis can be expected from them alone. Since the roots of our trouble are so largely religious, the remedy must also be essentially religious, whether we call it that or not. We must rethink and refeel our nature and destiny.

Lynn White, Jr.[1]

A fateful encounter with snakes stimulated Lynn White, Jr. (1907–1987) to begin thinking about how the attitude toward nature varies with different religions. In 1926, while visiting Ceylon (now called Sri Lanka), he observed mounds of earth left on a new road under construction. Workers explained that each mound surrounded a snake's nest. The workers were local Buddhists who believed that the snakes should not be disturbed, but left alone to exit their homes on their own accord. White speculated that the snakes would probably have been harmed if the colonial supervisors from Scotland, who were likely Presbyterians, wielded the shovels instead of the locals. This incident eventually led to his famous essay.[2]

In an article titled "The Historical Roots of Our Ecologic Crisis," White argued that Christianity is a major cause of the environmental crisis. His essay was published in the journal *Science* in 1967. It is supposed to be the single most frequently cited article in the entire history of that periodical. Part of the reason White's essay attracted so much attention is the venue in which it was published, that of the American Association for the Advancement of Science, the premier scientific organization in the United States of America. Another reason for the attention it received is simply the cogency and force of the bold argument that White marshaled. However, probably the most important reason is its critique of Christianity; it ignited a controversy that continues to this day more than four decades later.

White's critique did not stem from any antagonism toward religion as an atheist or agnostic. He was a Christian and earned an MA from the Union Theological Seminary in 1928. Subsequently he was awarded an MA and PhD in history from Harvard University, the latter in 1934. White taught at the leading universities of Princeton, Stanford, and UCLA. His scholarly books *Medieval Technology and Social Change* in 1962 and *Medieval Religion and Technology* in 1978 as well as his other works gained the highest respect from historians and others, yet he is best known by far for the 1967 essay.

In his now-classic article White adopts a mentalist or idealist position: "What people do about their ecology depends on what they think about themselves in relation to things around them. Human ecology is deeply conditioned by beliefs about our nature and destiny."[3] In other words, what people think about nature and their relationship to it has a significant influence on their behavior, and that, in turn, has practical consequences for the natural environment. This contrasts with a materialist position that would place the emphasis instead on the environmental impacts of population, technology, and economy.

White wrote that "especially in its Western form, Christianity is the most anthropocentric religion the world has seen."[4] In particular, he pointed to the biblical mandate in Genesis 1:26–29 and 9:1–3 to be fruitful and multiply, and to fill the earth and subdue it. However, White did not actually quote these or other biblical passages, although other authors did so in responding to him.

In White's view the environmental crisis was the result of a combination of factors and was the product of the synergy among Christian religion (particularly Protestantism), Western science, technology, economy, and culture. Nevertheless, he stressed that the primary cause was the prevalent interpretation of particular passages in the Bible by Christians. This led to a theocentric and anthropocentric environmental ethic stressing dualities (e.g., human/animal), hierarchy (human superiority over other animals), and utility (extrinsic value of animals and other aspects of nature). In turn, this worldview, in tandem with science, made possible the objectification, commodification, desacralization, and exploitation of nature as nothing more than merely resources for human extraction and consumption.

Christianity replaced, or at least suppressed, pre-existing local religions, according to White. As Christianity spread into new areas, it often appropriated sacred sites of prior religions by building on them its own churches and other religious structures. All of this contributed to the desacralization of nature and removed any religious constraints on its exploitation to the point of resource depletion and environmental degradation to a far greater extent than ever before. In White's words: "By destroying pagan animism, Christianity made it possible to exploit nature in a mood of indifference to the feelings of natural objects."[5] These attitudes were reinforced by developments in Western science and technology since the Enlightenment. It is noteworthy that other prominent scholars—including Arnold Toynbee and Aldo Leopold—had thoughts similar to those of White.[6] Curiously White didn't seem concerned about the ecological relevance of the other Abrahamic religion, Islam.[7]

White also suggested possible solutions for the environmental crisis. He argued that "more science and more technology are not going to get us out of the present ecologic crisis until we find a new religion or rethink our old one."[8] He entertained three alternatives: a reversion to Animism, a turn toward some Asian religion, or a reinterpretation of Christianity and Judaism. He didn't think that the first two were viable in modern Western society.

For the Eastern alternative, White pointed to Zen Buddhism in particular, and especially its stance on the unity of humans and nature. He recognized the beatniks and counter-culture movement of the 1950s and 1960s, which included some elements of Asian religions and philosophies as potentially revolutionary, but had failed to engage much of American society in any fundamental transformation. He was skeptical that Buddhism would ever make much headway in the West because of the very different historical trajectories and cultural contexts of Western and Eastern societies. However, deep ecology was developed initially by Norwegian philosopher Arne Naess, who was influenced in part by Asian philosophy and religion including Buddhism. The American pioneer who contributed most to deep ecology is the Zen Buddhist, essayist, poet, and environmentalist Gary Snyder.

In his essay White actually devoted only two sentences to Zen Buddhism as an alternative, whereas Saint Francis of Assisi was discussed in six paragraphs. White advocated a more feasible transformation of human-nature relations in the West through a reinterpretation of Christianity following the lead of Saint Francis: "We must rethink and refeel our nature and destiny. The profoundly religious, but heretical, sense of the primitive Franciscans for the spiritual autonomy of all parts of nature may point a direction. I propose Francis as a patron saint for ecologists." White described Saint Francis as "the greatest radical in Christian history since Christ . . ."[9] Although Saint Francis attracted a considerable following in Medieval Europe and beyond, and although his legacy endures to this day in various manifestations, he did not revolutionize Catholicism let alone Christianity or Western society as a whole. Still, Pope John Paul II declared him the "Heavenly Patron Saint of Ecologists" in 1979.

Responses to White's essay range from warmly positive and constructive to virulently negative and destructive. Some critics even stooped to personal attacks, accusing White of being anti-Christ, a communist, one who was destroying Christianity, or even threatening Western civilization.[10] In addition to academia, White's article was discussed and debated in the popular press (such as the *Christian Century*, *New York Times*, *Sierra Club Bulletin*, and *Time* magazine).[11] Basically there were four different responses to his thesis: demonstrate that other interpretations of the Bible were feasible; pre-Christian societies also degraded their habitat; adherents to other religions have done likewise; the environmental crisis did not become serious until the nineteenth century with the Industrial Revolution. Nevertheless, the prevailing interpretation of the Bible was despotic in relation to nature.[12] Some of the scholarly responses and subsequent developments can be found in a book edited by Eugene C. Hargrove titled *Religion and the Environmental Crisis*. Ian Bradley argued that Christianity is intrinsically green and has just been misinterpreted by most of its followers. In 1996 Robert Whelan, Joseph Kirwan, and Paul Haffner marshalled a critique of green spirituality with an agenda of defending Christianity against White and fearful of a possible reversion of some to Paganism. In 2008 the *Green Bible* was published with over a thousand passages highlighted in green to point out reverence for nature, stewardship, and other environmentally friendly ideas.[13] By now dozens of other works have gone beyond a critical reaction to White to reconsider and advocate the green potential of Christianity.

Although White's essay was only five pages in length, the ensuing discussion and debate contributed substantially to the development of a whole new field of scholarly inquiry called *ecotheology*, much of it devoted to a reactionary defense of Christianity. White also stimulated an initial surge of interest in the relationship between religions and ecology more generally. When David Kinsley published the first textbook on spiritual ecology in 1995 he included Chapters 8 and 9 respectively to address the question as to whether Christianity is harmful or beneficial to the environment. In 1996 a whole new academic journal emerged called *Ecotheology*. (In 2007 this periodical was transformed into the *Journal for the Study of Religion, Nature and Culture* with far broader scope and more diverse contents.) White is still frequently referenced, as for example by several different contributors to the benchmark *Handbook of Religion and Ecology* edited by Roger S. Gottlieb in 2006. White's ideas continue to be reflected in numerous works in philosophy, ethics, history, religion, and other studies related to the environment and ecology.[14] In short, his article was also a major catalyst in the development of spiritual ecology, especially its intellectual component.

In 1986, however, there was a seminal turning point toward a new direction in spiritual ecology. The Basilica of Saint Francis in Assisi was the venue for the twenty-fifth anniversary celebration of the international conservation agency called the World Wildlife Fund (WWF). First, instead of blaming one or more religions for the environmental crisis, this conference looked to religions for solutions, a far more constructive and broader approach than White and much of ecotheology. Second, the international conference facilitated interfaith dialogue and collaboration. H. R. H. Prince Phillip, then President of WWF, welcomed the participants with a charge: "Come, proud of your own tradition, but humble enough to learn from others." Third, the meeting engaged scientists, environmentalists, conservationists, and government officials as well as religious leaders and adherents.[15] One concrete result was the publication of a booklet called *The Assisi Declarations* in which leaders from Buddhism, Christianity, Hinduism, Islam, and Judaism each offered a brief statement on environmental ethics for their own followers.[16]

The format of the Assisi meeting provided a model emulated by subsequent conferences sponsored by WWF and later independently by other organizations. In 1995 another WWF conference at Windsor Castle in England yielded additional declarations on environmental ethics from Baha'i, Jainism, Sikhism, and Taoism. A similar WWF conference was held that same year in Ohito, Japan. It produced the interfaith "Declaration on Religion, Land and Conservation" and added statements by representatives of Shintoism and Zoroastrianism.[17] Subsequently, independent conferences at Middlebury College in 1990 and Harvard

University, 1996–1998, followed the precedent set by the Assisi meeting.[18] All involved a more constructive approach to the relationship between religion and ecology—encompassing interfaith dialogue, and also meaningful interaction between religious and secular leaders, the latter including scientists, scholars, environmentalists, conservationists, and others—thereby developing spiritual ecology in new directions beyond White, albeit clearly indebted to him.

The WWF conferences contributed to another important development, the Alliance of Religions and Conservation (ARC), initially based at Manchester Metropolitan University under the leadership of Martin Palmer. He pursued Theology, Religious Studies and Chinese from 1973 to 1976 at Cambridge University, England, gaining his MA in 1979. Currently he is Secretary General of the Alliance of Religions and Conservation (ARC) which he co-founded with HRH Prince Philip Duke of Edinburgh in 1995. Palmer is also Director of the International Consultancy on Religion, Education and Culture (ICOREC) established in 1983. By now Palmer and his team at ICOREC have been working on Chinese culture and religion for more than a quarter of a century and have produced many translations and presentations of Chinese Classics and other works.[19] In addition, he is a regular contributor to BBC World Service and BBC Radios 3 & 4 as well as television programs for the BBC including the series *Exploring Planet Earth*. Furthermore, Palmer is author or editor of over 50 books as well as a popular lecturer in over 50 countries including the United States, Turkey, India, and Mongolia.

ARC outreach generated a pioneering book series for the general public, each on a different religion in relation to ecology.[20] These foreshadowed the later more ambitious academic series from the Forum on Religion and Ecology published by Harvard University Press.[21]

The vision of ARC is to reduce the environmental impact of people through greater adherence to ecologically relevant aspects of their religious beliefs. The strategy of ARC is to help faiths realize their potential to be proactive on environmental matters and to help secular groups to become active partners in collaboration with religious organizations. ARC encourages and assists religious groups in the application of their powerful influence and resources for the widest possible environmental benefits through a focus on six key areas: stewardship of land and assets; education at the community level and beyond; information campaigns in the print, radio, television, and internet media; relating human and environmental health; promoting lifestyle changes that take advantage of consumer power; and advocacy in environmental practices and policies. For example, ARC recognizes that about 7 percent of the habitable surface of the earth is owned by just 11 faiths. Accordingly, they could contribute significantly to reducing human environmental impact.

Among the various initiatives implemented by ARC are Sacred Land, Living Churchyards, Sacred Gardens, Pilgrimage Trails and Shrines, Sacred Gifts for a Living Planet, International Interfaith Investment Group, and the ARC website and Bookshop. For instance, the Churchyards Project encompasses 6,000 sacred ecosystems in Britain without the use of pesticides and mowing grass only once a year in order to allow birds, bats, reptiles, and insects to thrive. In addition, 6,000 saplings from 2000-year-old churchyard trees were planted in churchyards throughout Britain. Many of them will still be alive in another 1,000 years.[22]

The Sacred Land Project was changed to become the Sacred Sites Programme in 2007, thereby shifting from Britain to a global focus and also consulting with national governments and others besides faiths. By now thousands of religiously based environmental projects have been implemented. As one example, the Association of Forests, Development and Conservation in Lebanon was initiated in 1993. It pursues the conservation of 13 forest areas in that country, most notably the Harissa Forest, a sacred area for Maronites. It has also sponsored interfaith conferences.[23]

In contrast to White's approach, largely remembered, although unfairly, for only placing the blame on Christianity for the environmental crisis, the conference in Assisi marked a major turning point in the history of spiritual ecology. Yet it built on the legacy of White. As K. S. Shrader-Frechete remarks, it remains true that "how to view man's relationship to the environment is one of the great moral problems of our time."[24] In this regard, religions of the world have a special role to perform in contributing toward more sustainable, greener, just, and peaceful societies. Historian White initiated a conversation with far reaching consequences that continues to this day, in the process making history himself.[25]

CHAPTER 12. SUPERNOVAS

Humanity may destroy the possibilities for life on earth unless the free-dom and power that we have acquired are channeled in new creative directions by a spiritual awareness and moral commitment that tran-scend nationalism, racism, sexism, religious sectarianism, anthropocen-trism, and the dualism between human culture and nature. This is the great issue for the 1990s and the twenty-first century.
Steven C. Rockefeller and John C. Elder[1]

Among scholars contributing to spiritual ecology, five stand out because of their exceptionally high creativity, productivity, and impact: Steven C. Rockefeller, Mary Evelyn Tucker, John Grim, Bron Taylor, and Roger S. Gottlieb. Each of them has cultivated their own niche in this emerging field of academic thought and pragmatic action. Taken together they may be best considered as mutually reinforcing in synergy. *There is obviously a very substantial qualitative difference in the status of spiritual ecology prior to and since their work.* They are supernovas in the sense of each generating a rapid burst of scholarly energy, creativity, and luminosity on an unprec-edented scale. No doubt their most constructive and far-reaching contri-butions and influence will continue well into the future as a major component and catalyst of the quiet revolution that is spiritual ecology in the twenty-first century. Here the work of each is briefly considered in turn, although only an entire book on each would do them justice.

Our environment is one subject that should readily generate dialogue and collaboration among a multitude of individuals and groups of diverse backgrounds and persuasions for the elemental reason that we are all pas-sengers on the same spaceship called Earth. The first major interfaith dis-cussion on spiritual ecology in the United States was held at Middlebury College in Vermont in the autumn of 1990.[2] Buddhist, Christian, indige-nous, Islamic, and Judaic religions were represented. The proceedings are documented in an edited book and film, both titled *Spirit and Nature*. The main speakers were John C. Elder, J. Ronald Engel, Tenzin Gyatso (His Holiness the 14th Dalai Lama of Tibet), Sallie McFague, Seyyed Hossein Nasr, Robert Prescott-Allen, Steven C. Rockefeller, Imar

Schorsch, and Audrey Shenandoah. They are authors of chapters in the edited book generated from the conference and portions of their speeches appear in the historic film.[3]

The principal organizer and director of the conference as well as the first co-editor of the book was Steven C. Rockefeller, a Professor of Religion at Middlebury College. In the Introduction the editors identify the goal of this conference:

> Its purpose was to foster ways of imagining and living in the natural world that promote sustainable development, joining scientific understanding with life-affirming moral values and world-affirming religious values."[4] Some of the seminal questions explored in the conference were: "In what sense does the environmental crisis reflect a crisis of moral values and religious faith? What spiritual resources do the various religious and ethical traditions of the world hold for us at such a time? What do the different traditions have to say to one another today that may clarify what it means to have a proper respect for the earth in our personal and social choices? And how do religious traditions need to be reevaluated and reconstructed in light of our increasing environmental difficulties?[5]

Rockefeller begins his own chapter with this statement: "Humanity's search for its spiritual center and the quest for a new way of life in harmony with ecological stability are converging today. The environmental crisis cannot be addressed without coming to terms with the spiritual dimension of the problem, and the spiritual problems of humanity cannot be worked out apart from a transformation of humanity's relations with nature. The integration of the moral and religious life with a new ecological worldview, leading to major social transformations, is a fundamental need of our time."[6] He reflects further on this: "The split between the head and the heart in Western culture has found expression in the divisions between science and faith, fact and value, spirit and nature, ultimate meaning and everyday life, the sacred and the secular, the individual and community, the self and God, male and female, and oppressor and oppressed."[7]

To resolve the ecocrisis Rockefeller asserts that an anthropocentric perspective and utilitarian value toward nature, as exemplified by Gifford Pinchot's wise-use, needs to be replaced by an ecocentric perspective and intrinsic value toward nature, as exemplified by Aldo Leopold's "land ethic."[8] The moral community must be extended, nonhuman beings and things have their own values and rights as do future generations. Community encompasses kinship, identity, interdependence, shared destiny, and the common good. Most of all experience of the sacred in nature is needed to generate the radical personal and social transformations that are needed to restore balance and harmony between humanity and nature. This includes recognizing that human domination, exploitation, and abuse of other humans and of nature are interrelated, thus both social and environmental justice must be pursued.[9]

Rockefeller concludes:

> One might call what is happening a new kind of 'Great Awakening.' It is in part a response to the acute environmental degradation, social fragmentation, international conflict, and psychological stress that mark the times. On the positive side, it is the result of the convergence of a variety of social, scientific, international, ethical, and religious movements that all point to the urgent need for a transformation in our way of life based upon a new sense of interdependence, community, and responsibility that is global and intergenerational, including women and men, all races and religions, all life forms, and the Earth as a whole. People are led to embrace this new way of imagining the world and living by traveling diverse pathways, which are often interconnected. They include diverse religious visions, moral democracy, various holistic philosophies, the new physics, the science of ecology, reverence for life, deep ecology, the practice of I and thou, feminism, and the ethics of sustainable development.[10]

In his chapter, J. Ronald Engel, Professor of Social Ethics at Meadville/ Lombard College, perceptively identifies six more or less successive phases in the exploration of the nexus of religion and ecology:

1. Critical assessment of any influence of religions in the development of the ecocrisis;
2. Recovery and affirmation of areas and points of positive relevance of different religions;
3. Dialogue among religious and secular individuals and organizations including from conservation and science;

4. Specific environmental action projects the number of which has grown exponentially;

5. Identifying specific ways in which religions can learn from each other; and

6. International coalitions of religiously motivated individuals addressing the ecocrisis.[11]

This historic conference with the resulting edited book, and especially with the film televised on PBS, brought to the attention of a large public audience throughout the United States the question of why the environment is a religious issue. It also demonstrated the possibilities for pursuing common interests in a mutually respectful and constructive dialogue and effective collaboration among individuals from very different religions and organizations, possibilities that the other extraordinary academics discussed in this chapter have effectively pursued.

Mary Evelyn Tucker and John Grim, individually and as a team, have edited numerous books and published their own monographs as well; organized more than two dozen major international interdisciplinary conferences and edited the resulting book series and some individual volumes; developed a unique website with a wealth of most useful information; and collaborated in various organizations and practical projects, all of this on the relationship between religion and ecology. Also Tucker and Grim were among the founders of the special journal *Worldviews: Environment, Nature and Culture* that started in 1997. Each is a Senior Lecturer and Research Scholar at Yale University in the School of Forestry and Environmental Studies, Divinity School, and Department of Religious Studies where they are developing an MA program in Religion and Ecology.[12]

Tucker and Grim co-edited one of the earliest anthologies on religion and ecology with contributions from leading academic specialists on Confucianism, cosmogenesis, ecofeminism, environmental ethics, deep ecology, Hinduism, Jainism, and Native North American worldviews and ecology. They continue to build on this initiative, but far more broadly and ambitiously, through serving as Editorial Advisors for the Ecology and Justice book series of Orbis Press as well as in organizing a series of ten conferences on the world's religions and ecology hosted in the Center for the Study of World Religions at the Harvard University Divinity School during 1996–1998.[13]

These international and interdisciplinary conferences were collectively attended by more than 800 individuals. Most of the conferences focused on a particular religion in relation to ecology and environmentalism: Buddhism, Christianity, Confucianism, Daoism, Hinduism, Indigenous Traditions, Islam, Jainism, Judaism, and Shinto. Subsequently a substantial anthology with an extensive bibliography was published as a result of each conference by Harvard University Press, although the volume on Shintoism was only published in Japan in Japanese. The Islamic volume was translated into Arabic, Urdu, and Turkish, while the ones on Confucianism, Daoism, and Buddhism were translated into Chinese. The Hinduism and Jainism volumes were also published in India. The primary goal of these conferences and books is to outline the contours of a whole new multidisciplinary field of study on religion and ecology that also has implications for contemporary environmental ethics, public policy concerns, and related matters.

In addition three culminating conferences in the autumn of 1998 were held at the American Academy of Arts and Sciences (AAAS) in Cambridge, Massachusetts, the United Nations in New York City invited by the UN Environmental Programme (UNEP), and the American Museum of Natural History (AMNH) in New York City. The museum venue drew an audience of around a thousand people. Subsequently Tucker and Grim initiated the first research project on world religions and global climate change consisting of two conferences and a resulting co-edited issue of the journal *Daedalus* in Fall 2001.[14]

The primary principle behind much of the work by Tucker and Grim is most concisely stated by Tucker:

> Clearly religions have a central role in the formulation of worldviews that orient humans to the natural world and the articulation of rituals and ethics that guide human behavior. In addition, they have institutional capacity to affect millions of people around the world. Religions of the world, however, cannot act alone with regard to new attitudes toward environmental protection and sustainability. The size and complexity of the problems we face require collaborative efforts both among the religions and in dialogue with other key domains of human endeavor, such as science, economics, and public policy.[15]

Many of the pivotal questions in this arena of spiritual ecology are identified by Tucker:

Theoretically, how has the interpretation and use of religious texts and traditions contributed human attitudes regarding the environment? Ethically, how do humans value nature and thus create moral grounds for protecting the earth for future human generations? Historically, how have human relations with nature changed over time and how has this been shaped by religions? Culturally, how has nature been perceived and constructed by humans, and conversely how has the natural world affected the formation of human culture? From an engaged perspective, in what ways do the values and practices of a particular religion activate mutually enhancing human-earth relations? What are the contributions of ecofeminist or ecojustice perspectives to a sustainable future?[16]

Tucker goes on to ask:

Should religion and ecology simply be a scholarly field of historical or theoretical research apart from contemporary issues? How should it relate to science and policy concerns? Should it pursue engaged scholarship such as ecojustice? What, if any, is the role of advocacy within academia? Can academics be engaged scholars or public intellectuals in the environmental field within academia and beyond?[17]

In their Series Foreword to the conferences and books, Tucker and Grim caution about the difficulties in the task ahead:

Some of the key interpretive challenges we face in this project concern issues of time, place, space, and positionality. With regard to time, it is necessary to recognize the vast historical complexity of each religious tradition, which cannot be easily condensed in these conferences or volumes. With respect to place, we need to signal the diverse cultural contexts in which these religions have developed. With regard to space, we recognize the varied frameworks of institutions and traditions in which religions unfold. Finally, with respect to positionality, we acknowledge our own historical situatedness at the end of the twentieth century with distinctive contemporary concerns.[18]

Since 1998, Tucker and Grim have been developing and maintaining the website called Forum on Religion and Ecology (FORE) with the objectives of facilitating teaching and outreach as well as further research.

The outreach extends within academia to interdisciplinary programs in environmental studies and outside of academia to religious and policy groups.[19] The associated *Religion and Ecology Newsletter* is circulated widely by email with more than 11,000 subscribers. After more than a decade the website has become the world's leading resource for information about the relationship between religions and ecology as well as a catalyst in religious environmentalism in particular. Furthermore, elsewhere at least two similar organizations have developed since 2003: the Canadian Forum on Religion and Ecology, and the European Forum for the Study of Religion and Environment.

Of special interest is the collaboration between Tucker and Brian Swimme in producing an awesome new documentary film titled "Journey of the Universe." It describes the evolutionary coherence of the universe, Earth, and humans. In addition, a companion book has been published and there is an Educational Series in the form of a video of interviews with leading scientists, environmentalists, historians, and educators.[20] The film is reaching a broad national audience, and eventually it will be circulated internationally. The film website received 30,000 visits during the month of December 2011 alone.[21]

In a recent essay titled "Daring to Dream: Religion and the Future of the Earth" Tucker and Grim address what is referred to in the present book as the quiet revolution of spiritual ecology: "Among environmentalists, a conviction deepens: though science and policy approaches are clearly necessary, they are not sufficient to do the job of transforming human consciousness and behavior for a sustainable future. Values and ethics, religion and spirituality are important factors in this transformation."[22] They go on to say that "this is not only about stewardship of the Earth, but about embracing our embeddedness in nature in radical, fresh, and enlivening ways."[23]

The oceanic perspective on spiritual ecology pursued by Bron Taylor stems at least in part from his recognition that many different kinds of environmental activists are ultimately motivated by some kind of extraordinary experiences in nature that can only be described as spiritual or religious. For example, Taylor writes that "religious perceptions and practices *have* decisively shaped American environmentalism and to such an extent that much environmentalism can be considered a nature religion."[24] His own spiritual experience in nature stems at least in part from surfing along the coast of California, and he has researched and written about the ecospirituality of surfing, among many other topics.[25] His main research approach integrates social science through fieldwork and grounded-theory with normative reflection. A book in preparation, *On Sacred Ground: Earth First! and Environmental Ethics*, is a synthesis of one of his long-term projects.

As Professor of Religion at the University of Florida, Taylor is preoccupied with environmental philosophy, ethics, sustainability, and, in particular, the moral and religious dimensions of environmentalism, including its connection with social justice. This is more than intellectual curiosity. As a social scientist Taylor is dedicated to testing in specific situations how ideas and perceptions may influence behavior. Promoting critical thinking about environmental issues may lead to wiser environmental behavior by individuals and institutions.

Environmentalism has usually been considered to be principally, if not exclusively, a sociopolitical movement. However, environmental concerns are not simply a matter of a competition between nature preservation and economic concerns like jobs and development, or only about political ecology. Instead, elements of religion and spirituality as well as morality and ethics can be involved in various ways and degrees, depending on the particular individuals and organizations involved.[26] For instance, Taylor observers that "what animates most Earth First!ers are their own spiritual experiences in nature which convince them of the interrelatedness and sacrality of all life."[27] He has highlighted the spiritual aspects of environmentalism beyond the so-called world religions, a relatively neglected phenomenon.[28]

Taylor suggests possible alternative future scenarios for the practical nexus of religion and nature, which amount to these three:

> traditional world religions are radically transformed to become more environmentally relevant and responsible as well as more compatible with contemporary science;
>
> they are largely replaced by reversion to nature religions such as Animism, Paganism, and Pantheism; or
>
> new syncretic green religions emerge integrating the most progressive elements of previous religions while discarding the anachronistic and worst elements.[29]

The Encyclopedia of Religion and Nature was incubated mainly in the Religion and Ecology interest group of the American Academy of

Religion in which Taylor has been very active.[30] It is the product of intensive labor from 1998 to 2005 with Taylor as Editor-in-Chief. This was a multidisciplinary collaborative enterprise as well, with over two dozen editors assisting in various degrees. Altogether the two volumes have 1,000 peer-reviewed entries by 520 expert authors and total 1,877 pages. Authors include activists as well as scholars. The great breadth and diversity in the subjects surveyed in this historical benchmark reference work is far more inclusive than previous approaches in this emerging academic field of religion and ecology.[31]

Taylor was also the prime mover in the development of the International Society for the Study of Religion, Nature and Culture founded in 2006 as well as in its official quarterly periodical first published in 2007, the *Journal for the Study of Religion, Nature and Culture*. These appear to be a natural outgrowth of the *Encyclopedia of Religion and Nature* and are as oceanic in scope. The historic inaugural meeting of this multidisciplinary professional organization was held on April 6–9, 2006, at the University of Florida in Gainesville.[32] About 150 participants from two dozen countries presented papers and served as discussants while around the same number of observers attended. Several of the conference papers were subsequently revised for publication in the early issues of the organization's journal. So far membership has reached around 200. By now this society has held five international meetings, including in Mexico, Australia, the Netherlands, and Italy.[33]

In the first article introducing the new journal, Taylor as editor envisions it as a wide-ranging, interdisciplinary, and inclusive ("taboo-free") scholarly exploration of the pivotal question: What are the relationships among human beings, their diverse religions, and the earth's living systems? The vast scope and variety of entries is characteristic of Taylor's openness to exploring anything that might be informative and insightful in understanding the web of interrelationships among religion, nature, and culture. There is even a special issue devoted to the film *Avatar*. This periodical, like the encyclopedia, embraces a wide range of approaches from the humanities, social sciences, and natural sciences. The scope extends beyond the so-called world, major, or mainstream religions, countering what might be viewed by some as unjustified exclusionism.[34]

Dark Green Religion: Nature Spirituality and the Planetary Future is Taylor's most recent book, a synthesis of the foregoing publications in

many respects. Therein he explores the pivotal question: How can spiritually motivated environmentalists, both individuals and movements, be
viewed as religious when many reject traditional religious and supernatural
worldviews? He surveys "green religions" as spiritual practices that believe
nature is sacred. Many of them have replaced traditional religions in the
belief and value systems of numerous individuals. The variety of groups
considered includes radical environmental activists, bioregionalists, surf-
ers, new-agers, ecopsychologists, and scientists. Taylor demonstrates that
many aspects of the green revolution are, indeed, also a religious revolution. Taylor explicates further points that he discussed in previous publications. These points include the possibility that traditional world religions
are declining, whereas nature religions, such as neo-paganism as well as
forms that are entirely naturalistic based solely on scientific understandings, are increasing.[35]

Last, but not the least, Taylor was instrumental in the development of the
track on Religion and Nature in the doctoral program in Religion at the
University of Florida.[36] Among the questions explored in the program are:

In what ways have religions been environmentally beneficial or
detrimental?

How are religions being transformed as they respond to environmental
concerns?

How do natural environments influence religions?

Are some aspects of environmental sciences and environmentalism
religious?

What trends and patterns are emerging globally in the nexus of
religion and nature?

The current website of the Department of Religion reveals how such
questions are being explored while Taylor's websites offer an extraordinary
abundance of related information.[37]

Taylor's work has highlighted the religious and spiritual aspects of
environmentalism, and in many other ways it has greatly expanded the
study of the relationship between religion and nature, thereby significantly
advancing this new field of research and teaching. In the process, beyond
his own substantial research and publications, Taylor has edited a monumental encyclopedia, established a whole new professional organization
and its captivating journal which he edits, evolved an exceptional doctoral

program focused on the subject, and created very informative websites, among other initiatives.

Integrating philosophy, ethics, Judaism, Marxism, and environmentalism is not an easy task. However, it has been accomplished in a most impressive and significant manner by Roger S. Gottlieb, Professor of Philosophy at Worcester Polytechnic Institute in Massachusetts. The bottom line for Gottlieb is that ultimately the health and rights of humans are related to the health and rights of the environment because in reality everything is interconnected and interdependent. Justice and liberation demand both critical inquiry and activism. This guiding orientation is articulated in one of Gottlieb's recent publications: "There is no part of the earthly web of life that is not affected by human beings; no social relation of oppression that does not have some role in ecological degradation; and no form of ecological degradation the effects of which are not made worse by social inequality. To honor nature we need not only new prayers and rituals, but a radical alteration in our basic social structures. We cannot heal social injustice without transforming our relations to nature."[38]

Such concerns generate a more progressive stance for many religious adherents who are often critical of capitalism including at least some corporate practices as well as rampant materialism and consumerism.[39] Accordingly, Gottlieb identifies a major contribution of religion to environmentalism: "Finally, at their most moral and socially engaged, religious traditions can offer models of humane and compassionate activist politics that are particularly appropriate to environmentalism. For environmentalism to succeed, it must offer a universal vision of community, one which includes all people and all of life, not mere interest group politics applied to old-growth forests."[40]

Gottlieb also notes that religious environmentalism creates new environmentalists and new environmental initiatives that offer hope in a world that is increasingly depressing with its manifold problems. But to be more successful environmentalism needs to be more diffuse, involving communities—not only central governments formulating policies, laws, and regulations, and not just aloof nongovernmental organizations targeting specific issues like wilderness preservation or some endangered species.[41] From this perspective, Gottlieb concludes that academics need to apply their roles as teachers, researchers, and writers to critically analyze the particulars of environmentalism. What is significant should be determined by real-world problems and issues rather than by mere academic traditions and fashions of individual disciplines. Environmental and other sociopolitical problems and issues are simply far too serious and urgent. Gottlieb writes: "We are members of an ecologically murderous civilization which must be replaced by a sustainable one."[42] This is the vital difference between ecocide which is suicide for humanity, and ecosanity which involves creating and maintaining sustainable, green, and just lifestyles and societies.

One of Gottlieb's edited books, *This Sacred Earth: Religion, Nature, and Environment*, is recognized internationally as the premier comprehensive anthology on the subject.[43] The second edition incorporates more than 90 contributors in 762 pages. Editor Gottlieb provides a fairly balanced religious, topical, spatial, and temporal coverage of the subject matter.[44] In 2006, Gottlieb edited yet another seminal reference work, *The Oxford Handbook of Religion and Ecology*.[45] In this anthology prominent authorities and leaders in what Gottlieb refers to as religious environmentalism contribute 25 chapters totaling 662 pages. Furthermore, in 2006, Gottlieb published his own monographic synthesis in this new field, *A Greener Faith: Religious Environmentalism and Our Planet's Future*.[46] His own writing in these and other publications is unusually clear, informative, passionate, compassionate, compelling, and inspiring. If an individual had the dedication and stamina to only read all three of these books, then a very thorough and deep knowledge of spiritual ecology would be acquired.[47]

In the Introduction to the handbook Gottlieb asserts that the heart of the subject of religion and ecology involves two primary questions: What have the world's religions believed about nature? How must their beliefs and actions change to cope with the ecocrisis? He points out that as religions have confronted the ecocrisis a new level of dialogue and collaboration among them, as well as between them and the sciences, has emerged. In turn, as religions have added ecology to their interests this has stimulated a reassessment of their traditions and the invention of new ones as well. Thereby religions have become "theologically revitalized and politically energized" in pursuing environmental problems and issues.[48]

Religions are compelled to confront the ecocrisis simply because it is also a spiritual crisis. For instance, if for Christians, Jews, and Muslims the Earth is God's creation, then surely for them environmental degradation is sacrilegious and consequently sinful. Furthermore, religion can be a powerful force in environmentalism, given its values, institutional resources, influential leadership, multitudes of adherents, and strong motivating potential.[49]

Gottlieb's synthetic overview of the unprecedented emergence of religious environmentalism and related matters in his own book, *A Greener Faith: Religious Environmentalism and Our Planet's Future*, provides some hope when one considers the multitude of diverse positive actions on behalf of the environment implemented by individuals and organizations that are motivated and guided by some variant of spiritual ecology. Indeed, this is starting to change for the better the ways that many people relate to both their natural habitat and their religion, in some instances restoring forgotten elements of their traditions while in others transforming them or creating new ones. Religious leaders and institutions also recognize that attending more closely to nature enhances their meaning and significance for individual adherents and society in general.[50]

As a skillful philosopher, Gottlieb contributes a systematic, precise, and incisive critical analysis of religious environmentalism that goes a long way toward helping to lay the conceptual foundations for spiritual ecology. Several themes in his book are especially pertinent:

Religion has a unique and crucial contribution to make to environmentalism.

Ultimately environmentalism, including religious environmentalism, challenges society to change profoundly in response to the ecocrsis.

Religious environmentalism is changing religions.

Religion has to be political, if it is to be moral. Environmentalism itself evinces some characteristics of religion and spirituality.

Religious environmentalism is a sociopolitical movement that is growing exponentially, has great potential, and provides hope for a more positive future.[51]

Religion implicates deep conviction and concern that can add a significant positive influence to environmentalism.

Gottlieb revealingly asserts that "Religion is, quite simply, the single strongest alternative to government, corporations, and consumerism."[52]

Several additional perceptive observations are provided by Gottlieb:

Activist religious environmentalism goes beyond theology and public declarations. It is directly aimed at changing the world: by making new laws, stopping harmful practices, creating better ways to produce and consume, healing the earth, and nurturing human beings in their relations with the rest of life. *Politically* it seeks to generate a collective force of voters, demonstrators, long-term activists, tree planters, and energy conservers. *Ecologically* it treats the earth with care and respect, hoping to replace our current system with organic agriculture, habitat restoration, the conservation of biodiversity, alternative technology, and renewable energy. *Morally* it pursues justice in the distribution of negative ecological effects.[53]

The quiet revolution that is spiritual ecology is reflected in various statements by Gottlieb. "It is the task of religious environmentalism to set itself against the reigning social vision, putting forward values that will ultimately serve people and the earth far better than the ones currently in place."[54] "The fusion of religion and politics at the heart of much of the world's environmentalism is a prophetic alternative to modernity's current reigning faith, the one that stresses the "holiness" of economic growth, ever more complicated gadgets, and hyperstimulating media spectacle."[55]

Gottlieb observes: "Religious environmentalism has given rise to prayers, rituals, and forms of meditation that embody celebration, concern, and contrition. These include Christian prayer services for Earth Day, new Buddhist meditations, fresh significance given to old holidays, and the creation of innovative and original observance."[56] He affirms that "ultimately, however, I believe that two related and profound values permeate all of these rituals: the reality of our *kinship* with the rest of earth community and the importance of finding a way to *balance* our needs, desires, and lives with theirs."[57]

In spite of all of the doom and gloom about the ongoing and worsening ecocrisis, Gottlieb remarks: "Religious environmentalism is a diverse, vibrant, global movement, a rich source of new ideas, institutional commitment, political activism, and spiritual inspiration."[58] He says that "religion is now a leading voice telling us to respect the earth, love our nonhuman as well as our human neighbors, and think deeply about our social policies and economic priorities."[59] Accordingly, Gottlieb mentions that he is deeply encouraged, and one might add, his work is deeply encouraging as well.[60]

In conclusion, since the 1990s there has been a burst of vital creativity and productivity in academic thought and practical action on the relationship between religion and ecology. The scholars briefly discussed here are the contemporary supernovas in the quiet but accelerating and hopeful revolution that is spiritual ecology. While there are differences in their approaches, together they move in the same direction, which Thomas Berry so aptly identifies as crucial: "The present urgency is to begin thinking within the context of the whole planet, the integral earth community with all its human and other-than-human components."[61]

PART IV. LEAVES

The leaves of a tree are elemental in generating energy from the sun through the process called photosynthesis. This applies metaphorically to such luminary personages as W. S. Merwin in his ecopoetry and forest restoration ecology, Joanna Macy's systems and Buddhist thinking as a major catalyst in the Great Turning transforming lifestyles and societies from ecocide to ecosanity, and the Green Patriarch Bartholomew I in his many initiatives highlighting the pollution of the great rivers of the world as sacrilegious. Such charismatic individuals help energize the activist component of spiritual ecology. Others who should be at least mentioned include founder of deep ecology Arne Naess, Matthew Fox for his creation spirituality, Zen ecopoet Gary Snyder, desert spiritual ecologist Edward Abbey, James A. Swan for his seminal work on sacred places in nature, and James Lovelock with his Gaia hypothesis. All of the above individuals realize both intellectually and emotionally the synergy and sacredness of the interconnections and interdependencies of all beings in nature.

CHAPTER 13. CAN A POET SAVE NATURE?
W. S. MERWIN

What I really believe is the only hopeful relation between our life and the whole of life is one of reverence and respect and of feeling at one with it. The other attitude which is the one our society is based on is devastating and it is killing the earth and it is killing us too.

William Stanley Merwin[1]

The above quote from William Stanley Merwin reflects his profound eco-poetry, commitment to Buddhism and deep ecology, extraordinary sensitivity to nature, special attachment to place, and awesome work in restoration ecology on the Hawaiian Island of Maui, among other influences. Merwin moved to Maui in 1976 to study with Zen Buddhist Robert Aitken at his Maui Zendo, which had been established in 1969. There Merwin resided for a period in an outbuilding.[2] In Hawai'i Merwin became increasingly aware and sensitive to nature as reflected in his poetry over the years.[3] He is keenly cognizant of the fact that the human species is gradually impoverishing and poisoning all of life on the planet including its own.[4]

Merwin's extraordinary environmental sensitivity and attachment to place developed from an early age and throughout his life. As a child he enjoyed the freedom, beauty, and exhilaration of hiking in the mountains near his second home in Scranton, Pennsylvania. However, on his eleventh birthday, during a hike with a friend, he reached a ridge to discover that an entire valley had disappeared through strip mining. He says that six decades later he remembers "the horror and grief and rage and unspeakable emotions that I felt at that destruction, the complete obliteration of a place that would never be there again."[5] Merwin relates: "What turned me into an environmentalist, on my eleventh birthday, was seeing the first strip mine. To treat the earth like that, to me, is like murder. Rape. I just hate it. I don't think we have any right to treat the living world like that. We have to do something about our needs in that case. My house has been solar for thirty years."[6] Most tragically, by today such scenes of environmental devastation are becoming common in Appalachia and elsewhere such as the Alberta tar sands in Canada.[7]

Over the decades Merwin has developed a remarkably successful project in local restoration ecology in a secluded area along the northern coast of Maui in the Haiku area. He could not stop deforestation in the tropics, but he could restore a forest locally. On some 18 acres of land that was formerly a pineapple plantation in the 1930s he gradually developed a forest community of 850 species of palms, 30 of them are Hawaiian. He estimates that there are four to five times as many individual trees in the forest. One species, *Hyophorbe indica*, may have been saved from extinction from the seeds of a last remnant tree from Reunion Island. Merwin sent seeds from this species to a palm nursery on the Big Isle and they are available for distribution now. During rainy periods Merwin tries to plant one palm tree each day.[8]

Originally Merwin had hoped to restore a rain forest community like that of the pre-1840 ecology of the area. However, soil and other environmental conditions remaining from the devastation reeked by the monocrop pineapple plantation was just too much of an obstacle.[9] The wasteland was covered by scrub brush, guava trees, and Christmas berries.[10] Nevertheless, the palm forest he created is surely a miracle and exemplar of restoration ecology. It is also a demonstration that ecopoetry can impact reality as well as imagination, even to the extent of preserving a portion of nature. (Contemplate the facts that palms have been evolving for over 80 million years into the some 3,000 species extant, and Merwin conserves 850 of these species.) Merwin says, "I've always wanted to take a ruined piece of land and restore it."[11] The Merwin Conservancy has been established to further this work in what is clearly spiritual ecology.[12]

Some biographical background helps appreciate Merwin. He was born in New York City in 1927. His father was a strict Presbyterian minister and his mother a pacifist. He grew up in nearby Union City, New Jersey, and then in 1936 the family moved to Scranton, Pennsylvania.[13] His mother cultivated a love of poetry in Merwin through reading to him during his childhood poems by Alfred Tennyson and Henry W. Longfellow among others.[14] Also, a tree in the backyard of their home was a special childhood friend where he found refuge when he became upset, such as when his strict father scolded him. On one occasion workers from the telephone company wanted to trim the branches of the tree, but

Merwin, then only around five years of age, made such a fuss screaming at them not to harm the tree, that they backed away and left.[15] Merwin continues to love trees, he feels a special closeness to them.[16]

Merwin studied on a scholarship at Princeton University. However, suddenly life changed for him in August 1945 when the United States bombed Hiroshima and Nagasaki. He graduated in 1947. Merwin went to Europe where he became a freelance translator of Latin, French, Spanish, and Portuguese. Also he worked as a tutor, during one period for the children of poet Robert Graves in Majorca, Spain. During the 1960s he resided in a long-abandoned stone house in a farm village in southwestern France. There Occitan was spoken among the people, the language of twelfth- and thirteenth-century troubadours known for lyric poetry.[17] The village of Lacan de Loubressac, located in the Dordogne River region in southwestern France near Bretenoux, was made famous by the Lascaux cave paintings from the Upper Paleolithic period.[18] Merwin developed the land into an organic garden and bird sanctuary, foreshadowing his later work with nature in Hawai'i.[19] Next he moved to Chiapas, Mexico, restored an old house, and translated indigenous poems from that area.[20]

When Merwin eventually returned to the United States he became critical of Western colonial expansionism with its doctrine of Manifest Destiny and the attitude of the human domination of nature derived from the predominant interpretation of the Bible.[21] The Cuban missile crisis in October of 1962 was another event for his critical introspection with the fear and militarism it generated in the nation. When he received the Pulitzer Prize in 1971, he donated the $1,000 award to the Draft Resistance movement of the Vietnam War.[22] Merwin outlined his objections to the Vietnam War in an essay in the *New York Review of Books*.[23] Much later he joined a multitude of poets worldwide against George W. Bush's war in Iraq, viewed by so many as unnecessary, incompetent, and disastrous. Their organization, Poets Against the War now has a collection of 30,000 poems by 26,000 poets.[24] In an interview with Ed Rampell, some lines from Merwin's "Ogres" of 2003 are quoted: "the frauds in office, at this instant devising their massacres in my name." Merwin then says: " ... I was thinking about the invasion of Iraq, and I was thinking about organized violence. It's always to some degree effected by lies. Because we justify what we are doing, and the justifications, as we keep finding out, are very often not true. There was no Gulf of Tonkin incident, which was one of the reasons for the Vietnam invasion. And there were no weapons of mass destruction."[25]

Ideally spirituality, ecology, and peace are necessarily mutually reinforcing in a kind of synergy.[26] An intelligent person who professes and practices respect and reverence for life is unlikely to favor warfare and any other forms of violence, unless he or she is a hypocrite.[27] Speaking in an interview about Zen Buddhist ethics, Robert Aiken observes: "When we look closely at the word *beings*, in both Asian and Western languages, we find that beings are not limited to that which we ordinarily consider sentient. Indeed, storms, clouds, unicorns, and so on are beings. So the precept not to kill is really a fulfillment of our vow to save all beings, and the protection of the environment is an essential part of that vow."[28]

According to the American Academy of Poets: "The rigorous practice of Buddhism and passionate dedication to environmentalism that Merwin devoted himself to in Hawaii has profoundly influenced his later work, including his evocative renderings of the natural world in *The Compass Flower* (1977), *Opening the Hand* (1983), and *The Rain in the Trees* (1988), as well as *The Folding Cliffs*, a novel-in-verse drawing on the history and legends of Hawaii."[29] H. L. Hix observes: "Hawaii has become 'the last place' for Merwin, since apparently he plans to reside there until his death, and for humanity, symbolizing the last chance for humans to learn to live within the limits of the natural order instead of self-destructively attempting to overcome nature by manipulation, possession, and control."[30]

In July 2010, Merwin hesitatingly accepted the invitation from the U.S. Library of Congress to serve as the 17th Poet Laureate from October through May. This recognizes his six decades as a prolific author with 26 anthologies of his own poetry. His book *Migration: New and Selected Poems* won a National Book Award for poetry in 2005. In 1971 he was awarded a Pulitzer Prize for *The Carrier of Ladders*, and in 2009 another for *The Shadow of Sirius*. Indeed, Merwin has received almost every major award for poetry. Furthermore, he published translations of the poetry of Pablo Neruda, Federico Garcia Lorca, and others, nearly 20 books. Beyond poems, he has authored essays, fables, plays, fiction, and travel and history writing.[31]

Merwin explains that in his poems he " ... tries to convey some inner experience that there is no way of expressing. Language evolved not to convey information so much as to convey some inner experience that there was no way of expressing. It was an attempt to convey an inner sense of passion—although it did have information in it—but the feeling was more powerful."[32] This is reminiscent of one attribute of spirituality in general and spiritual ecology in particular, grappling with the challenges of the ineffable.[33] Furthermore, Merwin observes: "There is a feeling in which the natural world that includes us is sacred. Because we know, if there's anything sacred, that's it. You go out and spend two hours with the other forms of life around us, and you come back elated, feeling a great charge because this is basically what you want to be doing. Not to be cut off from it, but to be part of it."[34]

A great admirer of Henry David Thoreau, Merwin was a naturally engaged environmentalist before it became popular. He started composting and growing vegetables in the 1960s while dwelling in southern France. Then in 1976 he built his own house in a secluded rural place along the volcanic slope of Haleakala on the island of Maui. He was able to purchase the land relatively cheaply at the time using the inheritance from the life savings of his parents. His house relies on solar energy for power. The mornings he devotes to Buddhist meditation and to his writing. In the afternoon he gardens in his palm forest where he feels the presence of just being.[35]

For Merwin poetry and nature are mutually reinforcing, reflective of the unique place he has discovered and created. As he reflects with his usual wisdom and insight: "We as a species define ourselves by our relation to the rest of life."[36] His perspective applies to his own life on Maui as well. In the same interview, Merwin says: "A garden for me asks the question, if you have a piece of earth, what would you want to do with it, how would you treat it?" He has transformed the piece of earth he dwells on initially into a palm garden and then into a palm forest, a place where previously only land degraded by a pineapple plantation remained.[37]

Merwin devoted a dozen years of research to write an epic poem, *The Folding Cliffs*. This book-length poem focuses on Koolau, an outlaw leper who opposed the illegal overthrow of the last monarch of Hawai'i, Queen Liliuokalani. He took refuge in Kalalau Valley on the island of Kauai. The masterful and moving verses of this poem expose some of the horrible aspects of Western colonial expansion in the 1890s in the Hawaiian Islands. At the same time the poem illustrates the spiritual ecology of Native Hawaiians.[38]

Merwin's interests in what amounts to spiritual ecology have also fed his environmental activism, including support of Native Hawaiian causes such as helping to sponsor a statewide conference on the importance of keeping the waters of streams flowing. This may reflect in part the condition of the Peahi Stream on his land, which dried up through previous land misuse and degradation.

The title of the present chapter on Merwin was inspired by John Felstiner's book title *Can Poetry Save the Earth?* He traces the development of Western ecopoetry from the Bible through history to contemporary times. Felstiner argues that poetry can touch the heart and soul as well as the mind, and that this can translate into environmental activism. He includes chapters on Merwin and Snyder as well as William Wordsworth, Walt Whitman, Emily Dickinson, Robert Frost, Ted Hughes, and many others. Felstiner writes: "Science, policy, and activism point the way toward solutions, but something deeper must draw us there. It can be found in poetry's musical lift, attentive imagery, and shaping force, which stem from prehistory and live on in today's magazines, slim volumes, readings, slams, songs, Web sites, blogs. In country or city, poems make a difference by priming consciousness."[39] Felstiner concludes his book with these last two sentences: "Can poetry save the earth? For sure, person by person, our earthly challenge hangs on the sense and spirit that poems can awaken."[40] In short, poetry is one path to and from spiritual ecology. As Elizabeth Lund remarks about Merwin, deep ecology, and poetry: "Tree by tree and poem by poem, however, this master craftsman will save what he can."[41] Thereby he is a witness to the intrinsic value of nature.[42] Here Merwin has the last word: "On the last day of the world I would want to plant a tree."[43]

CHAPTER 14. RECONNECTING, JOANNA MACY

The central purpose of the Work that Reconnects is to help people uncover and experience their innate connections with each other and with the systemic, self-healing powers of the web of life, so that they may be enlivened and motivated to play their part in creating a sustainable civilization.

Joanna Macy[1]

Urbanization, industrialization, and other forces have alienated many humans from nature. They and nature suffer from this alienation. Ecopsychology recognizes that healing one's self is intricately connected to nature.[2] Joanna Macy is a most extraordinary pioneer in this healing. She is a student and practitioner of Buddhism, systems theory, deep ecology, and ecopsychology, which are all interrelated in *The Work That Reconnects.*[3] Her life, writings, and activities are an awesome synergy of these interests. She is the primary source of this project and also its main teacher. The theory and practice involved are explained in her book *Coming Back to Life: Practices to Reconnect Our Lives, Our World;* there is also a website and a documentary film along with her lectures and workshops.[4] Macy is also an instructor at the California Institute for Integral Studies in San Francisco.

An activist as well as a philosopher and theorist, Macy has been engaged in the related peace, justice, and environmental movements for more than four decades. She has been influenced by Mohandas Gandhi and Sarvodaya, the commumity-based self-help movment in Sri Lanka. Her profound ideas are put into practice in workshops that train individuals to transcend the pain and despair that they experience in observing the social and environmental crises in the world, to change personally, and to strive to change their society and the world. She has trained thousands of people in small workshops and talked to many more throughout the world. Others have pursued and developed her experiential group methods in diverse institutions such as educational, religious, and grassroots activist organizations. For many her work helps create a new way of seeing the world and interacting with it as an integral part of the great web of life. Interconnectedness helps individuals feel the pain of others and the world, and explicitly facing this pathology in turn generates strength and courage to act effectively to try to reduce suffering and improve the situation. Craig S. Strobel remarks: "Her work is designed to cut through illusions constructed by the individual mind and society that serve to deny the reality of the environmental crisis."[5]

Macy's work is part of the third revolution beyond the previous agricultural (Neolithic) and industrial revolutions, a transformation to a life-sustaining society. Like a growing number of other individuals in a diversity of contexts, she recognizes the fundamental fallacy of modern industrial, capitalist, and consumer society; that infinite growth is possible on a finite base.[6] The latter includes not only space and resources, but also the capacity of ecosystems and the planet to absorb pollution and other insults. Acid rain, the ozone hole, and global climate change are among the symptoms that the capacity of earth systems to absorb pollution is being exceeded. Treating nature as nothing more than a supply house and a sewer is suicidal for the human species. This third revolution is called "the Great Turning," a radical (as in root) transformation from the Industrial Growth Society to a Life-Sustaining Society. Its three components interact in synergy: holding actions to reduce damage such as the initiatives of environmental nongovernmental organizations; creating new institutions such as organic farming to produce healthy and environmentally friendly foods for local consumption; and changing worldviews with accompanying values, attitudes, and behaviors derived from the wisdom traditions of the world such as Buddhism.[7] Macy asserts: "These structural alternatives cannot take root and survive without deeply ingrained values to sustain them. They must mirror what we want and how we relate to Earth and each other. They require, in other words, a profound shift in our perception of reality—and that shift is happening now, both as cognitive revolution and spiritual awakening."[8]

Macy points out that this revolution is already well under way, although it is uncertain whether or not it will succeed. Nevertheless, Macy views the Great Turning as an auspicious period in history, as a profound change in mind and spirit that will eventually affect every human life in a multitude of diverse ways. This revolution has the potential to be the decisive influence on the fate of future generations of the human species and that of the planet as a whole. The basic ideas behind The Great Turning are not unique to Macy, but reflect an extraordinary convergence in thinking from diverse individuals and organizations, such as ecospsychologist Ralph Metzner (see Table 14.1).[9]

Table 14.1. The Transition to an Ecological Worldview[10]

INDUSTRIAL AGE	ECOLOGICAL AGE
Scientific Paradigms	
Mechanomorphic	Organismic
Universe as machine	Universe as process or story
Earth as inert matter	Gaia: Earth as superorganism
Life as random chemistry	Life as autopoiesis
Determinism	Indeterminancy, probability
Linear causality	Chaos: nonlinear dynamics
Atomism	Holism and systems theory
Epistemology	
Logical positivism	Critical realism
Operationalism	Constructivism
Reductionism	Reduction and integration
Role of the Human	
Conquest of nature	Living as part of nature
Dominion, control	Co-evolution, symbiosis
Heroic individualism	Ecological consciousness
Exploitation and management	Stewardship, restoration
Anthropocentric and humanist	Biocentric or ecocentric
Nature has instrumental value	Nature has intrinsic value
Human Relationship to Land	
Land use: farming, herding	Land ethic: thinking like a mountain
Competing for territory	Dwelling in place
Owning "real estate"	Reinhabiting the bioregion
Human Social Relations	
Sexism, patriarchy	Ecofeminism, partnership
Racism, ethnocentrism	Multiculturalism, diversity
Hierarchies of class and caste	Social ecology, ecojustice
Theology and Religion	
Nature as background	Animism
Nature as demonic	Nature as sacred
Transcendent divinity	Immanent divinity
Creation as fallen, corrupt	Creation spirituality
Monotheism, atheism	Polytheism, pantheism
Education and Research	
Specialized disciplines	Integrative disciplines
"Value-free knowledge" pursued	Unconscious values explicated
Science/humanities split	Unified worldview

(*continued*)

Table 14.1.   (Continued)

INDUSTRIAL AGE	ECOLOGICAL AGE
Political Systems	
Nation-state sovereignty	Multinational federations
Centralized national authority	Decentralized bioregions
Patriarchal oligarchies	Egalitarian democracies
Cultural homogeneity	Pluralistic societies
National security focus	Humans and environmental focus
Militarism	Commitment to nonviolence
Economic systems	
Multinational corporations	Community-based economies
Assume scarcity	Assume interdependence
Competition	Cooperation and competition
Limitless economic growth	Limits to growth
Economic "development"	Steady state, sustainability
No accounting of nature	Economics based on ecology
Technology	
Addiction to fossil fuels	Reliance on renewables
Profit-driven technologies	Appropriate technologies
Waste overload	Recycling, reusing
Exploitation, consumerism	Protect and restore ecosystems
Agriculture	
Monoculture farming	Polyculture farming, permaculture
Agribusiness, factory farms	Community and family farms
Chemical fertilizers and pesticides	Biological pest control
Valuable high-yield hybrids	Preservation of genetic diversity

Macy's work reflects a long journey with many spiritual experiences and influences. She was born in Los Angeles in 1929 but spent her childhood in New York City. Nevertheless, she loved nature from her earliest years and took special pleasure during summer vacations at her grandfather's farm in western New York State where her best friends were a horse and a maple tree. Her grandfather was a Presbyterian minister and she was profoundly influenced by his religious devotion. Later she pursed Biblical Studies as an undergraduate at Wellesley College graduating in 1950. She acted as interpreter for Albert Schweitzer during his visit to New York City and continued correspondence with him through her college years. Schweitzer was renowned, among many other things, for his principle of reverence for life inspired by South Asian religious philosophies and especially the concept of *ahimsa* (non-harm). Macy mentions that she learned about deep ecology from John Seed, Arne Naess, Starhawk, Choegyal Rinpoche, David Abram, Judi Bari, Paul Winter, Julia Butterfly Hill, Paul Shepard, Robinson Jeffers, Dolores La Chapelle, Francis of Assisi, and Gautama the Buddha among others. This, like so many facets of spiritual ecology, is reminiscent of the image in Buddhism of Indra's Net, a cosmic net strung with jewels each reflecting all others.[11]

In the 1960s, when her husband, Fran Macy, joined the administrative staff of the Peace Corps in India, Joanna accompanied him along with their three children. There she first encountered Buddhism through working with Tibetan refugees. Eventually she studied Buddhism with monks and even went on a retreat in the Himalayas. She also worked in Sri Lanka with A. T. Ariyaratna and other Theravada Buddhists in the Sarvodaya Shramadana Movement helping rural poor to develop economically and ecologically self-sustaining communities.

Back in the United States, Macy pursued graduate studies in Religion at Syracuse University earning her doctorate in 1978. Her dissertation focused on Buddhist ideas about interdependence and mutual causality in relation to general systems theory. A revised version was latter published.[12] In particular, the Buddhist principle of "dependent coorigination" (*paticca samuppada* in Pali) is at the core of her thought and action and her workshops. Janet W. Parachin observes: "If it is true that all things are interdependent and that a change in one part of a system causes changes in other parts of the system as well, then what we do, no matter how big or small, *does* make a difference!"[13] Macy maintains that the interest of the one is the interest of all.[14] This is reflected in the title of her book *World As Lover, World As Self.* Like others, such as His Holiness the 14th Dalai Lama of Tibet, Macy recognizes underlying convergent principles shared by Buddhism and Western science.[15]

Through her activist work with Nuclear Freeze and Disarmament from the 1960s through the 1980s, Macy developed the principles and practices that she called Despair and Empowerment, including practical group exercises, rituals, and role-playing.[16] The almost unimaginable possibility of nuclear war and the resulting nuclear winter would not only be massively devastating for humankind, but also for life on planet Earth. Furthermore, there is the long-term hazard of nuclear waste that can poison portions of nature and endanger humans and other beings for millions of years. Since everything is connected to everything else, radioactive contamination, like any chemical hazard, can circulate over enormous areas through the flows of the atmosphere and hydrosphere, as the accident at Chernobyl demonstrated. Unlike many contaminants that may eventually be absorbed and dissipated by natural processes, nuclear radiation lasts far longer, impacting many generations into the future.[17] Macy spearheaded the Nuclear Guardianship Project focused on nuclear facilities as centers for activist citizens to monitor and even as places for pilgrimage, meditation, and rituals of environmental stewardship. Macy includes in her memoir an appendix titled "An Ethic of Nuclear Guardianship: Values to Guide Decision-Making on the Management of Radioactive Waste."[18] The first principle is: "Each generation shall endeavor to preserve the foundations of life and well-being for those who come after. To produce and abandon substances that damage following generations is morally unacceptable."[19]

The Council of All Beings was developed by Macy with John Seed to ritually reconnect individuals with other species and forces in nature. It involves transcending anthropocentrism to experiment with cultivating empathy for other species. This ritual facilitates a deeper feeling, appreciation, and caring for the interconnectedness and interdependence of all beings. It expands the bounded egocentric self into the unbounded ecological self to realize that we are an integral part of nature rather than being apart from nature. It is an effective demonstration of the truth and sacredness of the wondrous web of life.[20]

Systems theory, developed by Ludwig von Bertalanffy, Ervin Laszlo, Gregory Bateson, Fritjof Capra, and others, is a way of viewing the world that focuses on relationships and processes. Systems are wholes composed of interacting components that are self-regulating and self-balancing, but they can also change and become more complex. Furthermore, each system is a *holon*, a whole within a larger whole. This systems perspective is similar to the Buddhist principle of dependent cooorigination: in various ways and degrees everything is interconnected and interdependent. All phenomena lack intrinsic being, as they depend on causes and conditions for their emergence and existence. Macy writes in her website: "Strong convergences are at play here, as Buddhist thought and practice interact with the organizing values of the Green movement, with Gandhian nonviolence, and humanistic psychology, with ecofeminism, and sustainable economics, with systems theory, deep ecology, and new paradigm science."[21]

In conclusion, Macy has been most successful in integrating and synthesizing a rich diversity of resources from science, religions, and environmentalisms in her thought and practice as a spiritual ecologist. Anita Barrows observes: "Joanna brings to her work a powerful combination of deep feeling, intellectual clarity and personal charisma. Joanna is a visionary: her vision consists of transformational possibilities that exist in human beings."[22] Synergist Macy is a vital catalyst in spiritual ecology as well as in the Great Turning.[23]

CHAPTER 15. GREEN PATRIARCH, BARTHOLOMEW I

... the ecological problem of our times demands a radical reevaluation of how we see the entire world; it demands a different interpretation of matter and the world, a new attitude of humankind toward nature, and a new understanding of how we acquire and make use of our material goods.

His All Holiness, Bartholomew I, Ecumenical Patriarch.[1]

His All Holiness, Bartholomew I, is Archbishop of Constantinople, New Rome, and Ecumenical Patriarch. According to his website: "The Ecumenical Patriarch has the historical and theological responsibility to initiate and coordinate actions among the Churches of Alexandria, Antioch, Jerusalem, Russia, Serbia, Romania, Bulgaria, Georgia, Cyprus, Greece, Poland, Albania, The Czech Land and Slovakia, Finland, Estonia, and numerous archdioceses in the old and new worlds. This includes the convening of councils or meetings, facilitating inter-church and inter-faith dialogues and serving as the primary expresser of Church unity as a whole. As Ecumenical Patriarch he transcends every national and ethnic group on a global level and today is the spiritual leader of approximately 250 million faithful world-wide."[2]

Popularly known as the Green Patriarch, Bartholomew I sees the environment not merely as a technological or political issue; instead, it is primarily a religious and spiritual matter. Thus, just a month after his election in 1991 as Ecumenical Patriarch he convened an environmental convention in Crete called "Living in the Creation of the Lord," although he had taken initiatives earlier on the environment as well. He co-sponsored with His Royal Highness Prince Philip (International Chairman of the World Wildlife Fund or WWF) international Religion, Science and Environment symposia in Patmos (1995), Black Sea (1997), Danube River (1999), Adriatic Sea (2002), Baltic Sea (2003), Amazon River (2006), Arctic 2007), and Mississippi River (2009). The Amazon and Arctic symposia were under the patronage of the Ecumenical Patriarch and Kofi Annan, the former Secretary-General of the United

Nations. The most recent spiritual ecology symposium, on the Nile Delta, has been postponed.

These international, interdisciplinary, and inter-religious symposia are intended to generate reflection on the fate of the rivers and seas as well as interfaith debate on the environment by visiting and discussing some of the most ecologically threatened areas on the planet.[3] In many cases, the voyage aboard a ship followed the route of pollution from its source to its point of impact, thereby vividly demonstrating the interconnectedness of the world's waters and associated ecosystems. It is also especially noteworthy that these conferences have pursued carbon offsets and other measures to reduce their ecological footprint.[4]

The symposia are not limited to informing the participants; they also discuss practical solutions and then lead to their implementation. Among these are the development of World Wide Fund for Nature Wetlands Conservation Programme in Greece; a Pew Fellowship in Marine Conservation awarded to Professor Laurence Mee, to develop public information materials on the Black Sea and to organize a 2-year program for training a group of teachers from all six associated countries; agreement by representatives of the Lower Danube countries of Bulgaria, Romania, Moldova, and Ukraine to sign a declaration for the creation of a Lower Danube Green Corridor for restoration and conservation of an interconnected network of floodplains along the Lower Danube; pressure from journalists for the Albanian government to clean up a toxic waste dump from abandoned chemical factories in Porto Romano; and a Bread and Fish initiative to bring together farmers and fishermen to consider environmental issues that connect these industries in the Baltic Sea region.[5]

The Halki Ecological Institute was organized in June 1999 by the Ecumenical Patriarch to promote broader regional collaboration and education among some 75 clergy, theologians, educators, students, scientists, policy makers, and journalists. It developed a new direction in interdisciplinary vision and dialogue about environment matters.[6]

For the Halki Ecological Institute as well as for the ecological symposia the Green Patriarch serves as a facilitator for people to transcend their differences through realizing their commonalities and complementarities for their common good in the context of facing the challenges of the environmental crisis. The many initiatives of the Patriarch generate interfaith dialogues and collaborations among leaders of different religions and likewise among religious and scientific leaders. This is a very constructive achievement, considering the tensions and conflicts that have often emerged over the centuries within and among these different interest groups. One of the significant attributes of spiritual ecology is to serve as a context to facilitate such dialogue among individuals and groups from diverse backgrounds, persuasions, and interests.

The Ecumenical Patriarch was a special participant in the International Summit on Religions and Conversation in Atami, Japan (Session I, 1995), and the subsequent meeting at Windsor Castle in Great Britain (Session II, 1996). Also, he attended the Santa Barbara Environmental Conference on "Caring for God's Creation" in 1997, and another called "Sacred Gifts of a Living Planet" in Kathmandu, Nepal, in 2000. For about two decades now he has given over 136 environmental addresses and issued an annual encyclical on the environment on the first day of each September, designated as a day of prayer for the protection of creation by the entire Orthodox Church.[7]

The Green Patriarch was the very first global religious leader to denounce environmental abuse as a *sin* against God, humanity, and nature.[8] For example, at the Santa Barbara conference in November 1997, Patriarch Bartholomew declared:

> To commit a crime against the natural world is a sin. For human beings to cause species to become extinct and to destroy the biological diversity of God's creation; for human beings to degrade the integrity of the earth by causing changes in its climate, by stripping the earth of its natural forests, or by destroying its wetlands; for human beings to injure other human beings with disease by contaminating the earth's waters, its land, its air, and its life, with poisonous substances—all of these are sins.[9]

The Ecumenical Patriarch's deep commitment to interfaith dialogue and collaboration is also exemplified by his signing common statements concerning the environmental crisis with Pope John Paul II in 2002 and Pope Benedict XVI in 2006. The first joint statement includes a fundamental principle: "An awareness of the relationship between God and humankind brings a fuller sense of the importance of the relationship between human beings and the natural environment, which is God's creation and which God entrusted to us to guard with wisdom and love (cf. Gen.:1–28) . . . In this perspective, Christians and all other believers have a specific role to play in proclaiming moral values and in educating people in *ecological awareness*, which is none other than responsibility towards self, towards others, towards creation."

The joint statement with Pope Benedict XVI reflects a common theme in the Green Patriarch's words and deeds, a preoccupation with our legacy to future generations: "As religious leaders, we consider it one of our duties to encourage and to support all efforts made to protect God's creation, and to bequeath to future generations a world in which they will be able to live." Serious concern for the environment to be inherited by future generations is one of the most fundamental tenets of any genuine environmental ethics.[10]

These joint statements likely influence many among the more than one billion Catholics and 250 million Orthodox Christians in the world. This and other initiatives demonstrate the tremendous power of religious leaders and organizations to address environmental concerns.[11]

The spiritual ecology and environmentalism of the Ecumenical Patriarch reflects the Orthodox perspective that humans are part of nature, and that God's intention for humans is to serve humbly as stewards or caretakers of all creation in communion with it. Accordingly, as John (Zizioulas) Metropolitan of Pergamon writes: " ... the Orthodox Church realizes that without a profound spiritual transformation of the human being there is no hope for salvation of the natural environment from the human interventions that threaten it with destruction, and that in order to achieve such a spiritual transformation *all* religious communities should cooperate, together with scientists, politicians, ethicists, etc."[12] (Incidentally, the Green Patriarch's predecessor, Ecumenical Patriarch Demetrios, was also deeply concerned about the natural environment.)[13] John Chryssavgis affirms:

> With reference to the environmental initiatives and actions, what is perhaps most characteristic of the Patriarch's initiatives is the mark of humility. The Ecumenical Patriarch is able to see the larger picture. He recognizes that he is standing before something greater than himself, a world before which he must kneel, a chain that long predates and will long outlast him. Therefore, he speaks of self-emptying (*kenosis*) (Phil. 2.4–11), ministry (*diakonia*) (Luke 10.40; Acts 1.17, 25; 6.4), witness (*martyria*, a term which also has the sense of martyrdom and suffering) (John 1.7, 19), and thanksgiving

(or *eucharistia*, a term which also implies liturgy) (Acts 24.3; 2
Cor. 4.15).

The emphasis is always on humble simplicity—the technical term in
Orthodox spirituality is asceticism (*askeo*—to work up raw material
with skill, to exercise by training or discipline; Acts 24.16) and on
liturgy (ministration, ministry, service) as the essential source of
Orthodox theology. The notion of liturgy leads us into what is perhaps the most distinctive feature of the Patriarch's vision, namely
the concept of *communion* (*koinonia*—which also means communication and fellowship; 1 Cor. 10.16; Phil. 6).[14]

Chryssavgis, furthermore, observes that Bartholomew I appreciates that
environmental issues are closely related to and dependent on various other
sociopolitical issues including war and peace, justice and human rights,
and poverty and unemployment. In this realm of ecojustice, it is also recognized that environmental degradation impacts on the poor most of all.
Moreover, not only is the environment primarily a religious and spiritual
issue; "a spirituality that is not involved with outward creation is not
involved with the inward mystery either."[15]

The Green Patriarch's persistent commitment and work has been recognized worldwide. He has been awarded honorary doctorates from dozens of universities, received honorary citizenship from several countries,
and been presented with awards from many organizations and countries
including the U.S. Congressional Gold Medal in 1997. In 2002, he was
awarded the Sophie Prize in Oslo, Norway. Then in 2008, the magazine
Time identified him among the "100 Most Influential People in the
World" for "defining environmentalism as a spiritual responsibility."[16]

In conclusion, a statement by Chryssavgis merits quoting at length
because it reflects much of the heart of spiritual ecology in a most clear,
concise, and forceful way: "We tend to call this an "ecological" crisis, and
this is a fair description insofar as its *results* are manifested in the ecological
sphere. The message is quite clear: our way of life is humanly and environmentally suicidal. Unless we change it radically, we cannot hope to avoid
or reverse cosmic catastrophe. Yet, the crisis is not first of all ecological.
It is a crisis concerning the way *we* perceive reality, the way we imagine
or image our world. We are treating our environment, our planet, in an
inhuman, god-forsaken manner—precisely because we see it in this way,
precisely because we see ourselves in this way. Therefore, before we can

effectively deal with problems of our environment, we must change our world-image, which in turn means that we must change our self-image. Otherwise, we are simply dealing with symptoms, not with their causes."[17] This reflects the radical and even revolutionary nature of spiritual ecology— namely, to diagnose the ultimate causes of the ecocrisis and then to prescribe the necessary cure which is no less than a profound transformation in the ways that humans relate to nature as well as to each other.[18]

PART V. FLOWERS, SEEDS, AND FRUITS

The nutrients that trees draw mainly through their roots in the soil ultimately nourish the flowers, seeds, and fruits, which in turn variously sustain a diverse multitude of other organisms. Here these metaphors apply to the remarkable environmental activities of Wangari Maathai in generating the Green Belt Movement for planting trees beginning in Kenya and eventually spreading worldwide; the extraordinary annual Burning Man celebration in the Black Rock desert of Nevada as a creative ritual expression of spiritual ecology; and James Cameron's unique movie *Avatar* illustrating for a worldwide audience the contrast between a militant imperialistic society engaged in ecocide and genocide on the one hand and on the other a kind of indigenous society epitomizing some of the highest values of spiritual ecology. While they cannot be discussed in detail, other extraordinarily creative and influential personages who should be mentioned at least include Native American environmental activist Winona LaDuke, the profound primatologist Jane Goodall, anthropologist Wade Davis and ecologist David Suzuki for their work on sacred nature, pioneer ecopsychologists Ralph Metzner and Theodore Roszak, courageous defender of redwood trees Julia Butterfly Hill of the Circle of Life Foundation, political ecological activist and Wiccan Starhawk, Christopher McCleod of the Sacred Land Film Project, and Martin Palmer of the Alliance for Religions and Conservation. They each enrich humanity and nature through their mindful actions.

Chapter 16. To Plant a Tree, Wangari Maathai

> *It gradually became clear that the Green Belt Movement's work with communities to repair the degraded environment could not be done effectively without participants embracing a set of core spiritual values.*
>
> Wangari Maathai[1]

Wangari Muta Maathai, a Kikuyu from Kenya, was honored in 2004 with nothing less than the coveted Nobel Peace Prize, the first African woman to receive the award. The Nobel Committee recognized her contribution to sustainable development, democracy, and peace. As Maathai observes: "At that time, as now, people wondered what all my activities had to do with the way they lived their lives, with politics, with economics, with spirituality. And I still hear people say: what have trees to do with the peace? What have trees to do with the economy? Yet the tree, for me, is a symbol of what we all can see in the environment, but it is also an entry point into understanding the link between the environment and all these other issues."[2]

The Nobel Prize recognition was one of the triumphs on a long, arduous, and sometimes dangerous path. It started with the planting of trees in rural Kenya for the very practical reason of promoting the welfare of women who faced increasing scarcity of fuel wood and water along with other symptoms of environmental deterioration, poverty, and hardship. Only 3 percent of the country's original forest was left, the result of colonial clearing for timber and plantations of coffee and tea crops for export.[3]

The Green Belt Movement (GBM) was launched on World Environment Day in June 1977. By now there are more than 6,000 tree nurseries and 150,000 women volunteers in Kenya. The planting of more than 40 million trees of indigenous species on private farms and community lands like schools and church yards has transformed the social as well as biophysical landscape of her country. Furthermore, by 1986 funds from the UN Environmental Programme facilitated the movement's spread to 36 organizations in 15 countries in Africa with the planting of more than 35 million trees and the establishment of the Pan-African Green Belt

Network.[4] Even more, the United Nations followed Maathai's example with the Billion Tree Campaign. At the time of this writing, already more than 10.5 billion trees have been planted in 170 countries.[5] In 1987 the United Nations Environment Programme recognized the GBM for its success in ecological restoration with the Global 500 Award. Perhaps more than anything else, this miraculous story reflects the famous dictum of anthropologist Margaret Mead: "Never doubt that a small group of thoughtful citizens can change the world. Indeed, it's the only thing that ever has."[6]

Behind the modern miracle of Maathai's GBM is the story of an extraordinarily intelligent, wise, determined, and courageous woman of modern Africa. She was born the third child of a farmer woman and a sharecropper father. She excelled in a convent high school. With a scholarship from the U.S. government she obtained a B.S. in 1964 at Mount St. Scholastica College, in Atchison, Kansas, later renamed Benedictine College. Next she earned a M.S. in Biological Sciences in 1965 at the University of Pittsburgh. Finally, in 1971 she received the Ph.D. in Biology at the University College of Nairobi, later renamed the University of Nairobi. Maathai was the first woman from East Africa to earn a doctorate.[7] By 2002 Maathai was appointed deputy to the head of the Ministry of Environment and Natural Resources in Kenya, serving until November 2005 in the new President Mwai Kibaki regime. In the patriarchal culture of Kenya Maathai broke gender barriers to become the first woman to receive a doctorate in East Africa, to become an associate professor at the University of Nairobi, and even to head one of its departments, Veterinary Anatomy.[8]

Maathai's environmental concerns developed in the mid-1970s as she witnessed the environmental deterioration of her Kenyan homeland with watersheds drying, streams disappearing, deforestation, and desertification. She imagined that these environmental problems could be relieved through the planting of trees that would not only hold and nourish the soil and help restore watersheds, but yield fuel wood, water, and also food for better nutrition of the rural poor. Her early efforts were discouraged by others, but she persisted, and in 1977 the GBM took off. Beyond planting trees it also facilitated cultivating indigenous food crops, appropriate technology, training in entrepreneurship, and education about reproductive health and HIV/AIDS prevention. By the 1990s, Maathai was leading campaigns to preserve forests like Karura Forest on the edge of Nairobi, and, in urban areas' green spaces, such as Uhuru Park in that city. She and her followers were harassed, beaten, threatened, and jailed by government security forces and hired thugs. Maathai herself was beaten unconscious and hospitalized during one nonviolent resistance demonstration. She was actually on a list of targets for political assassination. The successes of the GBM led to its engagement with the pro-democracy movement in Kenya which challenged the autocratic President Daniel arap Moi. In the campaigns for the 2002 presidential election, Maathai planted trees to encourage fair voting and a peaceful transition to democracy. She was elected to parliament and then appointed assistant to the Minister for the Environment and Natural Resources. She was a member of the Mazingira Green Party, which she helped establish in 2003.[9] Eventually even the Kenyan military collaborated with the GBM, realizing that trees and forests were a matter of national security, or more specifically, environmental security.[10]

The community-based GBM mobilizes and empowers women through facilitating village tree planting, sustainable organic farming of indigenous crops, and environmental conservation encompassing biodiversity and local species. Women were given a modest stipend to search nearby forests for seeds to grow native trees and establish nurseries. Through civic and environmental education seminars and practical activities like tree planting the movement pursues the improvement of the livelihood of rural communities, household food security, poverty alleviation, and women's rights. It tries to cultivate a value-driven society concerned with personal and communal improvement emphasizing social and environmental justice. Although the main force in the movement is women, men and children are involved too, as in planting trees in school and church yards.[11]

It should be noted that the GBM reflects many attributes of the green movement more generally, such as organic farming, sustainable development, small is beautiful, appropriate technology, decentralization, bioregionalism, green education, and ecofeminism.[12] It also reflects principles of ecopsychology, the most fundamental being the mutuality of healing nature and self.[13]

The GBM developed from the roots of traditional African culture and religion wherein trees and nature were usually valued and respected, even though colonialism, including Christian missionization, greatly weakened such concerns. However, the GBM also emphasized aspects of Christian stewardship of God's creation, given that about 90 percent of Kenyans are Christians and that the percentage is even higher among GBM members. The main Christian religions are Catholic, Anglican, and Presbyterian. Church leaders and members have increasingly become concerned and active in healing their natural environment, although Evangelicals were resistant until recently.[14]

At the same time African traditions must have had considerable influence on Maathai and the GBM. As Faith Warner and Richard Hoskins observe: "Traditionally, the gods are all around: present in the nature in which people are a part. Therefore to respect the spiritual is to respect nature. The converse is equally true. The rape of the land is traditionally seen as a violation of the spirit world, and only to be undertaken at peril." Furthermore, ". . . spiritual well-being depends on a harmonic relationship with the gods and with the environment. Life is a unity, a web of relationships extending outwards with all that is around: humans, flora, fauna, and gods. Indeed, even to separate those terms, as if distinct categories, is to miss the point that in African religious life everything is interconnected. As such, if one part suffers, all do." A diversity of landscape features and natural phenomena were considered sacred in many African traditions, and taboos often restricted resource extraction.[15]

Maathai started tree planting for a pragmatic reason, to help heal rural poor women and their environment. As Maathai writes:

> Upon reflection, it is clear to me that when I began this work in 1977, I wasn't motivated by my faith or by religion in general. Instead, the motivation came from thinking literally and practically about how to solve problems on the ground. It was a desire to help rural populations, especially women, with the basic needs they described to me during seminars and workshops. They said that they lacked clean drinking water, adequate and nutritious food, income, and enough energy for cooking and heating. So, when these questions were asked during the early days, I'd answer that I didn't think digging holes and mobilizing communities to protect or restore trees, forests, watersheds, soils, or habitats for wildlife that surrounded them was spiritual work or only relevant to the religious.[16]

Maathai was often asked why she was undertaking such an effort. Gradually she began to realize that, beyond practical needs, passion, and vision, underlying the GBM was a set of four basic core values, and that ultimately they were spiritual and shared by many religions. Maathai identifies these values as love for the environment, gratitude and respect for Earth's resources, self-empowerment and self-betterment, and the spirit of service and volunteerism. She adds that "These values encapsulate the intangible, subtle, nonmaterial aspects of the GMB as an organization. ... Such values are not unique to the Green Belt Movement. They are universal, but they can't be touched or seen. We cannot place a monetary value on them; in effect, they are priceless. They define humanity."[17]

Maathai came to appreciate the scope of human action: "In degrading the environment, therefore, we degrade ourselves and all humankind. The reverse is also true. In the process of helping the earth heal, we help ourselves."[18] This is the recognition of the fact that every being is interconnected and interdependent to some degree in various ways; this is a fundamental tenet of biological ecology, human ecology, spiritual ecology, and ecopsychology, as well as Buddhism and Hinduism, among other perspectives. Thus, Maathai asserts:

> Human beings have a consciousness by which we can appreciate love, beauty, creativity, and innovation or mourn the lack thereof. To the extent that we can go beyond ourselves and ordinary biological instincts, we can experience what it means to be human and therefore different from other forms of life. We can appreciate the delicacy of dew or a flower in bloom, water as it runs over pebbles, or the majesty of an elephant, the fragility of a butterfly, or a field of wheat or leaves blowing in the wind. Such aesthetic responses are valid in their own right, and as reactions to the natural world they can inspire in us a sense of wonder and beauty that in turn encourages a sense of the divine.[19]

Interestingly, Maathai identifies the existence of "our inner ecology, our soul and sense of being human."[20] Throughout her book, *Replenishing the Earth: Spiritual Values for Healing Ourselves and the World*, she uses the word "God" in connection not only with the monotheistic Abrahamic traditions of Christianity, Islam, and Judaism, but also with the Kikuyu religious worldview. However, she also applies the term "the Source" as "the place of all knowledge and awareness" and the "repository of all that we cannot explain."[21] She writes: "I came to identify trees as the answer to the environmental problems the Kenyan women faced, partly because I grew up in the countryside surrounded by trees and green vegetation. . . . I can also point to the Source as the wellspring for all of the ideas that came."[22]

Alluding to the ongoing environmental crisis, and to global climate change in particular, Maathai concludes:

> The questions we have to ask ourselves are these: Will we have the foresight now to stop the worst from happening, or will we wait until it is too late? We have the power to guide the earth toward a goal that's beneficial for our own goals too. Will we adjust our practices and values in time to stop our own destruction? These questions insist on more than a scientific answer, which is why the ecological crisis is both a physical crisis and a spiritual one. Addressing it requires a new level of consciousness, where we understand that we belong to the larger family of life on Earth. If we were able to achieve this consciousness, we'd see that the planet is hurting, and internalize the spiritual values that can help us move to address the wounds. We'd recognize that it should be in our nature to be custodians of the planet and do what's right for the earth and, in the process, for ourselves.[23]

One source that Maathai discusses frequently in the book is the traditions of her own Kikuyu culture, such as sacred trees inhabited by spirits.[24] Another is the Holy Bible of Christians which she quotes. However, her attention to ecologically relevant aspects of religion is much broader and more diverse, extending to references from Judaism, Buddhism, Hinduism, and Shintoism, among other traditions.[25] It is also noteworthy that, although a scientist, Maathai finds no incompatibility with spirituality: ". . . [one] can be committed to the scientific method and still experience ecstasy at the great mystery of the cosmos." Later she writes: "We need to remind ourselves, however, that for all of its extraordinary sophistication, there are many issues that modern science can't explain."[26]

At the same time, Maathai does not hold back criticisms of Christian religion, particularly in the earlier context of European colonialism. One example is that the missionaries insisted that God had to be worshipped in the church, not outside in nature.[27] Nor does she hold back criticism of former European colonial nations that, although now concerned with environmental conservation, previously exploited resources and degraded the environments of their colonies.[28]

Maathai points to several different sources of inspiration for her life and work with the GBM: her family; Catholic schooling; other spiritually motivated heroes and heroines including in the civil rights movement in the United States and Kenya; liberation theology in Latin America and beyond; the Source; leaders in the spiritual ecology revolution like Mary Evelyn Tucker, John Grim, Al Gore, and Terry Tempest Williams; the Earth Charter initiative; and members of the GBM. She was also deeply influenced by the civil rights, women's, and environmental movements in the United States.[29]

A history of Wangari Maathai on the website of the Wangari Maathai Institute for Peace and the Environment sums up much of her unique contribution:

> ... when she was awarded the prestigious Nobel Peace Prize (2004), becoming the first African woman and the ninth African to be so honored, the entire world had to sit up and take notice. Besides being an accomplished scholar, Professor Wangari Muta Maathai has made her mark as an uncompromising environmental conservationist, an ardent human rights crusader, a tireless Non-governmental Organization net-worker, a champion for democracy as well as a principled politician. She has emerged as a leader who thinks globally but acts locally and one that knows the way, shows the way and goes the way. Professor Maathai has also reasserted the place of Kenya on the global map and secured our pride as a nation.[30]

From the above, it should be no surprise that Maathai was recognized in 2005 by *Time* magazine as one of 100 most influential people in the world, and by *Forbes* as one of 100 most powerful women in the world. She has received many awards, such as the Goldman Environmental prize in 1991, and several honorary doctorates, such as from Yale University in 2004.[31]

In conclusion, although until recently the GBM was viewed, at least by outsiders, as largely a women's social, economic, political, and/or environmental movement, clearly it also has a spiritual component as reflected in the subtitle of her book *Replenishing the Earth: Spiritual Values for Healing Ourselves and the World*. Indeed, this book provides a very useful overview of many aspects of spiritual ecology in general as well as the

GBM in particular. Maathai ends her book: "If my work with the Green Belt Movement had evolved as I had hoped, tree-planting would be a national activity throughout Africa, people would be required to plant a certain number of trees on their land, soil erosion would be a thing of the past, and environmental education would be taught in every Africa school."[32] Perhaps that hope is still being realized. Tragically Maathai died of cancer at the age of 71 on September 25, 2011. Yet her saintly legacy lives on in the multitude of lives, human, arboreal, and ecosystemic, that she greatly benefited in Kenya and far beyond.

CHAPTER 17. DESERT SPIRITUALITY, BURNING MAN

Burning Man is an interactive stage on which to perform, interrogate, and negotiate the meanings of religion, spirituality, ritual, identity, and culture, alongside a multitude of concurrent themes and possibilities.

Lee Gilmore[1]

Black Rock Desert in northwestern Nevada is a flat, hot, dry, and dusty ancient lake bed. This barren area comes alive with tens of thousands of pilgrims from many parts of the world every year during the week before Labor Day weekend. The people attending are not just spectators of some event. They actively participate in a carnivalesque bonding into a community of pilgrims. Performances include a rich variety of highly creative, fanciful, eclectic, colorful, and rebellious self-expression through theater, art, dance, and music. The performances are permeated with ritualistic and other elements that often generate personal transformations of a kind that many would identify as spiritual or mystical. The grand climax of this largely spontaneous festival is the sacrificial burning of a giant wooden effigy over 40 feet high standing on a raised platform together with a pyrotechnic spectacle. The festival is called Burning Man, participants are referred to as Burners, and the desert locale as the *playa*. When it first started in this locale in 1990, fewer than a hundred individuals came.[2] The attraction of tens of thousands in recent years surely reflects something quite extraordinary that people consider as a genuine experience worthy of the time, money, and effort required for travel and for temporary residence in the otherness of a harsh desert. The overwhelming majority of participants are Caucasians who can afford to travel and stay for the week of adult play, fantasy, and comedy. A rock opera has even been produced: *How to Survive the Apocalypse: A Burning Opera.*[3]

The humanoid effigy has no gender and is not assigned any particular meaning by the organizers of the festival. Indeed, in a somewhat anarchic fashion each participant is at liberty to construct their own individual meaning out of their personal observations and experiences during the festival. The event is thus something of a pilgrimage.[4] While there are

religious elements in the festival, such as traditional motifs used creatively in some art work, organizers and most participants reject any
established religious dogma or organization in association with the festival.[5] Instead, the performances challenge the traditional concepts and
boundaries of religion. They emphasize spirituality as distinct from religion, although some participants even deny that any spirituality is
involved for them.[6] The festival also emphasizes the nature of culture
as a dynamic, flexible, and adaptable construction.[7] The event is an
expression of "countercultural" resistance to the dominant and dominat-
ing aspects of American culture, an antistructural ritual challenging
structure.[8] As part of their antistructural performances, Burners also
engage in parody and rituals of reversal in which ". . . normative symbols,
meanings, and hierarchies are deliberately inverted or otherwise dis-
torted."[9] In short, Burners creatively engage experimentally in individual
interactions and community social dynamics that can be entertaining,
cathartic, and liberating, but also deeply spiritual. There is skydiving
from a small airplane, a taxi service, and even an ice cream truck circulat-
ing in the desert.[10]

Anthropologist Lee Gilmore illuminates aspects of the spiritual ecology
of the Black Rock Desert: "This dramatic landscape can seem like the
surface of an alien planet and presents numerous physical challenges. In
its seemingly endless expanse and otherworldly terrain, the Black Rock
playa evokes feelings of both fantastic and limitless possibility, and the
austerity of the desert stirs up the themes of hardship, sacrifice, mystery,
and boundlessness that are deeply ingrained in the Western cultural
imagination. It is not without significance that deserts have a long history as loci of transformative possibilities—from Moses to Muhammed
and from Christ to Carlos Castaneda—and Burning Man plays to these
ideational sensibilities. Participants today often speak of being "on the
playa" in a way that references this sense of environmental and cognitive
otherness, helping to set the stage for transformative experiences."[11]
In other words, the desert offers a crucible for personal ritual catharsis,
renewal, and transformation.[12] The desert environment, with extremes
of temperature from noon to night as well as wind, dust, and storms,
raises awareness of the vulnerability of the human organism to nature,
and it can push individuals to the limits of endurance and even survival.
It often generates community bonding and personal transformative
experiences.[13]

Through the years Burners have developed "Ten Principles" that identify and sustain an ethos of their shared values and standards providing guidelines for the community of participants:

1. radical inclusion—anyone is welcome;
2. gifting—participants are encouraged to freely share their resources and creativity without any assignment of value or expectation of return;
3. decommodification—corporate and independent sponsorship, advertising, and vending are strictly prohibited;
4. radical self-reliance—every individual must supply all of their own survival needs including water, food, and shelter which at least temporarily removes them from the corporate and consumer aspects of American culture and emphasizes responsibility, autonomy, freedom, and inner resources;
5. radical self-expression—individuals are encouraged to engage in their own creative and reflexive interactions with others and the larger community as a whole but respect the rights and liberties of the recipients of their actions;
6. communal effort—individuals interact in synergy to create and maintain the whole community and celebratory character of the event through creative cooperative and collaborative activities;
7. civic responsibility—consideration for the welfare, rights, and freedom of others as well as for local, state, and federal laws;
8. leave no trace—make every effort to erase as much as possible any material evidence and environmental impact of the activities during the festival including removing any refuse;
9. participation—deep active engagement is expected and promoted by everyone and no one should be merely a passive spectator; and
10. immediacy—being in the moment and spontaneous in the celebratory and contemplative activities of the festival and in transcending any barriers to the recognition of the inner self and communion with nature.[14]

Radical inclusiveness is reflected in the religious backgrounds of participants, which range from so-called world religions to Paganism, New Age, and idiosyncratic spirituality to nonreligious, agnostic, and atheist.[15] Cultural and religious themes are appropriated and manipulated in the artistic performances from Balinese, Buddhist, Christian, Islamic,

Mayan, Shinto, Vodou, and other sources.[16] There are also classes in Kabbalah, meditation, and yoga as well as a Balinese Monkey chant, marriages, memorial ceremonies, Shabbat services, and Wicca circles, among other events.[17]

Many of these principles reflect common attributes of spiritual ecology. For instance, at the end of the festival participants and organizers do their utmost to remove every trace of their activities in the temporary city they created in order to restore the desert environment to its previous natural condition. They even have the special term "moop" meaning matter out of place. This reflects an ethical environmental awareness, conscience, and responsibility. Furthermore, many participants take this and other attributes of the festival back to apply in their mundane existence in the larger society.[18] One documentary film opens with these phrases: "once a year a city rises & falls leaving no trace ... during its brief existence, 25,000 people gather to celebrate life, passion & art ... a visionary world where no money changes hands."[19]

The extent of environmental concern is illustrated in the detailed guidelines on the official Burning Man website. For instance, here are even guidelines for just digging holes: "Do not excavate holes in the playa. Small holes (6 inches or less in diameter & less than 2 feet deep) used for structural support are the sole exception. When digging such a hole it is best to use an auger or a posthole digger, NOT a shovel. Bag the dirt you are removing so that it does not blow away in the wind. Refill the hole by carefully tamping the soil back into place. Repeat this process every few inches while dampening the soil. An inverted sledgehammer works well for this. Experience has shown that the larger holes easily erode within a year's time, even when carefully backfilled. They leave a visible mark and create a serious safety hazard to drivers throughout the rest of the year."[20]

Burners are searching for something more real, true, or genuine than they usually experience in their mundane existence and the larger materialistic consumer society.[21] Linguistic anthropologist Edward Sapir's (1924) distinction between genuine and spurious culture appears to the present author to be quite pertinent here. Basically, a genuine culture encompasses meaningful active participation of individuals in a society, whereas spurious is just the opposite.[22] Many involved in spiritual ecology are also engaged in something of a personal vision quest in pursuit of a more genuine culture ecologically as well as socially, psychologically, and spiritually. Gilmore notes: "Yet for many of these individuals there remains a desire for a spiritually informed life, a connection to a larger, or ultimate, reality, meaning, or purpose, as well as a deepened, expanded, and reflexive sense of self."[23] The ritualized space and the chemistry of the festival facilitates individual experimentation with alternative experiences, identities, and spiritualities that may be more meaningful than those encountered in the mundane world.[24] The desert naturally generates spirituality at the Burning Man pilgrimage—as it has done in so many other cases.[25]

CHAPTER 18. AVATAR, OPENING PANDORA'S BOX, JAMES CAMERON

We still have time to fix this [ecocrisis] and we still have time to make it better, but really what is needed here is that the human race needs to wake up and look forward with the sense that we've got to change the way we live. ... What we have to do is to transform ourselves yet again into something that has never existed on this planet before, which is a kind of techno-indigenous people. ... We will use high technology and science to provide us with the energy we need, but they'll be sustainable solutions. Nature is not our enemy, it is our sustenance and we need it, and we need nature healthy for us to be healthy and to survive long-term, and that's the realization we have to come to and that's the next stage in evolution that we have to reach.

James Cameron.[1]

Avatar, an unprecedented epic of science fiction, has become the greatest of all blockbusters movies so far, attracting a record number of viewers and fans worldwide while grossing a record 2.7 billion dollars or more, including from its spin-off books, video game, action toys, and the like.[2] In many respects it is the most innovative and spectacular movie ever, as well as the most successful and expensive one so far. Many viewers shed tears, some become depressed, and a few even suicidal. What is this all about? The appeal of the movie as popular culture is surely influenced by several factors, the combination varying to some degree with different members of the audience.[3] Indeed, the reactions to *Avatar* have been compared to a Rorschach test.[4]

Certainly *Avatar* has great entertainment value with its allegorical hero's journey, romantic love story, and epic battle between good and evil. The main hero, Jake Sully, is a paraplegic ex-marine. He joins an expedition to an exotic planet called Pandora to help mine its rare mineral, which has a value far higher than gold and is called unobtanium. The Na'vi are the indigenous inhabitants of Pandora, 10-foot-tall blue-skinned humanoids with some feline features including their yellow eyes, ear shape, and long tail.[5]

Avatara is a Hindu concept regarding the terrestrial manifestation of a deity such as Vishnu in human or animal form to save the world from imminent destruction.[6] In this film the scientists of the invading empire design avatars, Na'vi-human hybrid bodies that resemble Na'vi but with a human mind. Jake is assigned to become an avatar in order to gather intelligence about the Na'vi for the purposes of the mining and associated military operations. However, in the process he is attracted to their life-style and to the beautiful heroine named Neytiri.[7] Moreover, Jake begins "going naïve" by identifying more with the Na'vi than with his fellow humans."[8] Eventually Jake rebels against his own kind as they attempt to forcefully exploit the rare and highly valued mineral wealth of Pandora through warfare. Some of his Terran (human) colleagues, including scientists, also rebel in their empathy for the innocent Na'vi, enchanted by their seemingly idyllic life and wondrous edenic environment. Kevin Patrick Mahoney interprets the role of Jake as following the archetype of the hero's journey and rebirth in the work of comparative mythologist Joseph Campbell.[9]

The most obvious attraction for many viewers is the brilliant technological wizardry that so skillfully engineered this extraordinary film. A whole new generation of visual effects combine computer-generated images and live action to create the virtual world of Pandora, something referred to as performance or motion capture.[10] James Cameron was the movie's script writer, director, and producer. Many of the basic ideas in the film germinated over a period of more than 15 years in Cameron's mind and the production took four years, starting in 2005. He developed appropriate technology to realize his epic futuristic vision. He had the ideas much earlier, but had to await technological advances.[11]

Many viewers are deeply moved emotionally by the beauty and majesty of the landscape of Pandora. Its powerful aesthetic appeal stems from the colorful and captivating grandeur of the apparently primeval landscape. The latter is reminiscent of the paintings of Maxfield Parrish (1870–1966) that were once extremely popular in the United States.[12] The Pandora landscape includes mountainous tropical rain forest with towering island-like pinnacles resembling parts of China's Guilin region and the tepui's (isolated table-top mountains) of Venezuela's Gran Sabana and Amazon regions. The bioluminescence of some of the plants is awesome.

The colorful ecology of Pandora is sharply contrasted with the drab buildings, uniforms, equipment, and vehicles of the invading human colonists. Furthermore, the Na'vi are appealing because their society and life appear to be more humane, peaceful, harmonious, spiritual, and natural than that of the invading empire from Earth. Nevertheless, the Na'vi are portrayed as having some elements of a warrior tradition.[13]

Avatar mirrors fascinating elements including tropes from previous films that touch fond memories for many movie goers, such as *Apocalypse Now*, *At Play in the Fields of the Lord*, *Dances with Wolves*, *Emerald Forest*, *Fern Gully*, *Jurassic Park*, *Kundun*, *Last of the Mohicans*, *Last of His Tribe* [Ishi], *Little Big Man*, *Pocahontas*, *Princess Mononoke*, *2001: A Space Odyssey*, *Star Wars*, *Whale Rider*, and *Zulu*. Likewise, the movie is reminiscent of classic literature, perhaps most of all novels such as *Green Mansions* by William H. Hudson, *Lost World* by Arthur Conan Doyle, and *The Word for World Is Forest* by Ursula LeGuin. Many of these films and novels exemplify attributes of spiritual ecology, such as an intimate spiritual and ecological connection of indigenes with nature.

The film starts with a series of images that introduce the main themes: wondrous mountainous tropical rain forest, highly advanced technology and space craft, vast mining pits with enormous extractive machinery, mercenary personnel and their military equipment, an innocent and idyllic indigenous society, and the brutality typical of much of colonialism. The juxtaposition of these images also exposes a forthcoming ideological message on the far left; namely, a radical critique of the American empire, the greed of rapacious corporate business, belligerent militarism and mercenaries, environmentally destructive and inhumane technology, and rampant consumerism.[14] The society of the human invaders is sharply contrasted with the spiritually motivated and environmentally friendly Na'vi society, which possesses a combination of Animistic and Pantheistic worldview, values, and attitudes while struggling to retain its sovereignty, land, culture, and identity. This is obviously a metaphor for the recurrent processes in colonial history.[15]

Apparently Cameron is well aware of the long history of the militarism of the United States of America and, perhaps, also the Human Terrain System initiative which embeds social scientists with the American military to collect cultural and political intelligence data in the wars in Afghanistan and Iraq.[16] Cameron refers to these contemporary

American wars through well-known phrases from the George W. Bush presidency like "war on terror," "shock and awe," "embed," and "win hearts and minds."[17] The enormous mining pits are reminiscent of the environmentally and socially devastating practices in many places of the world, including the mountain top removal for coal mining in Appalachia.[18] This is all a contemporary illustration of General Dwight D. Eisenhower's concern in his farewell speech as president of the United States warning about the dangers of the industrial-military complex, a phenomenon which is now more appropriately recognized as the industrial-military-media-academic complex. The subplots of resources and militarism in the movie reflect their frequent complementary association in American and other industrial societies throughout history to this day.

Another subplot is that of Jake Sully, the main hero, as a paraplegic marine veteran who is liberated and reborn by becoming a Na'vi avatar. Accordingly, Kevin Patrick Mahoney insightfully observes that: "... Cameron is utilizing Jake Sully as a metaphor for the West itself, to show that it is possible for our Nation States to change the way they behave, so that they become (at the very least) more caring and considerate to other peoples, and more economical in the utilization of finite resources, as the ultimate price for smashing and grabbing what you want is only ever going to get higher."[19]

The Na'vi and the Terran invaders can be better appreciated as representing equilibrium and disequilibrium societies following the heuristic conceptual framework of ecological anthropologist John W. Bennett (see Table 18.1).[20] These are polar extremes along a continuum from equilibrium societies, which are sustainable and in a relative dynamic balance and harmony with their natural environment, to disequilibrium societies, which are just the opposite. Population-environment interactions in small-scale, subsistence-based, equilibrium societies are often regulated by religious worldviews, values, attitudes, institutions, practitioners, and customs. Many traditional indigenous societies throughout the world, such as the Desana in the Colombian Amazon, were in dynamic equilibrium as they were almost entirely dependent on local land and resources for their survival and well-being.[21]

Contemporary industrialized societies involve the state level of sociopolitical organization enforced by police and military institutions, a market economy obsessively pursuing predatory capitalism, and expansion and

Table 18.1.   Ideal Types of Societies Based on Degree of Ecological
Equilibrium

	Equilibrium	Disequilibrium
Population dynamics	Small, controlled	Large, expanding, and weakly controlled
Contact with environment	Direct contact by maximum number of people	Direct contact by minimum number of people
Range	Restricted to local resources	Resources available from external sources
Sustenance needs	Close to minimal	Maximal
	Defined largely by physiological needs	Defined largely by cultural wants
Gratification expectations	Low, controlled	High, promise of continued expansion
Technological capacity	Low	High
Feedback loop	Functioning to control resource use	Functioning only to promote resource use

control of distant lands and resources to meet culturally created materialistic consumer demands. This is the inevitable clash of incompatible cultural worlds represented in *Avatar*. The movie is a metaphor for
European colonial empires in the Americas, Australia, and elsewhere and
the interconnected issues of environmental destruction, environmental
justice, and human rights more broadly.[22] The base of the human colony
on Pandora is appropriately named Hell's Gate. Post–World War II disequilibrium societies are spiraling out of control like a cancer destroying
its host that, in this case, is the entire planet Earth. In contrast, in some
ways the Na'vi represent futuristic "ecologically noble savages."[23]

In the extreme the fundamental differences between the equilibrium
and disequilibrium types of societies are, respectively, satisfying need or
greed, spiritual or material focus, and ultimately, supposed utopia or dystopia. In other words, the Na'vi are focused on satisfying basic needs and
on active spirituality resulting in a utopia, while the Terrans are focused
on materialism and greed resulting in a dystopia. This binary opposition is
neat and clear in the movie *Avatar*, but, of course, far less so in reality.[24]
Nevertheless, the opposition is very useful as a provocative metaphor to
convey one of Cameron's messages, the connection between the denigration
of indigenous rights and their environment by the industrial-military-
media-academic complex of contemporary American imperialism, a matter
sometimes referred to as ecojustice and often involving genocide, ethnocide,

and ecocide, such as in the entire colonial history experienced by Native Americans.[25]

Most of all, whereas the Na'vi may appear to be a "primitive" tribal society with a low technological capacity to exploit resources and impact on their environment in sharp contrast to the alien invaders, actually the Na'vi are far more advanced in their spirituality and ecology.[26] They are not just an environmentally friendly and sustainable mostly foraging society in biophysical balance and harmony with nature in Pandora; they are intimately tuned into its spiritual forces and processes including sacred places (Hometree, Tree of Souls, Tree of Voices, forest sprites, and so on). Hometree is the physical and spiritual residence of the Omaticaya clan of Na'vi. Many clans live in trees that are several times higher than redwoods on Earth.[27]

Again, this ecospirituality parallels to some degree the reality of many traditional indigenous societies in the Amazon and elsewhere on planet Earth with their sophisticated and penetrating traditional environmental knowledge and their profound religion of Animism with shamans as part-time religious practitioners.[28] Animism is a belief in spiritual beings and forces in nature including kinship with other-than-human persons.[29] The jellyfish-like luminous wood sprites are such spirit beings in Pandora. There are also elements of Pantheism in the Na'vi religion wherein the divine and the natural are isomorphic in Pandora—the divine represented by "The Great Mother" called Eywa.[30] She reflects the Na'vi's deep connection with the network of various kinds of energies encompassing spiritual ones that flow through everything in Pandora, a phenomenon reminiscent of some interpretations of Gaia, the Earth as a giant superorganism with spiritual consciousness.[31]

Here is an especially apt description of Eywa and related phenomena: "On Pandora there is only one greater entity. She spreads beneath the ground in a complex root system like the neural pathways of the human brain, with every tree being a single brain cell or dendrite. And all the roots are commingling . . . those are the synapses. One vast sentience, covering all the land."[32] Eywa is also described as: "Guiding force and deity of Pandora and the Na'vi. . . . The Na'vi believe that Eywa, in turn, acts to keep the ecosystems of Pandora in perfect balance."[33] (This is also somewhat reminiscent of James Lovelock's Gaia hypothesis.) The Na'vi literally plug into this organic network by using their queue, a braid of hair hanging down their back. It is a sheath for neural tendrils that can be connected to similar structures of other life forms: "It is believed that the queue also allows the Na'vi to access the neural network that envelops the entire moon [Pandora], and thus the collective wisdom of all Pandoran life."[34]

Yet another attraction of *Avatar* is the intensely intimate interconnections between the Na'vi and their habitat, which caters to the broad and diverse craving of various sectors of the public for spiritual ecology.[35] This points as well to a nature deficit experienced by many modern humans, one especially pronounced in urban and industrial societies where people are alienated from nature.[36] One of the fundamental tenets of ecopsychology is that the health of humans, both emotional and physical, is closely linked with the health of their natural habitat and regular intimate interaction with it. Thus, to heal oneself and be healthy, one must heal nature and keep it healthy as well; the two are inextricably interrelated.[37] This may be one factor appealing to the people in the popular movement for learning the Na'vi language.[38] This attraction to the spiritual ecology of *Avatar* may also reflect the hypothesized phenomena of biophilia and topophilia, respectively—an affective attraction for biotic life and landscape.[39]

Here Cameron's own description of the Na'vi is illuminating: "The Na'vi are humanoid because the audience is invited to relate to them, not as aliens but as creatures which express some aspect of ourselves which we admire and aspire to. . . . They are emotional, spiritual, and physically accomplished. They are brave and unafraid of death because they know it is part of a greater cycle. They live in harmony with nature, not in some idyllic hippie fantasy but in a realistic way, meaning they know that they can be hunted as well as being the hunter, and they know they must not use technology to disturb the balance and must only take what they need."[40]

Indigenous people have been among the international audience viewing *Avatar*. Most revealing, for many of them the film resonates with their spiritual ecology. It also mirrors similar experiences that they have had with colonial and/or neocolonial empires invading their territory to exploit their land and resources including religious, environmental, and academic colonialisms.[41]

Given the ecospirituality of the Na'vi, the matter of Cameron's religious and/or spiritual beliefs arises. His biographer, Rebecca Keegan, provides the answer: "Cameron's interest in religion was driven as much by intellectual curiosity as by any kind of spiritual questing. As an adult, his movies would be full of religious imagery. Today he calls himself a "converted agnostic." "I've sworn off agnosticism, which I now call cowardly atheism," Cameron says. "I've come to the position that in the complete absence of any supporting data whatsoever for the persistence of the individual in some spiritual form, it is necessary to operate under the provisional conclusion that there is no afterlife and then be ready to amend that if I find otherwise."[42] Keegan also mentions that "*Avatar* is Cameron's spiritual and ecological call to arms disguised as an adventure about a planet with ten-foot-tall blue aliens."[43] The eventual movie sequel may focus even more on Na'vi spiritual ecology.[44] However, for Cameron the spirituality of the Na'vi appears to be a kind of global organic Internet driven by electrochemical energy and systems feedbacks; that is, something that actually may be purely biophysical.

After *Avatar* the Hollywood titan was invited to speak at a conference on sustainability in Manaus, Brazil. In addition, on April 12, 2010, he joined the protest in Brasilia against the proposed Belo Monte hydroelectric dam in the Xingu region of the state of northern Para in Brazil. Previously he had visited under a giant tree with the leaders of 13 tribes in the region who were discussing the impending environmental and social crisis that would be precipitating by the dam. Cameron is reported as saying that the dam is a "quintessential example of the type of thing we are showing in 'Avatar'—the collision of a technological civilization's vision for progress at the expense of the natural world and the cultures of the indigenous people that live there."[45] In other words, this is the reality of greed versus nature, and of viewing nature as a warehouse rather than a sanctuary. Just as the Amazon had been an inspiration for the tropical forest ecology depicted in the movie, now it has become an inspiration for Cameron to personally engage more actively in environmental issues.[46]

Cameron spoke to 200,000 people attending the Earth Day rally in Washington, D.C., on April 25, 2010.[47] He mentioned that the first Earth Day in 1970 was a major influence on his environmental concerns. Cameron reflected that "I think the success of the movie is a measurement of the fact that consciousness is raising out there." He challenged the audience to become earth warriors, to each learn about the scientific facts of the reality of global climate change, and then to disseminate the information to at least ten other individuals. Furthermore, Cameron and others launched the Avatar Home Tree Initiative for Earth Day 2010 with the goal of planting one million trees in 15 countries by the end of the year. As of December 10, 2011, 293,884 trees had been planted world-wide, a very significant number, even if the ultimate goal had not been reached.[48]

Biographer Keegan remarks: "Each James Cameron movie is a warning against his darkest childhood fears and a kind of how-to-guide for living through catastrophe with humanity and spirit intact."[49] Cameron spent his early childhood in rural Ontario, Canada, where he explored the forests, rivers, and gorges with their associated wildlife. He also enjoyed rafts and tree houses. He was enamored with the television series exploring the world of the oceans by Jacques Cousteau.[50] Later he was to pioneer several documentaries about the marine environment. Cameron became more concerned about environmental issues after his family moved to California and learned about the Santa Barbara oil tanker spill in 1969. He says that through this disaster he realized that the modern technological world was overwhelming and destroying the natural world.

Cameron is not simply a largely self-taught genius in the film industry, he is a profound thinker deeply concerned with the suffering of humans and nature in the present and future, and in an activist as well as philosophical manner.[51] With the enormous worldwide audience for his film, together with his fame, fortune, and connections, he can be, and appears to be becoming, a very powerful influence for environmentalism in the world. For example, in June 2010, he was one of the consultants meeting in Washington, D.C., to explore possible solutions to the disastrous oil leak of the BP Deepwater Horizon in the Gulf of Mexico. Within a few years he plans to produce two sequels to *Avatar* to form a trilogy; thus he will continue to be influential in many ways and levels.

Judging from his monumental accomplishments so far, as a futurist, Cameron the writer, artist, scientist, engineer, visionary, and filmmaker, is making a significant contribution to bringing public attention to environmental, indigenous, and other sociopolitical problems and issues. Keegan remarks: "Cameron's movies provide us a place to imagine a path to a better future. 'Yes, we're all doomed,' Cameron told that Santa Barbara crowd. 'But on the positive side, we created this impending doom ourselves, with our brains, with our technology, and we can damn well uncreate it.' Cameron's career has been built on questioning accepted wisdom and believing in the power of the individual. His outlook, that we can take fate in our own hands, has implications far beyond making entertaining movies. It determines the very future we face."[52]

In conclusion, *Avatar* is far more than a purely escapist epic adventure from Hollywood. It is also a wake-up call concerning the environmental and human destruction caused by the voracious greed of rapacious capitalism as a component of the military-industrial-media-academic complex of the American empire. Cameron powerfully reaches a worldwide audience by emotionalizing environmental issues in a mythic narrative about the future. *Avatar*, like many of his other films, is an apocalyptic narrative, specifically about future environmental catastrophe after key resources on Earth are depleted and its environment poisoned with widespread pollution. However, only after the film did Cameron engage more actively in environmentalism. Previously he was an environmentalist mainly through his personal lifestyle with organic gardening, recycling, a hybrid car, and solar and wind energy to power his home.[53]

Avatar reached many millions of people with emotionally as well as intellectually compelling messages, thereby generating a lot of useful discussion and even activism. About halfway through the movie Jake muses: "Everything is backwards now, out there is the true world [Pandora], in here is the dream [human world]." Indeed, in viewing *Avatar*, it is not always clear what is fantasy and what is reality. In some respects, contemporary industrial society, with its materialistic consumer mentality and pursuit of continual growth, is fantasy in the sense that materialism has not been very satisfying and unlimited growth on a limited base is simply logically and pragmatically impossible. As Keegan says, "Based on Cameron's track record as a futurist operating in a fictional world, it's entirely likely that 2029 will require our best survivalist skills."[54] As Neytiri's mother admonishes Jake in the film, "learn well, then we will see if your insanity can be cured."[55]

PART VI. HAZARDS

Trees face pests, diseases, and other hazards that threaten their ability to flourish if not even their very survival. Likewise, spiritual ecology is challenged by an array of critics and obstacles, not the least of which are militant atheists with their myopic worship of scientism. Yet there are also atheist spiritual ecologists like philosopher Donald Crosby, who finds the sacred to be inherent in nature itself. Moreover, there are top scholars with graduate degrees in both religion and science from major universities who champion the re-enchantment of nature for the survival of the human species and the biosphere, such as Alister McGrath and his reworking of aspects of natural theology. Finally, there is the most tragic case of Tibet which, under an atheistic communist regime invading from China since the second half of the twentieth century, has suffered ecocide as well as geonocide, ethnocide, and religiocide. The secularization of sacred Tibet and the resultant deterioration of its ecosystems is part of this disastrous invasion and colonization, mirrored in some respects by the movie *Avatar*. However, the passage of time may reveal that the magnitude, momentum, and influence of the quiet revolution of spiritual ecology are far more powerful than any noisy critics and other obstacles.

CHAPTER 19. ATHEIST SPIRITUAL ECOLOGY, DONALD A. CROSBY[1]

We must learn to reverence and hold in awe the sacredness of the earth as our beloved community and household rather than view it merely as the backdrop or setting for self-contained, self-regarding human enterprises. Deeply rooted religious sensibilities and commitment are required.

Donald A. Crosby[2]

Atheists, agnostics, secular humanists, and the like in some way and degree may still be at least spiritual, if not also somehow religious, as reflected in the above quote. Accordingly, some of them can be considered as another aspect of spiritual ecology. Indeed, the Crosby quote might well have been written by Thomas Berry or another theist.

In his book *A Religion of Nature* philosopher Donald A. Crosby provides one atheist's perspective in answering these perennial, elemental, and pivotal questions: What is nature? What is human? What is the place of humans in nature? What should be the place of humans in nature? Crosby affirms in concluding his book: "Nature itself, when we rightly conceive of it and comprehend our role within it, can provide ample context and support for finding purpose, value, and meaning in our lives."[3]

In the Preface Crosby succinctly lays out his thesis that spirituality is immanent in nature itself:

This book, in contrast, makes a sustained case for nature itself as a proper focus of religious commitment and concern. For it, nature—envisioned as without God, gods, or animating spirits of any kind—is religiously ultimate. It also argues that nature is metaphysically ultimate, that is, self-sustaining and requiring no explanation for its existence beyond itself. Moreover, humans are viewed as an integral part of nature, natural beings in the fullest sense of the term. They are at home in the natural world, their origin, nature, and destiny lie here and not in some transcendent realm, and their moral and religious responsibilities extend not only to one another and to the human community but to the whole of nature and to all living beings. This book urges us to grant to nature the kind of reverence, awe, love, and devotion we in the West have formerly reserved for God.[4]

Crosby makes a basic point that is an important consideration for spiritual ecology in general at some stage of its development. No fundamental intellectual or spiritual outlook can be taken for granted; instead, each must be subjected to critical scrutiny in the context of opposing viewpoints.[5] This reflects his personal history. Crosby pursued his undergraduate education at a Presbyterian institution called Davidson College in North Carolina, then the master's degree at the Princeton Theological Seminary, and finally the doctorate in religion at the Union Theological Seminary and Columbia University in New York. His doctorate focused on Western philosophy and world religions. But eventually he personally rejected theism and anthropomorphism of any kind in favor of a religion of nature.[6] Thus, Crosby asserts: "We need not go any further than nature to probe the depths of our existence and the powers that sustain our being. Nature, then, is a fit object of religious concern. It is holy."[7] At the same time, Crosby thinks that nature has no sentience, consciousness, or purpose.[8] (This is a position contrary to the views held by many in spiritual ecology, such as those of Pierre Teilhard de Chardin and Thomas Berry.)[9]

The natural sciences alone, however, are not sufficient for a comprehensive vision of nature in Crosby's opinion. Through the centuries scientific thinking has changed fundamentally and will probably do so in the future as well. Science is not completely objective, infallible, and absolute. Furthermore, according to Crosby, science and other kinds of thinking are not readily distinguishable, nor are emotion and reason.[10] He writes: "So inexhaustibly mysterious is nature and so multifarious its guises that we need a great variety of methodologies, perspectives, and modes of expression for probing its depths."[11] Moreover, he notes: "Exclusive reliance on the natural sciences for our understanding of nature leaves us with a nature devoid of values."[12] The idea that only science is objective, and everything else is subjective, is invalid.[13] In short, Crosby rejects scientism, the myopic faith in science as the only source of knowledge, understanding, truth, and reality.[14]

In considering the so-called New Atheists like Richard Dawkins, Sam Harris, and Christopher Hitchens, another philosopher, Roger S. Gottlieb, recognizes the difficulty of collaboration: "Ultimately, there may be no way to bring religious believers and militant atheists together. The former cannot conceive of a universe without a higher power, the latter can't believe the universe has one!"[15] His constructive suggestion is to set aside the issue of whether or not God exists, and deal instead with other matters, especially where they have common interests, like the environment—all people have basic needs like clear air and water, whether they are theists or atheists. Gottlieb asserts that no single approach, whether scientific or religious, has a monopoly on rationally and usefully addressing socio-political issues. Many problems like the environmental crisis are so serious that a constructive dialogue should be pursued to solve them rather than automatically excluding some perspectives.[16]

A similar point is emphasized in introducing *The Oxford Handbook of Religion and Science* when Philip Clayton affirms: "We have assumed that the scientific and the religious quests are likely to be permanent features of human existence, and that humanity will be much better positioned successfully to navigate the threats that it faces if it draws constructively on *both* dimensions. If ways can be found for science and religion to work together in a complementary and productive fashion, perhaps humankind will have a better chance of overcoming the momentous challenges of the twenty-first century than otherwise"[17]

Among the venues in which representatives of religion and science have found common concern and collaborated is the environmental crisis.[18] As an example of such collaboration, leading religious, scientific, and government persons from 83 countries met at the Global Forum in Moscow in January 1990 and concluded with a joint statement titled "Preserving and Cherishing the Earth: An Appeal for Joint Commitment in Science and Religion." Among the scientific luminaries were astronomers Freeman J. Dyson and Carl Sagan, geologist Stephen Jay Gould, botanist Peter Raven, and climatologist Stephen H. Schneider. Part of the statement is especially relevant to quote here:

> The Environmental crisis requires changes not only in public policy, but in individual behavior. The historical record makes clear that religious teaching, example, and leadership are powerfully able to influence personal conduct and commitment. As scientists, many of us have had profound experience of awe and reverence before the universe. We understand that what is regarded as sacred is more likely

to be treated with care and respect. Our planetary home should be so regarded. Efforts to safeguard and cherish the environment need to be infused with a vision of the sacred.[19]

It is noteworthy that several of the participating scientists were atheists or agnostics, yet they did not automatically dismiss the validity and significance of religion, but explicitly recognized its salience for the ecocrisis and as complementary in some ways to their science.[20]

Another commonality between science and some religions that may also help facilitate dialogue and collaboration among them is mentioned by Gottlieb. Believers in God's creation can appeal to reverence for life, maintain a sense of awe and mystery about nature, and recognize kinship with other species, all of which are important contributions to environmentalism. Yet these same things could also be involved in a purely secular view such as that of nature religion.[21] This is exemplified by Crosby's book.

It is not surprising, then, when Gottlieb observes the case of religious environmentalism: "Never in religious history has a religious movement been so intimately connected with and dependent on science."[22] After a discussion of various statements by religious leaders and organizations on environmental matters, Gottlieb goes on to say: "These statements, it should be emphasized, are more than just new theology. By joining forces with scientific leaders, widely considered our society's arbiters of rationality and its best sources of sound public policy, religious leaders are announcing a decisive intention to influence social life in a way that *combines* a spiritual vision with empirical science. Faith here is not a substitute for or alternative to science, but a way of understanding and working with it."[23]

Returning directly to Crosby, he characterizes religion as serving basic functions in an individual's life. Religion is unique, primary, pervasive, valuative, permanent, mysterious and awesome. However, he argues that nature can also serve these functions, and therefore a religion of nature alone is possible without any reliance on God, gods, spirits, and the like. The ultimate mystery is the very existence of nature; it remains completely inexplicable. There is also wonder in the exploration and discovery of aspects of nature. Nature is awesome because we can only partially grasp it, and that includes ourselves as part of nature.[24]

The religious experience in nature can be cultivated in natural sacred places in particular. Like the ecopsychologists, Crosby believes that the beauty, sublimity, vastness, and power of nature can inspire, heal, and humble the human spirit and thereby lead to respect, reverence, and care for it. He cites Mount St. Helens as reflecting nature as source, sustainer, and restorer of life.[25]

It is pertinent here to note that the Gaia idea originated by James Lovelock and Lynn Margulis lends itself to another vision of spiritual ecology that is not necessarily religious, although it can be. Their theory is that planet Earth is a single, self-regulating complex system that maintains the range of specific conditions for life on the planet in equilibrium or homeostasis.[26] However, many have interpreted Gaia as having religious or spiritual implications, given that the term derives from the Greek goddess who personified the Earth as Mother Nature and linking this to Neo-paganism and/or Pantheism.[27] In any case, although many scientists were initially very skeptical about the idea, in more recent times it has gained credence among a growing number, especially in considering the crisis of global climate change. A new field of geophysiology or Earth System Science has developed. Incidentally, there is growing literature from religious and ethical perspectives on global climate change, some of which connects with the principle of Gaia.[28]

At the same time, some of Crosby's characterization of a religion of nature is compatible with some other varieties of spiritual ecology. He cites Taoism, Shintoism, and Native American religions as close to a religion of nature, given their fascination and awe with the powers of nature as sacred. Accordingly, while his perspective on a religion of nature may be newly emerging, it does not need to do so in a vacuum and it may even be in part a transformation of previous religions like the aforementioned.[29] Crosby's work is useful in pointing to the possibilities of spiritual ecology beyond any particular religion and that even a nonreligious person may experience spirituality in nature. Accordingly, he offers a counter to the potential critics of spirituality who may be atheists, agnostics, secular humanists, adherents of naturalism, Marxists, and the like.[30]

A statement from Albert Einstein, an avowed agnostic, is most appropriate to conclude this chapter: "The most beautiful thing we can experience is the mysterious. It is the source of all true art and science. He to whom this emotion is a stranger, who can no longer pause to wonder

and stand rapt in awe, is as good as dead: his eyes are closed. This insight
into the mystery of life, coupled though it be with fear, has also given rise
to religion. To know that what is impenetrable to us really exists, mani-
festing itself as the highest wisdom and the most radiant beauty which
our dull faculties can comprehend only in their most primitive forms—this
knowledge, this feeling, is at the center of true religiousness. In this sense,
and in this sense only, I belong in the ranks of devoutly religious men."[31]

Chapter 20. Natural Theology, Alister E. McGrath

> *To reenchant nature is not merely to gain a new perspective for its integrity and well-being; it is to throw open the doors to a deeper level of existence.*
>
> Alister E. McGrath[1]

Why has religion been denied? What are the causes of the ecocrisis? How can nature be reenchanted? These basic questions are the focus of Alister E. McGrath's book *The Reenchantment of Nature: The Denial of Religion and the Ecological Crisis*.[2] In essence, McGrath's answers are that many scientists have tended to deny religion since the Enlightenment of the seventeenth and eighteenth centuries. Science has contributed to the disenchantment or descralization of nature and that has contributed to the ecocrisis. However, science and religion are not necessarily incompatible, and both are needed to reenchant nature and resolve the ecocrisis.[3]

Before exploring further McGrath's ideas in the domain of spiritual ecology, it is useful to consider his qualifications. He is eminently qualified to wrestle with the above questions because he holds two doctorates from Oxford University, one in Molecular Biology in 1977, and the second in Divinity in 2001. Also, while previously an atheist, now he is an ordained priest. He is one of the world's leading Christian theologians and authorities on natural theology, a prolific author of dozens of books. Currently he is Professor of Theology, Ministry, and Education at King's College in London. McGrath is among several prominent scholars who are highly trained and sophisticated in the study of both scientific and religious fields.[4]

Returning to McGrath's ideas related to spiritual ecology, he agrees with the mentalist view of Lynn White, Jr. (1967) when the former states: "The way we *see* our world shapes the way we *treat* that world."[5] However, McGrath's book is in part a critical response to White's basic thesis, which he refers to as a misinterpretation of Christianity that has been misleading generations and that provided Christianity as a scapegoat for the environmental crisis.[6] McGrath asserts that an important counter-example to

White's thesis is the severe environmental degradation that occurred under Joseph Stalin's regime in the Soviet Union where atheism was one factor. For McGrath that case also demonstrates the ultimate poverty of an exclusively secular approach to nature via science, technology, and economy alone.[7]

McGrath devotes occasional pages and then an entire chapter to refuting Richard Dawkins's scientism or naturalism, identifying it as militant, fundamentalist, atheistic, imperialistic, and totalitarian.[8] McGrath rejects Dawkins's view of science and religion as simplistic, arrogant, and elitist. He asserts that it utterly fails to recognize the limits of science, expertise, and authority.[9] In McGrath's view scientism tends to reduce nature to an exclusively scientific view and thereby sacrifices its magnificent beauty and awesome mystery.[10] There is simply much more to reality than what is detectable by ordinary sense perception and the scientific method. We need to accept and cherish the divine origins of nature through its wonder in order to resacralize it and thereby rescue it, according to McGrath.[11] He thinks that atheism is philosophically inconsistent, morally inadequate, and actually on the decline, although many would vehemently dispute this.[12]

Enchantment refers to a transcendent awe or wonder with nature that leads to respect, reverence, concern, and care for it.[13] The ecocrisis is caused by the disenchantment of nature that began with the Enlightenment.[14] It championed an anthropocentric rather than theocentric view of nature; secularized, objectified, mechanized, and commodified nature facilitating the almost exclusive concentration on its extrinsic or utilitarian value; advocated the human domination and exploitation of nature as a mere resource through science and consequent technology for economic progress; considered that reason, science, technology, and nature itself have no limits; and assumed that these will lead to human liberation and fulfillment.[15] But technological advance led to amoral progress, merely better and more efficient ways of achieving power, and the competitive quest for dominance threatens to destroy humanity as well as nature.[16] Moreover, solving old problems through science and technology often creates new ones, thereby further complicating and even worsening matters.

McGrath points to the environmentally benevolent Christian monastic traditions of the Egyptian and Syria deserts in the fourth century; Celtic

Christianity in Ireland, Scotland, and Wales during the seventh to ninth centuries; and Franciscans of the thirteenth and fourteenth centuries.[17] He asserts that the Christian doctrine of the Creation could impart intrinsic value to nature and call for responsibility and stewardship.[18] He notes recent environmental initiatives by Christians.[19] McGrath observes that already at an early stage of industrialization there were romanticists, like the American transcendentalists, who craved a reenchantment of nature.[20] Furthermore, McGrath argues that secularization is a myth, referring to the idea that inevitably science will progress to eventually replace religion in modern society. He observes that there has been a marked increase of interest in spirituality in recent times.[21] McGrath envisions an integration of science and religion as mutually complementary in exploring and preserving the wonders of nature—part of what spiritual ecology is ultimately all about in the present author's opinion.

To some degree McGrath's book also illustrates the obstacle of dualities that spiritual ecology faces—namely, the tensions and competition between science and religion; within academia the dichotomies and antagonisms between the sciences and the humanities, and within the former between the natural and social sciences; and the seemingly inevitable hostile and irreconcilable relationship between theists and atheists.[22] At the same time, spiritual ecology offers a special opportunity for engaging individuals of different backgrounds and persuasions who are willing to seek common ground and explore their complementarities in addressing the environmental crisis in a collaborative and constructive manner for the welfare of humankind and the planet as a whole. But obviously the legacy of lingering antipathies on all sides will restrict such endeavors, although they need not exclude them altogether, as witness numerous collaborations in conferences, publications, and other venues.

Since 2006, McGrath has focused on exploring the possibilities of renewing natural theology, especially in critical but positive dialogue with the natural sciences. He developed the intellectual foundations for this approach in his trilogy of books on *A Scientific Theology*, which he recently summarized in one volume titled *The Science of God: An Introduction to Scientific Theology*. There he argues for reworking natural theology as an initiative within the tradition of Christianity, this instead of an autonomous discipline seeking to prove the existence of God on the basis of nontheistic assumptions. McGrath is developing this approach in dialogue with the cognitive sciences. The results so far have been published in his book *The Open Secret: Renewing the Vision of Natural Theology*.

McGrath organized a conference titled "Beyond Paley: Renewing the Vision for Natural Theology," held at Oxford University June 23–25, 2008. William Paley was the most prominent proponent of natural theology. He developed the image of God as the "divine watchmaker" who constructed and set the cosmos in motion. He argued that divine wisdom could be inferred by studying the structure of nature. Natural theology flourished in the eighteenth and nineteenth centuries, but was generally refuted by theologians, philosophers, and scientists in the twentieth century, although Paley continues to have some supporters. The Oxford conference aimed to explore current thought about natural theology and the possibilities of revising and reviving it, particularly in relation to the natural sciences and Darwinism.[23] Participants surveyed historical, philosophical, theological, and scientific aspects of natural theology as a basis for considering the potential for its future development in new ways. The results of the conference are in preparation for publication in various forms. It was supported by the John Templeton Foundation.[24]

The apparent "fine-tuning" of the cosmos and its relevance for natural theology are explored by McGrath in another book, *A Fine-Tuned Universe: The Quest for God in Science and Theology*. There he surveys a broad range of physical and biological phenomena, and in particular draws on the most recent investigations in biochemistry and evolutionary biology. He reviews science's new understanding of the natural world and considers the implications of this for traditional debates about the existence of God.[25]

McGrath is by no means alone in his orientation and pursuits, nor are these limited to Christianity. For example, one of the leading experts on Islamic science and spirituality, Seyyed Hossein Nasr, independently opines: "One of the chief causes for this lack of acceptance of the spiritual dimension of the ecological crisis is the survival of a scientism which continues to present modern science not as a particular way of knowing nature, but as a complete and totalitarian philosophy which reduces all reality to the physical domain and does not wish under any condition to accept the possibility of the existence of non-scientistic world-views."[26] The position of Nasr, McGrath, and many others may reflect a healthy historic trend. After centuries of mutual antagonism between Western science and Christian religion finally there is in some important arenas a convergence in the thought and action of these two fields, catalyzed by the continuing and worsening global environment crisis. They believe that neither science nor religion alone is capable of adequately facing up to this gravest of challenges that threatens the extinction of the human species itself not to mention the devastation of the whole biosphere after more than four billion years of evolution. Many would concur including the present author.

CHAPTER 21. SECULARIZATION OF THE SACRED, HIS HOLINESS THE 14TH DALAI LAMA OF TIBET[1]

It is my dream that the entire Tibetan plateau should become a free refuge where humanity and nature can live in peace and in harmonious balance. It would be a place where people from all over the world could come to seek the true meaning of peace within themselves, away from the tensions and pressures of much of the rest of the world.

His Holiness the 14th Dalai Lama of Tibet[2]

What happens when a secular approach to nature replaces a religious one? While secularization, scientism, atheism, Marxism, and/or communism do not necessarily lead to ecocide, it is clear to many that these have contributed to the devastation of nature in the particular case of Tibet since the invasion and occupation by China.

Often Tibet has been envisioned as a Shangri-La in the form of an ancient, stable, homogeneous, nonviolent, peaceful, and highly spiritual society existing as an isolated independent sovereign nation for many centuries. While there is considerable truth to this characterization, often it is exaggerated through idealizing or romanticizing.[3] However, it is accurate to characterize Tibet as the "Roof of the World." With an average altitude of more than 4,000 meters (14,000 feet), 14 of the world's peaks above 8,000 meters (over 5 miles high), and an area of 1.2 million square miles (half the size of the lower 48 states of the United States), Tibet is the highest and largest plateau on earth. Tibet has also been described as the "Land of Snows." Yet the environmental zones range from tropical forests in the east to the high snow-capped mountains of the Himalayas. Tibet's biomes (different types of ecosystems) include forest, scrub, grasslands (70%), desert, water (15,000 lakes), and the headwaters of many of the major rivers of Asia. These rivers, and the countries they feed into, include the Brahmaputra or Tsangpo (Nepal, Bengal, and Bangladesh); Sutlej and Indus (Pakistan and Indian Punjab); Yangtse and Yellow (China); Salween (Burma); Karnail and Ganga (central India); and Mekong (Cambodia, Laos, Thailand, and Vietnam). Thus, Tibet is the "water storage tower" of Asia for 3.7 billion people, or about half of all humanity.

Consequently, Tibet and its environment, including the impact of deforestation as well as the reduction of glaciers and snowfields with global climate change, should be a major international concern, to say the very least.[4]

Tibet is also especially impressive and important in its biological diversity. For example, in the specific area of the so-called Tibetan Autonomous Region, here is the number of species in each category of animals: 2,307 insects, 488 birds, 142 mammals, 64 fishes, 55 reptiles, and 45 amphibians. Birds and mammals, respectively, comprise 28 and 60 percent of the endemic species for China. A combination of factors contributes to this biodiversity, such as variations in geology, topography, altitude, and climate. Also, Tibet is in a transition zone between the Palearctic and Indo-Malayan biogeographical realms in terms of its combination of floral and faunal species. However, all is not well: 163 species are rare and endangered.[5]

In a beautifully illustrated book titled *Across the Tibetan Plateau: Ecosystems, Wildlife, and Conservation*, R. L. Flemming, Dorje Tsering, and Liu Wulin assert: "In Tibet there is a long history of respect for living beings that grew from a religious reverence for life in all of its forms. In its hundreds of sacred places, strict no-hunting policies were the norm. . . . At the core of Tibetan beliefs is the enlightened idea of a balanced harmonious use of the environment, a tradition that gives Tibet tremendous scope and leverage to implement conservation."[6] Thus, the idea of Tibet as an international peace and ecological refuge.

In Tibet human antiquity extends back at least 30,000 years. As recently as only 5,000 years ago, farming emerged in regions that are arable, only about 1 percent of the land. Some one million people, or about 6 percent of the population, live by nomadic pastoralism. Farmers and herders limit their consumption mostly to subsistence, and in some cases pursue a modicum of trade. Thus, they satisfy their basic needs within the limits of the carrying capacity of their environment. Traditionally, energy resources are renewable, clean, and have a low impact on the environment. Also, the original Animistic religion called Bon and Tibetan Buddhism both promoted limitations on hunting and fishing; especially the latter with ideals of nonviolence, compassion, and loving-kindness toward all beings. Furthermore, the total population of Tibet was relatively small. Today there are only 5.5 million Tibetans with a population density of 3 to 4 individuals per square mile. The high proportion of the population participating in monasticism promoted the celibacy of 20 percent of males and 10 percent of females, which reduced population growth. These factors helped limit the environmental impact of traditional Tibetan society. Accordingly, early Western visitors in the mid-seventeenth century reported an awesome abundance of wildlife.

As early as 1642 the Great 5th Dalai Lama issued a "Decree for the Protection of Animals and the Environment." Since that year, each successive Dalai Lama has issued an annual "Decree for the Protection of Animals and the Environment" regarding wild and domestic animals. These decrees were dispatched to local leaders, observers were sent to monitor compliance, and local leaders sent reports back to top officials. Middle- and lower-level government officials issued periodic regulations as well. There was also a host of traditional environmental rituals such as those for Earth Conservation, Water and Rain, and Purification of the Environment. As much as 20 percent of the population in the form of monks and nuns were confined mostly to the monasteries during the seasonal period of retreat in connection with Buddhist custom.[7] All of this suggests the possibility that there was not only a very early interest in conservation, but that this may have been motivated by recognition of some decline in wildlife populations and/or other environmental problems.

In any case, nature in Tibet appears to have been relatively healthy until just a few decades ago when a significant decline coincided with the Chinese invasion and occupation of the formerly independent sovereign nation of Tibet.[8] Buddhism spread into Tibet in the fourth century CE In 822, a peace treaty delineating Tibet's borders was signed with China. But in 1244, the Mongols conquered Tibet, although they allowed autonomy thereafter. It was only in 1624 that the first contact with Europeans occurred. The reign of the Dalai Lamas started in the seventeenth century. In 1912, Tibetan independence was declared when Chinese encroachers surrendered. But in 1949, Mao Zedong founded the Peoples Republic of China (PRC) and threatened to "liberate" Tibet with military force. The subsequent Chinese military invasion and colonial occupation led to the death of at least 1.2 million Tibetans. The magnitude of this genocide can only begin to be appreciated if it is recognized that every one of these individuals had social, economic, and other relations as well as talents, hopes, and aspirations that were exterminated.

In 1965, the PRC established the so-called Tibetan Autonomous Region, just a portion of the former Tibet, and joined the rest of the original territory of Tibet to adjacent provinces of the PRC expanding the latter by one third. In 2006, the Chinese completed a new railroad linking Lhasa, the traditional capital of Tibet, with the capital of China, Beijing. Among other things, this railroad facilitates the transportation of military personnel, equipment, and supplies; the influx of Han immigrants with government encouragements; tourism; and the markedly increased extraction of natural resources including the trafficking of endangered wildlife species for furs and other purposes.

The central government of the PRC has worried that any resistance from Tibetans and granting of autonomy, let alone the return of independence, could have far-reaching repercussions, a domino effect elsewhere, possibly leading to the disintegration of China. The largest ethnic group in the PRC is the one billion Han composing 92 percent of the population. However, there are at least 56 "national minorities" collectively speaking 142 distinct languages and occupying 60 percent of the territory of the PRC, even though they comprise only 6 percent of its total population.

Another reason the government of the PRC has rejected any idea of independence or autonomy for Tibet is that it comprises one-third of the current country with a tremendous wealth of natural resources that can be freely mined by the government, business, and industry of China. Tibet appears to be an underpopulated, underutilized, and undeveloped region. Accordingly, the central government of the PRC invaded and occupied Tibet with the rationalization of liberating a feudal society that was considered to be stupid, ignorant, and backward, this supposedly in order to bring the populace economic development and progress through market socialism. In addition, religion was viewed as "poison of the mind" and, accordingly, religious leaders and institutions were "purged" in various ways. Catastrophically, in total disrespect for religion and human rights, some 6,000 monasteries were destroyed by the "civilized" Chinese. The wonderful sacred texts and art works in the monasteries were looted, if not just decimated. In the process, the monastic population was drastically reduced. Government agents have been placed in many monasteries to try to restrict and control religious activities and prevent any resistance. Government indoctrination programs have been imposed. Thus, the Tibetan society and culture that are so intricately interwoven with the Buddhist religion were attacked as well through mechanisms amounting to ethnocide.

The Chinese have increased the productivity of crops and livestock; improved communications, transportation, and commerce; and rapaciously extracted resources for the export market. This has transpired hand in hand with the militarization of Tibet through the invasion and occupation of over one million soldiers—about one soldier for every five Tibetans. In addition, the state sponsored migration of hundreds of thousands of Han Chinese into Tibet has reduced the Tibetans to a disadvantaged minority within their own traditional capital of Lhasa and in some other areas as well. In effect, this is a demographic version of the "final solution." Forced abortions and sterilizations among other horrible violations of the most basic human rights have caused tremendous suffering and numerous deaths. Furthermore, Han population growth has occurred in the regions and ecosystems that have the most productive ecosystems and are the richest in biodiversity. Land clearance for farming has sometimes led to devastating wildfires over large areas. Tourism has been unplanned and poorly managed. At the same time, the quality of life for Tibetans has declined markedly as they have become the lowest class in the new Han-dominated government and society. Among some portion of the Tibetan population, priorities have shifted from spiritual to material development. Yet also many Tibetans are becoming increasingly alarmed, frustrated, and rebellious, as evidenced in the last couple of years, among other symptoms, by the self-immolation of at least two dozen Buddhist clerics and others who sacrificed themselves in protest.[9]

All of this coincides with natural resource depletion and environmental degradation on an unprecedented scale. Wild plants and animals are exploited for export. At least 46 percent of the forests were cut within just two decades of the Chinese invasion and colonizaton. Livestock are overgrazed in many areas to increase productivity. The soil fertility has declined with greatly increased pressure from farming and herding, thereby leading to greatly increased soil erosion and the consequent siltation of waterways and degradation of their ecosystems. Some areas have suffered from flooding, while others experience desertification, all unprecedented. There has been pollution of soils, waters, and air by agricultural and other chemicals like never before. Even nuclear weapons and waste have been introduced as well, an anathema in a Buddhist society that was remarkably nonviolent and peaceful for the most part. There have even been changes in climatic and weather patterns.

As one specific example, owls, cats, weasels, and foxes have been extirpated locally in many regions for the fur trade to China among other reasons. Marked reduction of their predation pressure led to massive infestations of rats that destroyed grasslands and farm crops over millions of hectares, resulting in widespread famine and disease. This is only one example among a multitude of diverse instances of chain reactions in environmental degradation since the violent Chinese invasion and occupation of Tibet.

As the government of the PRC has become increasingly aware of the significant increase in environmental problems, it has imposed on locals top-down government-protected areas in collaboration with international conservation organizations, ignoring the traditional systems of community-based protected areas such as sacred groves. Within the so-called Tibetan Autonomous Region, Western-style conservation began in Tibet in 1985, but most initiatives have been since the mid-1990s. Now there is a total of seven national level preserves and five regional preserves as well as the integrated protection plan of the Four Great Rivers Ecological Environment Protection Plan for the Yangtze, Mekong, Salween, and Tsangpo. National level mega-preserves include the Qomolangma National Nature Preserve and the Chantang National Nature Preserve. By now 40 percent of the Tibetan Autonomous Region is supposed to be under conservation management; deforestation rates are said to have declined by more than 80 percent; large-scale tree plantations have been started along fragile river drainages; conservation partnerships are being developed among government, scientists, and the public; there is increased use of environmentally friendly solar, geothermal, and hydroelectric generated energy; and wild animal populations are supposed to be recovering for endangered species like the snow leopard.[10] However, other sources like the Tibetan Environment Watch and the Tibetan Environmental Network suggest a picture of environment and conservation that is far less positive, to say the least. From them it appears that ecocide has accompanied ethnocide and genocide in Tibet by the government, military, and Han colonists of the PRC.

Tibet, however, has several attributes that may well favor its cultural survival in the long term. Among these are its relatively isolated and marginal location; self-sufficiency of much of its population such as herders; a resistant population that may rebound and increase if given a chance; historical memory of pre-Chinese Tibet; ethnic identity and pride; religious integration and vitality; political unity and mobilization, especially under the leadership of His Holiness the 14th Dalai Lama of Tibet; selectivity in acceptance of external influences; and conscious counter-cultural strategies, especially on the part of the Tibetan diaspora that flourishes in exile.[11]

His Holiness the 14th Dalai Lama of Tibet has proposed that Tibet be converted to an autonomous region and promoted as a Peace Zone. It would serve as a geopolitical buffer between the giants of China and India, as the largest nature reserve on the planet, and as a unique region of spiritual pilgrimage for the world. His Five Point Peace Plan was proposed during a speech to the Human Rights Caucus of the United States Congress on September 21, 1987. His aspirations for this visionary initiative are echoed in the initial quote in this chapter.[12]

What a wonderful idea is the Peace Zone. How great it would be for the people, culture, religion, and ecology of Tibet. How great it would be for the world. How great it would be for the international image and relations of China. But this noble vision of integrating ecology, peace, and spirituality seems unlikely to be realized—at least in the near future, given the mentality and immorality of the central government of the PRC combined with Tibet as a frontier for Han exploitation through demographic, economic, cultural, and military expansion. Yet we should not believe that the idea of the Peace Zone could never be realized. In time the PRC will change and so may Tibet, hopefully for the better. For another thing, there are ample historical precedents throughout the world of previously unimaginable radical transformations, sometimes surprisingly rapidly, such as the abolition of slavery in the United States; the abandonment of the apartheid system in South Africa; the disintegration of the former Soviet Union; and the pro-democracy victories in Poland, Czechoslovakia, and many other countries in Europe, and most recently the Arab Spring.

It is also noteworthy that in many of these situations traditional religion had been severely repressed but quickly rebounded when government restraints were relieved. Most of all, the Tibetan people inside and outside of their homeland have repeatedly demonstrated truly extraordinary courage, endurance, patience, compassion, resiliency, and optimism. They give hope to dire circumstances in many parts of the rest of the world as well as to anyone genuinely concerned with Tibet.

Most tragically, however, it appears that although many political leaders of countries are willing to host His Holiness the 14th Dalai Lama of

Tibet, ultimately they are hypocrites when it comes to any serious action that might be effective in protecting the human rights and other concerns of Tibetans, something like a Faustian compact with the PRC because of its economic power. Accordingly, inescapably such leaders are to some degree complicit in the Chinese ecocide, genocide, ethnocide, and "religiocide" of Tibet, so much for their rhetoric about human rights. However, impermanence is one of the pivotal concepts of Buddhism. In time, social networking, both traditional and through the Internet, may generate enough people power of Tibetans and others to force a transformation of the government of the PRC, nonviolently, one hopes.

EPILOGUE

No important change in ethics was ever accomplished without an internal change in our intellectual emphasis, loyalties, affections, and convictions.

Aldo Leopold[1]

This intellectual pilgrimage through visiting some of the main pioneers in the rich history of spiritual ecology is concluding. Undoubtedly the coverage is far from complete (see Appendix 1). Nevertheless, on route many points of interest and significance have been explored. Furthermore, a wealth of resources has been cited for readers who may wish to continue the pilgrimage.[2]

At this juncture of the journey a few generalizations are offered in conclusion. Of course there are significant differences among the many pioneers in spiritual ecology. They come from different historical periods and different ecological, religious, cultural, linguistic, and national backgrounds. These pioneers also come from different lifestyles, professions, and experiences. Each has developed a personal path of thought and action in pursuing spiritual ecology. Each has made a distinctive contribution to the development of what is here called spiritual ecology, no matter how they may have identified themselves or how others may identify them.

At the same time, among most of these pioneers there are commonalities, although these are not identities. Many of these pioneers developed a profound concern for the environment as a result of some epiphany or mystical experience in nature, often in youth. Thereafter they continued to experience spirituality in nature, although more often than not they do not explicitly reveal this in any detail. Many have a special affinity for a particular aspect of nature, especially trees, mountains, or rivers. Many reflect elements of deep ecology in their thinking, such as an ecocentric rather than an anthropocentric worldview, values, and attitudes. Many also mirror elements of ecopsychology where nature is healing for people and in this process there is some healing of nature as well. Most are environmental activists in some manner and degree.

This all bodes well for spiritual ecology and its vital contribution in helping reduce, if not fully resolve, the ecocrises of the world, from the local to the global levels. The diversity among the pioneers in spiritual ecology can be adaptive. After all, diversity is the basis of evolution and diversity and adaptability are the basis of future evolution. At the same time, the commonalities among these pioneers, including their experiences in nature, are primary and synergetic in generating the direction and accelerating the momentum of this quiet and nonviolent revolution in spiritual and ecological thought and action.

Behind this revolution in developing a new spiritual and ecological consciousness and ensuing responsibility are several catalytic forces:

the challenge of new ecocrises including global climate change;

new narratives of the place of humans in nature;

new leaders, organizations, and networks;

new social, cultural, economic, political, scientific, and religious developments and movements; and

new modes and venues for information and education not the least of which is the internet.

This is a revolution in the sense of an accumulating series of changes that are profoundly transformative with far-reaching consequences for individuals and societies, but not in the sense of anything rapid or unified with a single leader. Yet this Great Turning is gaining momentum. Now the main reservation is whether or not it will be soon enough and powerful enough to avert a global environmental catastrophe if ecocrises reach some dangerous and essentially irreversible tipping point. Only in the long term will the passage of time reveal the destiny of the human species and the planet. But ultimately the matter is simple: a choice between ecocide or ecosanity!

Within the last two decades research and dialogue on the environmental relevance of each of the world's major religions has advanced to the point that some attempts have been made to discern general common denominators among them. For instance, in the last chapter of the first real textbook on spiritual ecology, David Kinsley identifies these ten basic principles:

1. Many religions consider all of reality, or some of its components, to be an organic whole or a living being.

2. There is an emphasis on cultivating rapport with the local environment through developing intimate knowledge about it and practicing reverence for its beauty, mystery, and power through ritual celebrations of recognition and appreciation.
3. The human and nonhuman realms are directly interrelated, often in the sense of some kind of kinship, and in certain cases, even to the extent of animals being viewed as another form of persons or humans.
4. The appropriate relationship between humans and nature should be reciprocal—that is, humans do not merely recognize interdependence, but also promote mutually beneficial interactions with nature.
5. Ultimately, the dichotomy between humans and their environment is nonexistent; humans are embedded in nature as an integral part of the larger whole or cosmos.
6. This nondualistic view reflects the ultimate elemental unity of all existence; nature and spirit are inseparable, there is only one reality, and this continuity can be sensed and experienced.
7. This underlying unity is moral as well as physical; humans and nonhumans participate in a shared moral system wherein environmental issues are first and foremost ethical concerns; and nature has intrinsic as well as extrinsic values.
8. Humans should act with restraint in nature by avoiding the anthropocentric arrogance of excessive, wasteful, and destructive use of the land and other resources, and in other ways they should exercise proper behavior toward plants, animals, and other aspects of nature as sacred.
9. Harmony or balance between humans and the rest of nature must be maintained and promoted, and, if it is upset, then it should be restored.
10. Frequently the motivation, commitment, and intensity of environmental concerns are essentially religious or spiritual.[3]

Incidentally, many of the above commonalities are reflected as well in deep ecology and ecopsychology. Each of these principles could be formulated as a hypothesis for exploration and testing through variously investigating religions, spiritualities, cultures, societies, institutions, lifestyles, and personages in terms of their relevance for ecology and adaptation.[4]

All of the above allows some optimism in what otherwise so often appears to be a rather dismal world with an ever more dismal future for humankind and Gaia. More often than not secular approaches to ecocrises have proven insufficient although certainly necessary. Perhaps a spiritual approach will serve as a catalyst to finally turn things around for the better because the ecocrisis is ultimately a spiritual and moral crisis.[5] As the profound thinker, writer, revolutionary dissident, and former president of Czechoslovakia Vaclav Havel testifies: "What could change the direction of today's civilization? It is my deep conviction that the only option is a change in the sphere of the spirit, in the sphere of human conscience. It's not enough to invent new machines, new regulations, new institutions. We must develop a new understanding of the true purpose of our existence on the Earth. Only by making such a fundamental shift will we be able to create new models of behaviour and a new set of values for the planet."[6] In essence, this is much of what spiritual ecology is all about. In this respect the reader may find it interesting and useful to contemplate the ruins of Ta Prohm in Cambodia on the front cover of this book.

Finally, it is most appropriate to end this pilgrimage with some brief excerpts from "A Prayer of Gratitude" for the Earth: "We live in all things. All things live in us. ... We are grateful. We rejoice in all life."[7]

NOTES

Foreword

1. Muir 1916/1997: 231, see also Taylor 2010: 61–70.
2. Leopold 1949/1966:262
3. Ibid.:xvii-xix
4. White 1967, 1973. (For more about White's views and their influence see Chapter 6 and 11).
5. Tuan 1968, Kellert 1995. For a contrasting view, see Callicott and Ames 1989.
6. Much more research is needed to ascertain the influence and possibilities; for my argument about how little we know of such influences and possibilities, and the need for more research see Taylor 2011. For my analysis of the most hopeful trends see Taylor 2010.
7. Kellert 2005, Wilson 1984, Kellert 2007, and Kellert and Wilson 1993.
8. Leopold 1949/1966:246.

Prologue

1. Best and Nocella 2006.
2. Some of the other authors who use the term *spiritual ecology* include Barton 2008, De Sercey 2007, Laszlo and Combs 2011, Merchant 2005:117–138, Montgomery 1997, Nollman 1990, Spring and Manousos 2007, Sullivan 1972, Sarah McFarland Taylor 2007, and Whitner and Grob 2009.
3. Here the word *ecology* is usually used in the sense of the scientific biological study of interactions among organisms and the ecosystems in their habitat. The word *spiritual* usually refers to some combination of these attributes in an individual's experience: awesome, cosmic, deep, ecstatic, epiphanic, extraordinary, high, ineffable, infinite, mysterious, mystical, numinous, oneness, peak, powerful, primal, serene, sublime, tranquil, transcendent, transformative, unforgettable, unity, unreal, ultimate, and/or wonder (see James 1902, Chang and Boyd 2012, and von Essen 2010). Sometimes the term *altered state of consciousness* is used as synonymous with spirituality (Winkelman and Baker 2010). However, spiritual may also refer to spirit beings and forces in nature, such as in Animism. It is quite possible to

scientifically study some aspects of the spiritual, such as trance states or spirit possession, by observing the actual behavior of the persons involved and/or by interviewing them as the situation allows or afterward (Milton 2002, Narby and Huxley 2001, Society for the Anthropology of Consciousness 2010, Turner 2006, and Young and Goulet 1994). The term and aspects of spiritual ecology are explained further in an anthropological context in several articles by Sponsel 2001a, 2007a,c,d, 2010a, 2011a.

4. Bassett, et al., 2000.
5. Gottlieb 2006a, Motovalli 2002, Taylor 2010a.
6. Taylor 2005.
7. Coates 1998, Curry 2011, de Steiguer 2006, Egan and Crane 2009, Pepper 1996, Thomas 1983, and Worster 1994.
8. Collett and Karakashian 1996.
9. Ayres 1999, Ehrlich 2008, Ehrlich and Ehrlich 2008, Foster, et al., 2010, Jensen and McBay 2009, Leslie 1996, McKibben 2006, 2010, Speth 2008, Starke and Mastny 2010, and Wilson 1999, 2003, World Meteorological Organization 2011, United Nations 2005.
10. Interfaith Power and Light 2011, Ostrow and Rockefeller 2007.
11. Gardner 2002, 2006. Also see English and Krueger 2010.
12. Hawken 2007, Kaza 2005, Payne 2010, and Starke and Mastny 2010.
13. Crosby 2002, Haught 2006, Houge 2010, Metzner 1999, Smith 2000, and Stone 2009.
14. Clayton and Simpson 2006, Edwards and Palmer 1997, Palmer and Finlay 2003, Pedersen 1998, and Swearer 2009.
15. Kearns and Keller 2007, and Tucker with Berling 2003.
16. Gardner 2002, 2006.
17. Anderson 2010, Barnes 1990, Gardner 2002, 2006, Haught 1990, Holm and Bowker 1994a,b, Moore and Nelson 2010, Milton 2002, Oliver 2009, Preston 2009, and White 1967.
18. Bourne 2008, Macy 1991, and Macy and Brown 1998.
19. Takacs 1996:256, 270, Taylor 2010, and von Essen 2010.
20. Appendix, Kumar and Whitefield 2006, Palmer 2001, and Rifkin 2008.
21. For a far more thorough sample see Taylor 2005.
22. Abram 1996, de Quincey 2002, Gibson 2009, Jensen 2004, Lerner 2000, Turner 2006, von Essen 2010, and Young and Goulet 1994.
23. Bookchin 1995, Dawkins 2006, Kimball 2002, and Whelan, et al., 1996.
24. Pakenham 2004.
25. For the most important background sources in spiritual ecology see Bauman, et al., 2011 Gottlieb 2006a,b, Kinsley 1995, Spring and Manousos 2007, Taylor 2005, 2010a, Tucker 2003, and Watling 2009. The present book

inevitably overlaps to some degree with such works, but it is designed to be complementary rather than competitive. Also, see Gottlieb 2007a, Taylor 2010b, and Tucker and Grim 2009b.
26. Hageneder 2001, Nadkarni 2008, and Tudge 2005.
27. Altman 1994.
28. Sponsel 2007b.
29. Sponsel 2011b.
30. Adams 2011, Brent 2011, and Luskin 2011.
31. Forum on Religion and Ecology 2011, and Taylor 2011.
32. Gottlieb 2011.
33. von Essen 2010:7. The website for the present book is http://spiritualecology.info. The author welcomes any comments from readers of this book at les.sponsel@gmail.com.

Chapter 1. What's in a Tree?

1. This chapter is integrated and revised from two previous publications with additional materials inserted (Sponsel 2005b, and Sponsel and Natadecha-Sponsel 2001). Portions of these previous publications have been used with the kind permission from the original publisher including Continuum in the case of Sponsel 2005b.
2. Rockefeller and Elder 1991:46.
3. Shyam, et al., 2010.
4. Altman 1994:9. Also see Circle of Life Foundation 2011, Guha 1995, Hageneder 2000, Hill 2000, Hill and Hurley 2002, Kaza 1996, Kynes 2006, Nadkarni 2008, Paterson 1996, Philpot 2004, Rival 1998, Suzuki and Grady 2004, Thomas 2000, Webster 2008, and Wolens 2000.
5. Sponsel and Natadecha-Sponsel 2001. For a description of Buddhist monks ritually protecting trees in Thailand see Darlington 1998, 2003.
6. Caldecott 1993:37–41.
7. Graham and Round 1994:31.
8. Pei 1993.
9. Altman 1994.
10. Bennett 1996:468.
11. On the various values of trees see Altman 1994, Henning 2001, Jones and Cloke 2002, Levitt 2010, Nadkarni 2008, Perlman 1994, and Shiva 1993:34–39.
12. Marchand 2000.
13. See Chandrakanth, et al., 1990, 1991, and Trudge 2005.
14. Wilson 1999:133–140.

15. Dawson 1993.
16. Weir 1991.
17. Sponsel, et al., 1998, cf. Dove, et al., 2011:6–10. On sacred groves see Ramakrishnan, et al., 1998; Sheridan and Nyamweru 2008; Sponsel 2007b; and Starkman 2011.
18. Skolimowski 1993:70.

Chapter 2. Enchanted Nature, Animism

1. This essay is substantially reworked and elaborated from Sponsel 2005a.
2. Harvey 2006:xi.
3. Pals 2006.
4. Harvey 2006:193.
5. Ibid,:206–207.
6. Solecki 1971, 1975. Also see Herzog 2011.
7. See Grim 2001.
8. Albanese 2002 ; Seed, et al., 1988/2007.
9. Kull, et al., 2003. Also see Swan 1990, and Verschuuren, et al., 2010.
10. Harvey 2006:109
11. Hughes 1983, McFadden 1991, and Narby and Huxley 2001.
12. Rose 1992.
13. Cunningham 1994, and Morrell 2005.
14. Reichel-Dolmatoff 1971, 1976, and Sponsel 2010a.
15. Ono 1962.
16. Broman and Warren 2005.
17. Hamilton 2003.
18. de Angeles, et al., 2005, Harvey 1997, Higginbotham and Higginbotham 2010, Howard 2009, Pearson 1998, and York 2003.
19. Posey 1999.
20. Taylor 2010.
21. Harvey 2006: xiv.

Chapter 3. The Original Spiritual Ecologists, Indigenous Peoples

1. Kunnie and Goduka 2004: xi. This chapter is substantially reworked and expanded from Sponsel 2005c. Some portions of this chapter previously appeared in Sponsel 2005c and have been used here with the kind permission of the original publisher Continuum.

2. Chun 2002, and Protect Kahoʻolawe ʻOhana 2011. For general background on Hawaiian spiritual ecology see Cuningham 1994, Kupihea 2001, and Sponsel 2001c.
3. Scupin 2000.
4. cf. Bennett 1976.
5. Cherniack 1999, DuBois 2009, Grim 1983, 2001, Harner 2011, Harvey 2003, Kehoe 2000, Kinsley 1995, Kozak 2000, Narby and Huxley 2001, Rajotte 1995, Townsend 1999, and Winkelman 1999. For the dark side of shamanism see Whitehead and Wright 2004.
6. Sullivan 1988, and Viveiros de Castro 1992.
7. Reichel-Dolmatoff 1971, 1976, 1999, and Sponsel 2008.
8. Sponsel 2006.
9. Beyer, et al. 2012, and Brent 2005.
10. Descola 1993, 1996, Perkins, et al., 2001, and Reichel-Dolmatoff 1971, 1976, 1999.
11. Sponsel 1986.
12. Slater 2002, and Smith 1996.
13. Reichel-Dolmatoff 1971, 1976, 1999; cf. Descola 1993, 1996.
14. Schefold 1988:212.
15. For similar cases in Southeast Asia see Schlegel 1998, Valeri 2000, and Wolff 2001, and for elsewhere see Berkes 1999, Nelson 1982, 1983, and Deborah B. Rose 1992.
16. McGee 1990, and Montejo 2001.
17. Abrams, et al., 1996.
18. Hart and Kottak 1999:160–161. For more on Rappaport see Messer and Lambek 2001.
19. Bodley 2008a,b.
20. Matthiessen 1984, McLeod 2002, 2011, Nabokov 2006, Sponsel 2007b, Swan 1990, and Verschuuran, et al., 2010.
21. Bodley 2008, and Elsass 1992.
22. Elsass 1992, Ereira 1990, 1993, 2009, Reichel-Dolmatoff 1990, and the Tairona Heritage Trust 2011.
23. Cajete 2000, and Verschuuran, et al., 2010.
24. Dudley, et al., 2005, Nelson 1982, 1983, Posey 1999, and Turner 2006.
25. Kunnie and Goduka 2004, and Turner 1992, 2006.
26. See, for example, de Quincey 2002.
27. cf. McNeley 1997.
28. Olupona 2004.
29. Kunnie and Goduka 2004, Schlegel 1998, and Wolff 2001. For environmental concerns by Native Americans see Beck, et al., 1996, Bierhorst 1994,

Grinde and Johansen 1995, Highwater 1981, Kawagley 1995, La Duke 1999, 2005, Mander 1991, McFadden 1991, and Weaver 1996. For other studies of indigenes as spiritual ecologists see Anderson 1996, Highwater 1981, Hughes 1983, McPherson 1992, Morris 2000, Myerhoff 1974, Deborah B. Rose 1992, Seeger 1981, Selin 2003, Swan 1990, Tanner 1979, Turner 2005, and Vitebsky 2005. Anthropological contributions to spiritual ecology are reviewed by Sponsel 2001a, 2007d, 2010a, 2011a
30. Rappaport 1979:97.

Chapter 4. Ecologically Noble or Ignoble?

1. This chapter is substantially reworked and expanded from Sponsel 2005c. Some portions of this chapter previously appeared in Sponsel 2005c and have been used here with the kind permission of the original publisher Continuum.
2. Sale 2000:52.
3. See Barnard 1999, Berkhofer, Jr. 1979, Buege 1996, Ellingson 2001, Fairchild 1961, Jahoda 1999, Johnson 2005, Lovejoy and Boas 1997, Pandian 1985, and Senior 2005.
4. Ellingson 2001.
5. Cooper 1999.
6. French 2005b:1429.
7. Ibid.:1428. Also see Grimsley 1968, 1970, and Rousseau 1762, 1782.
8. French 2005:1429.
9. Albanese 1990, 2002, Ereira 2001, Harvey 1997, 2006, Harrison 2004, Russell 2008, and York 2003.
10. See Oelschlaeger 1991.
11. Udall 1963:4. For one critical review of the relevance of indigenous religions for conservation see Tiedje and Snodgrass 2008.
12. See Ingram 2004 and Whitley 2008.
13. For example, see Diamond 1974, Hook 2004, Kroeber 1961, Sackman 2011, Shepard 1973, and Sponsel 1992a.
14. Sponsel 2010b. For the opposite representation of the Yanomami as "noble savages" see Donner 1982.
15. Turnbull 1961:89.
16. Ibid.:17.
17. Ibid.:17.
18. International Union for the Conservation of Nature and Natural Resources 1997.
19. Sponsel 1992b, 2001.

20. Posey, et al., 1999.
21. Krech 1999. Also see Krech 2005a,b. For a critical review of Krech's position see Deloria 2000, Harkin and Lewis 2007, and by implication Nabhan 1995.
22. International Union for the Conservation of Nature and Natural Resources 1997.
23. Whelan 1999.
24. Alvard 1993, Stearman 1992, 1994.
25. Rambo 1985.
26. Headland 1992.
27. See Conklin and Graham 1995, and Turner 1995.
28. Whelan 1999:42.
29. Redman 1999.
30. Whelan 1999:22, 27, 33, 42, 55.
31. Ibid.:25–26.
32. Ibid.:1999:27.
33. Whelan, et al.1996.
34. Sale 2000.
35. cf. Churchill 1997 and Klein 1997.
36. Sale 2000.
37. Johnson 2005:1419.
38. Bodley 2008, Hagan 1980. For further contributions to the debate on the "ecologically noble savage" see Balee 1998, Blackburn and Anderson 1993, Bodley 2008a, Booth 2003, Denevan 1992, 1996, Diamond 1986, 1992, Doane 2007, Edgerton 1992, Ellen 1986, Flannery 1995, Galvin 2001, Grande 1999, Grinde and Johansen 1995, Hagan 1980, Hames 1991, 2007, Headland 1992, 1997, International Union for the Conservation of Nature and Natural Resources 1997, Johnson 1989, Kalland 2003, Lohman 1993, Mann 2002, 2005, Martin 1978, Nadasdy 2005, Nelson 1982, Oelschlaeger 1991, Parker 1992, 1993, Pecore 1992, Pennybacker 2000, Posey 1982, 1985, 1989, 1992, Posey and Balee 1989, Redford 1990, 1992, Redman 1999, Rothenberg 1996, Smith and Wishnie 2000, Sponsel 1992b, Stearman 1992, 1994, Stevens 1997, Turner 1995, Vecsey and Venables 1980, Vickers 1991, and Waller 1996.
39. Blow 1998, Cote 2010, Happynook 2000, cf. Kalland 1993. Other examples of conflicts between indigenes and environmentalists are discussed by Redford and Stearman 1993, Waller 1996, and Whaley and Bresette 1994.
40. Balee 1998.
41. For example, see Cronon 1983, and Hackenberg 1974.
42. Sponsel 2001c. Also see Burney and Kikuchi 2006, and Burney 2010.
43. Cunningham 1994:11.

44. See White 1967.
45. Robinson 1994:11.
46. Carspecken 2012, Dobson 1991, Gould 2005b, Graeber 2004, Linkola 2009, Merkel 2003, 2005, 2011, Robinson 1994, and Zerzan 2008.
47. After Sponsel 2001b.

Chapter 5. Natural Wisdom and Action, The Buddha

1. This chapter is extensively reworked from previous publications by Sponsel and Natadecha-Sponsel 2003, 2008. Some portions from previous publications are included with the kind permission of Springer Science+Business Media B.V. The original articles contain far more detail and cite a wealth of additional resources. Brief surveys of general topics in Buddhism can be found in books by Carrithers 1996, and Keown 2000, 2005. Sangharakshita, an extraordinarily prolific author, has written a succession of separate books on various aspects of Buddhism with Windhorse Publications. *The Encyclopedia of Religion and Nature* is another very useful resource for brief articles on various aspects of Buddhism (Taylor 2005). Also see the superb films on the Buddha by Grubin 2010 and Meissonnier 2004. Among the more useful sources on Buddhist ecology and environmentalism are Johnston 2006, Kaza 2006, 2008, Kaza and Kraft 2000, Nhat Hahn 2008, and Tucker and Williams 1997. Williams (2011a,b) posted a course syllabus and an extensive annotated bibliography on Buddhism and ecology. Another useful annotated bibliography on "Buddhism and the Environment" was compiled by Richard Payne (2011) and is published in the series Oxford Bibliographies Online. The webite Ecobuddhism (2011) has a wealth of material on Buddhist environmentalism and especially in relation to global climate change.
2. Bodi 1987:vii.
3. Kabilsingh 1998:56.
4. Chicarelli 2004:59–60, 64.
5. Sivaraksa 1993:83.
6. Buddhadasa 1998:74.
7. On the Buddhist view of nature see Barnhill 2005, Ryan 1998, Schmithausen 1991a,b,Vajragupta 2011, and Visalo 2011.
8. Chapple 1996, 1997, Cowell 1895–1905, and Sahni 2008.
9. Erdosy 1998, Gadgil and Guha 1992:82, 87–90, and Thakur 2004.
10. Bilimoria 2001:1.
11. For the general historical context of the Buddha see Bailey and Mabbett 2003, and Ryan 1998:63–76.
12. For a discussion of ecological aspects of suffering see Kaza 2008:3–32.

13. Thanissaro 2006. Also see Kaza 2000, and Koizumi 2010.
14. King 1991, and La Fleur 2000.
15. Koizumi 2010.
16. Merkel 2003, and Rees and Wackernagel 1998.
17. See Harvey 2000.
18. Henning 2002a,b, Kvaloy 1987, and Macy 1991a,b.
19. For example, see Burger 2007.
20. Devall 1990, and Sponsel and Natadecha-Sponsel 1997.
21. Thanissaro 1994.
22. Suan Mokkh 2011.
23. Sponsel and Natadecha-Sponsel 1997, and Sponsel, et al., 1998. For the ecological practices of some other Buddhist centers see Fung 2011, Kaza 1997, and Yamauchi 1997.
24. See Burger 2007, Coleman 2006, 2011, Das 2000, Mackenzie 1998, Sponsel and Natadecha-Sponsel 2004, Tiyavanich 2003, and Watts 1968.
25. Escobin 2011.
26. Darlington 1998, 2003.
27. Boord 1994.
28. McKay 2006, Thurman and Wise 2000, and Vendetti 2006.
29. Queen 2000, and Queen and King 1996.
30. See Alliance of Religions and Conservation 2011, Association of Buddhists and Environment 2011, Buddhist Institute 1999, Chimedsengee, et al., 2009, Clippard 2011, Dharma Net International 2011, Kabilsingh 1987, 1997, Lumbini Crane Conservation Center 2011, Pauling 1990, Santikaro 2000, Schumacher 1973, Severson 2010, Sivaraksa 2009, 2011, Swearer 2003, Zen Environmental Studies Institute 2011, and Zsolnai and Johannessen 2006.
31. Kabilsingh 1987, 1997, 1998.
32. Namgyal 1986.
33. Martin 1997:176–177.
34. Escobin 2011.
35. Wat Lan Kuad 2010. For other examples see Alliance of Religions and Conservation 2011, Titubara 2010, Tongphanna, 2008, Vajragupta 2011, and Ziporyn, 2008.
36. Batchelor 1994, and Wilson 2001.
37. Mueller 1977.
38. His Holiness the 14th Dalai Lama of Tibet 2011, Dugdale 2008, Moyers 1991, and Rockefeller and Elder 1992.
39. Badiner 2002, Kaza 2005, Payne 2010, and Rees and Wackernagel 1998.
40. Timmerman 1992:74
41. Vendetti 2007.

42. Dobson 1991, and Kaza 2008.
43. See Intergovernmental Panel on Climate Change 2011.
44. EcoBuddhism 2011. Also, see Hout Bay Theravada Centre 2011.
45. See Loori 2000.
46. For example, Ward 1993.
47. Tuan 1968.
48. Martin 1997:176–177.
49. For example, Marten 2011.
50. See, for example, Harris 1991, 1994, 1995a,b,c, 1997; and Schmithausen 1991a,b, 1997, 2000.
51. See rebuttals by Cooper and James 2005:138–144, and Swearer 1997:37–40, 2005.
52. Berkwitz 2006.
53. Ekachai 2001, and Reynolds and Carbine 2000.
54. Clippard 2011.
55. See Buddhadasa 1987, His Holiness the 14th Dalai Lama of Tibet 1992, 1999, 2011, Nhat Hahn 2004, 2008, Plum Village 2011, Suan Mokkh 2011, Tangandvisutijit 1989, and the Tibetan Environmental Network 2011.
56. White 1967. For example, readers can judge for themself whether or not any of the writings of Ian Harris previously cited are defensive. For further discussion of this matter see Sponsel and Natadecha-Sponsel 2008.
57. Harris 1994. For a dialogue between Catholic and Buddhist monastics on the environment see Mitchell and Skudlarek 2010.
58. Among the superb biographies of the Buddha are those by Armstrong 2001, Carrithers 2001, and Nelson 2000.
59. Berkwitz 2006.
60. Sponsel and Natadecha-Sponsel 2010.
61. Nhat Hahn 2008:55–56.

Chapter 6. Medieval Radical, Saint Francis of Assisi

1. Unless otherwise indicated, the information in this chapter is extracted and synthesized from several excellent biographies of Saint Francis: Bobin 1999, Englebert 1965, Francke 2005, House 2000, LeGoff 2004, and Spoto 2002. For brief articles see French 2005a, and Linzey and Barsam 2001. Franke's book is a most informative and captivating journey following in the footsteps of Francis in his homeland and beyond. In addition, this chapter draws from two especially useful sources on the nature mysticism of Saint Francis: Armstrong 1973 and Sorrell 1988. Other helpful sources for general background are Robson 2011 and Spring Hill College 2011.

2. Skolimowski 1993:110.
3. Brockleman 1997:11.
4. Hollister 1998:219.
5. Bratton 1993:213 and Denis Edwards 2006:22.
6. See Fox 2000.
7. See Swimme and Tucker 2011a,b.
8. Le Goff 2004:43.
9. Engelbert 1965:136.
10. Boff 1997:211, Bratton 1993:218, 220, Delio, et al., 2007:68.
11. Hopcke and Schwartz 2006:56–58.
12. Franke 2005, Lionberger 2007.
13. Burrell and Malits 1997, and Harvey 2006.
14. Boff 1997:210.
15. Kinsley 1995:120–121.
16. White 1967:1206.
17. Ibid.:1967:1207
18. Bratton 1993:219.
19. Boff 1997:208.
20. Bratton 1993:218, and Hollister 1998. On deforestation and other environmental changes in the region see Hughes 1975, and Thirgood 1981.
21. Boff 1997:209.
22. Wirzba 2003:121–122.
23. Boff 1997:215. Voluntary simplicity is an attribute of spiritual personages such as the Buddha, Christ, and Thomas Merton as well as many Christian and Buddhist monks and nuns. It was also practiced by Henry David Thoreau at Walden Pond. Today Jim Merkel is notable for his lifestyle and work embracing radical simplicity. Obviously such a lifestyle minimizes a person's ecological footprint or environmental impact. See Harnden 2003.
24. Bratton 2007:157, 238.
25. Splain 2005:1406. For further discussion of Franciscan environmentalism see Delio, et al., 2007, Foley, et al., 2000, Institute for Contemporary Franciscan Life 2011, Mitchell and Skudlarek 2010, Mizzoni 2008, Nothwehr 2002, Sarah Taylor 2007, and Warner 2010. Also see *The Green Bible* edited by Maudlin and others in 2008, which, incidentally, reproduces the Canticle of the Creatures after the title page.
26. Swan 2000:188–189.
27. Assisi Nature Council, 2011.
28. Boff 1997:207.
29. For example, see Kienzle 2006.
30. Malone 2002, Winter 1982.

31. The famous Harvard biologist Edward O. Wilson (1984:1) defines biophilia as "... the innate tendency to focus on life and life processes. He goes on to note that "... our existence depends on this propensity, our spirit is woven from it, hope rises on its currents." Also see Milton 2002.
32. Linzey and Barsam 2001.
33. Murtagh 2002.
34. The popularity of Saint Francis to this day is reflected in the numerous films about his person and life including: Cavani 2003, HDH Communications 2006, Malone 2002, Rossellini 2003, Sbicca 1992, 2005; Seamans 1996, and Zeffirelli 1972. In addition, it should be noted that the Desert Fathers, Celtic Saints, and other Christians before and since Francis and his followers were also spiritual ecologists in many ways (Nash 1991:84–88). Early famous creation-centered ecomystics of special relevance here are abbess, artist, composer, and writer Hildegard von Bingen (1098–1179) and intellectual, theologian, and preacher Meister Eckhart (1260–1329). For information about von Bingen see Fox 2002, and Petri and van Damme 2003. For the broader historical context of Saint Francis see Fox 2000 in his primer on creation spirituality. Entries on these and related subjects can be found in Taylor 2005.
35. Boff 1997:205.

Chapter 7. The Spirit of Walden, Henry David Thoreau

1. Catherine L. Albanese 2002:12.
2. Clarke 1997:86–87.
3. Gould 2005:1634.
4. Dorman 1998:68, and Kinsley 1995:147.
5. Clarke 1997:85.
6. Walls 2001:108.
7. Thoreau 1854:80.
8. Dorman 1998:63.
9. Gould 2005a:1634. Also see Gatta 2004.
10. Emerson 1849:23.
11. Albanese 1990, 2002.
12. Clarke 1997:84.
13. Cronon 1983, Dorman 1998:55, 85, 89, and Marsh 1864.
14. Kinsley 1995:143.
15. Thoreau 1862:613.
16. Gould 2005:1635–1636.
17. Thoreau 1854:274.

18. Dorman 1998:50.
19. Worster 1994:83.
20. See Becher 2000, de Steiguer 2006, and Palmer 2001.
21. Albanese 2002:11.
22. Dorman 1998: 95–97.
23. Gardner 2006: 124.
24. Kozlovsky 1974:106.
25. Ibid.:106. Also see his DVD *Radically Simple* and his website on the Global Living Project at http://www.radicalsimplicity.org.
26. Merkel 2003:162–163.
27. Dorman 1998:87–88.
28. Ibid.:74.
29. Dorman 1998:74. Many of Thoreau's writings are being archived on a special website called The Thoreau Reader. Thoreau's legacy also continues in various organizations, such as the Thoreau Institute at Walden Woods, Thoreau Society, and the Walden Pond State Reservation. Also see Wawrzonek 2002.
30. Dorman 1998:97.
31. The best sources on the relevance of Thoreau for ecology and environmentalism are Dorman 1998:47–101, and Worster 1994:57–111. Kinsley 1995: 141–147 draws heavily on the latter to highlight Thoreau's spiritual ecology.

Chapter 8. Wilderness Discipline, John Muir

1. Muir 1896:282–283.
2. Brinkley 2009, Miller 2001.
3. Muir 2011.
4. Brinkley 2009, Dorman 1998:164–166, and Nash 2001:138–139.
5. Duncan and Burns 2009, 2011.
6. McKibben 2008:84.
7. Jones 1965.
8. Holmes 2005:1126.
9. Harnden 2007:8–9.
10. Dorman 1998:105.
11. Ehrlich 2000:18–19.
12. Dorman 1998:112, and White 1967. For example, see *The Green Bible* edited by Maudlin, et al., 2008.
13. Ibid.:120, 144, 151.
14. Ibid:115, 122, 128.
15. Albanese 2002:11.
16. Dorman 1998:116.

17. Also, see Nash 2001:126–127.
18. Oelschlaeger 1991.
19. Lionberger 2007. Also see Moon 2011.
20. Corcoran 2001:13.
21. Holmes 2005:1127.
22. Dorman 1998:111, 147.
23. Ibid.:110. Also see Shore 2009.
24. Ibid.:106. Also see Austin 1991, Highland 2001, 2008, and Williams 2002.
25. Albanese 2002:12.
26. Ibid:33.
27. For example, see Miller 2001.
28. de Steiguer 2006:11–12, Dorman 1998:130.
29. Dorman 1998:149, Nash 2001:161–181, Smith 1998, Williams 2002.
30. De Steiguer 2006:12.
31. Holt, et.al., 2008, Restore Hetch Hetchy 2009, Sierra Club 2011.
32. Marsh 1864.
33. Nash 2001:131.
34. Callicott and Nelson 1998, Coates 1998, de Steiguer 2006, and Pepper 1996.
35. See, for example, Adams 2001.
36. Keller and Turek 1998, and Spence 1999.
37. For example, see McNeely 1995.
38. Burton 2002, Matthiessen 1984, McLeod 2002, 2012, and Swan 1990, 2001.
39. Callicott and Nelson 1998, Coates 1998, Cronon 1995, De Steiguer 2006, Nash 2001, Pepper 1996, and Soule and Lease 1994.
40. See National Park Service 2011.
41. McKibben 2008, and Worster 2005.
42. The Sierra Club website has a wealth of information about Muir as well as about the organization. Also see Bade 1916, 1924, Brown 1988, Cohen 1984, Leonard 2008, Fox 1981, Gisel 2008, Holmes 1999, Johnson 2006, Meyer 1997, Miller 1995, 1999, Miller 2005, Muir 2011, Thurman 1995, Turner 1985, Wolfe 1938, 1945, and Worster 2005. Films on Muir include those by Clark and Tatge 2011, Duncan and Burns 2009, Holt, et al., 2008, and Panorama International Productions 1990.

Chapter 9. Spiritual Science, Rudolf Steiner

1. Barton 2008: 227.
2. Ellwood 2005, Goswami 1995, and Myerson 1984.
3. Barton 2008: 1–5.
4. General Anthroposophy Society 2011.

5. Taylor 2010:156.
6. Hindes 2010.
7. See Barton 2008: 58, 116.
8. General Anthroposophy Society 2011.
9. Quotes from Barton 2008: 36, 89, 160, 167, 168, 170.
10. For example, see Cohen 1997, Coleman 2006, Roads 1987, Swan 2000, Swimme and Tucker 2011a,b, and Tobias and Cowan 1996. For more on Steiner see Rudolf Steiner Archive 2011, Rudolf Steiner 2011, Steiner 1999, and Thomas 2005.

Chapter 10. Nature as Thou, Martin Buber

1. Buber 1970:58–59.
2. Gellman 2002, and Tirosh-Samuelson 2006.
3. Hill 2000, Hill and Hurley 2002, and Wolens 2000. Also see Kaza 1996 and Nadkarni 2008 for examples of other I-Thou relationships with trees.
4. Forum on Religion and Ecology 2004, Gottlieb 2006a:112–113, and Zuckerman 2004.
5. For Jewish environmentalism in general, see Coalition on the Environment and Jewish Life 2010, Elon, et al., 2000, Jacobs 2002, 2011, Kibbutz Lotan 2011, Aubrey Rose 1992, Schwartzschild 1984, Shalom Center 2010, Schwartzschild 1984, Solomon 1992, Tirosh-Samuelson 2002, 2006, and Waskow 2000.
6. Pick 1992:68. Also see Hareuveni and Frenkley 1984.
7. Harrison 2004, Harvey 2006, and Russell 2008.
8. Naess 1989:174. Also see Fink 2010 and Yaffe 2001.
9. Tirosch-Samuelson 2006:50.
10. Lerner 2000:138. For more on Buber see Martin Buber Homepage 2011, I-Thou 2011, and Margulies 2008.

Chapter 11. Challenging Christians, Lynn White, Jr.

1. White 1967:1207.
2. White 1973:55.
3. White 1967:1205.
4. Ibid.: 1205.
5. Ibid.: 1205.
6. Spring and Spring 1974:1, Toynbee 1972.
7. On Islam and ecology see Foltz 2006, Foltz, et al., 2003, Khalid and O'Brien 1992, and Nasr 1992, 1993, 1996, 1997.

8. White 1967:1206.
9. Ibid.: 1206.
10. White 1973:63.
11. Nash 1989:108–109.
12. Curry 2011:33.
13. Maudlin, et al., 2008.
14. Nash 1989.
15. Edwards and Palmer 1997.
16. World Wildlife Fund 1986.
17. Edwards and Palmer 1997.
18. Rockefeller and Elder 1992.
19. For example, Palmer 1996.
20. Breully and Palmer 1992, Khalid and O'Brien 1992, Prince 1992, Rajotte 1998, and Aubrey Rose 1992. Additional books influenced by ARC are Edwards and Palmer 1997, Palmer and Bisset 1985, Palmer and Finlay 2003, and Palmer and Palmer 1997.
21. See the Forum on Religion and Ecology (FORE) 2011.
22. Alliance of Religions and Conservation 2011.
23. See Association for Forests, Development, and Conservation 2011, and Verschuuren, et al., 2010.
24. Shrader-Frechette 1981:28. Also see Moore and Nelson 2010.
25. Among the extended critical analyses of White's article are Barbour 1973, Eckberg and Blocker 1989, Hall 1988, Hamlin and Lodge 2006, Hargrove 1986, Jenkins 2009b, Kinsley 1995, Nash 1988:87–120, Nash 1991, Spring and Spring 1974, and Whitney 1993. For subsequent discourses on the relationship between Christianity and environment see Berry and Clarke 1991, Breully and Palmer 1992, Burrell and Malits 1997, Chase 2011a,b, Cohen-Kiener 2009, DeWitt 2007, Edwards 2006, Hart 2004, Hessel and Ruether 2000, Hosenfeld 2009, Moyers 2006, National Religious Partnership for the Environment 2011, Religion and Ethics News Weekly (search under ecology or environment), Santmire 1970, Scharper and Cunningham 2002, Seamans 1996, and Wirzba 2003.

Chapter 12. Supernovas

1. Rockefeller and Elder 1992:2–3.
2. Rockefeller and Elder 1991, 1992.
3. It appears that in the United States the first interdisciplinary and interfaith collaboration on religion and environment was the Faith-Man-Nature Group, which organized six national and three regional conferences from

1963 to 1972 with loose sponsorship from the ecumenical Protestant organization the National Council of Churches. This organization also helped support the first Earth Day in 1970. Although primarily Christian, eventually the group also considered Buddhism, Judaism, and Native American religions. Theologians, church leaders, scientists, and environmentalists participated. Among the more prominent members were Ian G. Barbour (1973) and H. Paul Santmire (1970), who went on to publish books on ecotheology and environmental ethics. The group disbanded in 1974 because of inadequate funding. Nash (1988:102–106) provides the most extensive discussion of the Faith-Man-Nature Group. Also see Moyers 2006.

4. Rockefeller and Elder 1992:xiii.
5. Ibid.:1–2. Also see Rockefeller 1996, and Rockefeller and Elder 1991. It is noteworthy that since 1995 Rockfeller has been the seminal leader in the whole process of the development of the Earth Charter Initiative (2011).
6. Rockefeller and Elder 1992:141.
7. Ibid.:154.
8. Ibid.:142–144, 165–166.
9. 9Ibid.:144–146.
10. Ibid.:167.
11. Ibid.:182.
12. See the interview with Tucker and Grim 2009b.
13. Tucker and Grim 1993. Books from the Harvard conferences include: Chapple 2002, Chapple and Tucker 2000, Foltz, Denny, and Baharuddin 2003, Girardot, Miller, and Xiaogan 2001, Grim 2001, Hessel and Ruether 2000, Tirosh-Samuelson 2002, Tucker and Berthrong 1998, and Tucker and Williams 1997.
14. In 1998 a special issue of the periodical *Earth Ethics* summarized most of the conferences (Tucker and Grim 1998), and the articles from it are reprinted as introductory essays for each religion on the website of the Forum on Religion and Ecology (2011). For more detail on the conference initiatives see Tucker and Grim 1997, 1998, 2001, 2011, and Tucker 2006.
15. Tucker 2006:401.
16. Ibid.:406.
17. Ibid.:413.
18. Tucker and Grim 1997:xxi.
19. Tucker 2006:409, and Forum on Religion and Ecology 2011.
20. Swimme and Tucker 2011a,b.
21. Tucker, personal communication, December 21, 2011. The orientation of the film is foreshadowed in statements by Tucker in a previous book (Tucker 2003:7–8, 52).

22. Tucker and Grim 2007a:4.
23. Ibid.:a:6. Also see Tucker and Grim 2007b, 2009. It should be mentioned that Tucker and Grim were deeply influenced by the Jesuit Priest Thomas Berry as his graduate students at Fordham University and subsequently as a collaborating colleague and close friend. Tucker edited several of Berry's books, including *Evening Thoughts: Reflecting on the Earth as Sacred Community* which records his intellectual biography (Berry 2006). Berry in turn was influenced greatly by another Jesuit Priest, Pierre Teilhard de Chardin, who was a scientist, philosopher, and theologian. Tucker and Grim have both served as leaders in the American Teilhard Association. See Berry 1999; 2006a,b, 2009, 2011, Teilhard de Chardin 1959, Duffy 2001, Eaton 2001, King 2011, Laszlo and Combs 2011, Tucker 2007, and Webb 2007.
24. Taylor 2006:589.
25. Taylor 2007a.
26. Taylor 1995:6, 14.
27. Ibid.:15–16.
28. See Taylor 2010b.
29. Taylor 1995:346–349. Also see Taylor 2001a,b, 2004, 2010a.
30. American Academy of Religion 2011.
31. Matthews, et al. 2009, and Taylor 2005, Taylor 2009.
32. Taylor, et al., 2006.
33. Taylor (personal communication, December 23, 2011). This journal is a successor to the periodical called *Ecotheology: The Journal of Religion, Nature and the Environment* (1996–2006), which in turn was the successor of *Theology in Green* (1992–1995), all profoundly influenced by Lynn White's classic essay in *Science* in 1967. Taylor 2006, 2007b.
34. Taylor 2007a:5–7, 2012a,b. Also, Taylor is editing a book on Avatar and nature spirituality.
35. Taylor 2010a, 2006:598–599, 602–603. See Taylor 2009, which to some degree summarizes his book.
36. Monserud 2002.
37. Taylor 2012b.
38. Gottlieb 2007b:86.
39. Ibid.:86.
40. Ibid.:83.
41. Ibid.::88–89. See, for example, the project Ecotipping Points of Gerald Marten 2011.
42. Ibd.:90.
43. Gottlieb 1996, 2004a.

44. A somewhat similar anthology edited by Foltz (2003), although less ambitious, is also very useful.
45. Gottlieb 2006b.
46. Gottlieb 2006a.
47. Also see Gottlieb 2010.
48. Gottlieb 2006b:6–8.
49. Ibid.:11–14, cf. Gardner 2006.
50. Gottlieb 2006a.
51. Ibid.
52. Ibd.:82–83.
53. Ibid.:117.
54. Ibid.:13.
55. Ibid.:171.
56. Ibid.:174.
57. Ibid.:190.
58. Ibid.:215.
59. Ibid.:9.
60. See Gottlieb 2004b. Gottlieb's website includes an interview in the magazine *The American Prospect*. A most informative and stimulating guest lecture on "Religious Environmentalism" was passionately presented by Gottlieb (2007a) at Vanderbilt University, and is readily available on YouTube. It was sponsored by the new program on "Ecology and Spirituality in America: Exploring Possibilities for Cultural Transmission" in the Center for the Study of Religion and Culture. Also, see Gottlieb 2004b and 2012.
61. Berry 1999:150. See Bauman, et al., 2011, Jenkins 2009a, and Tucker and Grim 2007b. Gottlieb (2006a), Tucker and Grim 2009, 2012), and Taylor (2010) also published surveys synthesizing their previous publications. Their websites include their resume with a list of numerous publications.

Chapter 13. Can a Poet Save Nature? W. S. Merwin

1. W. S. Merwin in Wilcox 2011.
2. Aitken 1990, Aitken and Toms 1998, Kahn 2011, and Merwin 2011:11, 20.
3. Kraus 2005.
4. Frazier 1999, Hix 1997, and Rampell 2010:38.
5. Lund 2003. For a discussion of solastalgia, the distress generated by environmental change and loss, see Albrecht 2006, and Albrecht, et al., 2007.
6. Davis 2011:23.
7. For example, Butler and Tompkins 2009, Gudmundsson 2006, and Scott 2010.

8. Merwin 2011:23.
9. Ibid.:12, and Wilcox 2011.
10. Kubota 2010:G10, and Merwin 2011:12.
11. Ibid.
12. Merwin 2011. See Merwin Conservancy 2011, also for more on the historical ecology of Merwin's place
13. Rampell 2010:36.
14. Kubota 2010:G10.
15. Merwin 2011.
16. Rampell 2010:38. Also see Kaza 1996.
17. Kubota 2010:G10, and Merwin 2011: 18.
18. Hix 1997:3. Also, see Herzog 2011.
19. Merwin 2011:17–18.
20. Felstiner 2009:304.
21. Kubota 2010:G10, and White 1967.
22. American Academy of Poets 2011, and Kubota 2010:G10.
23. Merwin 1971.
24. Poets Against War 2011.
25. Rampell 2010: 37.
26. See the Buddhist Peace Fellowship 2011.
27. See the Center for Global Nonkilling 2011.
28. Aiken and Toms 1998:71.
29. American Academy of Poets 2011.
30. Hix 1997:124. For case studies of the spiritual ecology of Native Hawaiians see Cunningham 1994, and Sponsel 2001c.
31. Felstiner 2009:302. Also see Hix 1997. For interviews with Merwin, see Lynn and Baker 2010, Moyers 2009, and Wilcox 2011. For his own poetry readings, see Cameron and Carpenter 1997, Moyers 2009, Vitale 1991, and Wilcox 2011.
32. Lund 2003.
33. See von Essen 2010.
34. Chatenever 2011.
35. Kubota 2010, and Wilcox 2011.
36. Cameron and Carpenter 1995.
37. You can even walk with Merwin through his palm forest and observe his biophilic affinity for trees and birds (Mewin Conservancy 2011).
38. Kubota 2010:G10. Also see Cunningham 1994, Culliney 2006, Dudley 1990, Kupihea 2001, Sponsel 2001c, and Ziegler 2002.
39. Felstiner 2009:13–14. Also, see Herzog 2011.
40. Felstiner 2009:357.
41. Lund 2003.

42. Hix 1997:136.
43. Merwin 1988:64. For more on Merwin as ecopoet see Christhilf 1986, Cone 2005, Frazier 1999, and Hix 1997. Among documentary films about Merwin are Cameron and Carpenter 1997, Lynn and Baker 2010, Merwin 1991, Moyers 2009, Vitale 1991, and Wilcox 2011. His literary papers composed of 5,500 archived items along with 450 books are housed in the Rare Book and Manuscript Library at the University of Illinois in Urbana-Champaign. Also see information about Merwin on the Online Resources of the U.S. Library of Congress. American Academy of Poets 2011 and the Poetry Foundation 2011 include information on Merwin and his poems on their websites. For aspects of the arts and nature, see Bryson 2002, Goldsworthy 2004, Grande 2003, Green Museum 2011, Steiner 2007, and Weintraub 2006, 2007. In addition, see *The Journal of Ecocriticism* (a new journal of Nature, Society, and Literature).

Chapter 14. Reconnecting, Joanna Macy

1. Macy 2011.
2. Buzzell and Chalquist 2009, Chalquist 2007, Chase 2011a, b, Cohen 1997, Metzner 1999, Moore 2010, Roszak, et al., 1995, and Young 2011.
3. Macy 2006.
4. Macy and Brown 1998, 2006, 2011.
5. Strobel 2005:1019.
6. Meadows, et al., 1993.
7. Macy 2006.
8. Macy 2011. Also see Dobson 1991, Earth Charter Initiative 2011, and EcoBuddhism 2011, the latter for "A Buddhist Response to Global Warming."
9. Metzner 1999:171–182. For other examples related to the Great Turning see Bennett 1976: 139, Bourne 2008, Capra 1982, Capra and Steindl-Rast 1991, Darvich 2009, Deravy 2009, Dregson 1983, Fox 1988, Hartman 1999, Hawken 2007, Institute of Noetic Sciences 2010, Korten 2006, Lake 2010, Macy 2010, McKibben 2010, Metzner 1999, Roszak 1978, Speth 2008, and Starke and Mastny, 2010. Also, a number of periodicals and their websites consider aspects of the Great Turning including *EarthLight: The Magazine of Spiritual Ecology, The Ecologist, Ecopsychology Journal, Kosmos, Orion Magazine, Resurgence, ReVision: The Journal of Consciousness Transformation, Sacred Fire Magazine, The Great Turning Times, Trumpeter: Journal of Ecosophy,* and *Yes! Magazine.*
10. Extracted from Metzner 1999:171–182.

11. For deep ecology see Barnhill and Gottlieb 2001, Devall and Sessions 1985, Drengson and Devall 2008, Naess 2003, Sessions 1995, Tobias 1988, and van Boeckel, et al. 1997, the latter a superb film on Naess).
12. Macy 1991a.
13. Parachin 1999:117.
14. Barrows 2007:213.
15. Biographical information is extracted from Macy 2011, Parachin 1999, and Strobel 2005. Also see Macy 2007, 2010, and Vaughan-Lee 2011. See Tippet 2010 for an interview with Macy.
16. Macy 1983, Macy and Brown 1998.
17. Barker 2003, Johnston 2007, Johnston and Barker 2008.
18. Macy 2000:282–283. Also see Kraft 1997.
19. Seed, et al., 1988/2007. Also see Swimme and Tucker 2011a, b.
20. Macy 2011.
21. For an example of the application of systems thinking to human ecology see Marten 2003, 2011. For an indigenous perspective on human ecology see Cajete 1999. Also see Macy and Johnstone 2012.
22. Barrows 2007:213.
23. See Malkin 2007.

Chapter 15. Green Patriarch, Bartholomew I

1. Batholomew I in Chryssavgis 2003:106.
2. His All Holiness Bartholomew I 2011. For general background on Eastern Orthodox views on nature and the environment see Chryssavgis 2006, and Makrides 2005.
3. On sacred waters see Altman 2002, and Crabtree 2005.
4. The Patriarch's website contains a wealth of information about these symposia as well as the documentary films *The Green Patriarch*, *Arctic*, and *Amazon*. See His All Holiness Bartholomew I 2011.
5. See the website Religion, Science and Environment Symposia 2011 where there is a wealth of fascinating and valuable information on each of these symposia under categories such as overview, committees, itinerary, themes, presentations, field trips, conclusions, donors, photos, video clips, press, outcomes, and links, although these categories vary somewhat for different symposia. On the environmental health of the world's great rivers see Whol 2010.
6. Chryssavgis 2003:8, 11, 2007.
7. Ibid.: Environmental addresses by Bartholomew I are available on his website at His All Holiness Bartholomew I 2011.

8. Chryssavgis 2005:158.
9. Chryssavgis 2007.
10. His All Holiness Bartholomew I 2011.
11. Gardner 2006, 2010a, b. For the complete joint statements with Pope John Paul II and Pope Benedict XVI see His All Holiness Bartholomew I 2011. It should be noted that in 1990 Pope John Paul II issued the encyclical "The Ecological Crisis: A Common Responsibility."
12. Chryssavgis 2003:viii.
13. Ibid.:6.
14. Chryssavgis 2007.
15. Chryssavgis 2003:18.
16. This information was extracted from the website His All Holiness Bartholomew I 2011.
17. Chryssavgis 2003:23.
18. cf. Merchant 2005. Chryssavgis (2003) reprints many of the statements by the Green Patriarch and provides very useful background. However, the statements and a great deal of other interesting and useful information can also be readily found on the website of His All Holiness Bartholomew I 2011. Chryssavgis (2006), and Makrides (2005) write more generally about the Orthodox religion and ecology.

Chapter 16. To Plant a Tree, Wangari Maathai

1. Maathai 2010:27.
2. Maathai in Mazur and Miles 2009:215.
3. Breton 1998:11.
4. Mburu 2005:960–961.
5. UNEP Billion Tree Campaign 2010.
6. See Green Belt Movement 2010, also Marten 2011. On religious tree-planting elsewhere in Africa see Daneel 2001, 2005, 2006, and Gitau 2000, 2005.
7. MacDonald 2006:87.
8. Breton 1998:12–13. Maathai's (2006) autobiography details this story with many other fascinating details of her life and work. Also see Mazur and Miles 2009, and the award-winning film by Merton and Dater 2008.
9. MacDonald 2006:87, and Mburu 2005.
10. Maathai 2010:102–103.
11. Mburu 2005:958–959. The GBM is described in detail by Maathai 2004, and in Merton and Dater 2008.
12. Dobson 1991.

13. For example, Maathai 2010:140. For ecopsychology see Buzzell and Chalquist 2009, Chalquist 2007, Metzner 1999, Roszak 1992, and Rozak, et al. 1995a, b.
14. Mburu 2005:958. Also, see Gitau 2000, 2005, Mukanyora 2005, and Nyamweru 2005.
15. Warner and Hoskins 2005:26–28. Also see Castro 1991 and Ranger 2005.
16. Maathai 2010:13.
17. Ibid:16, 35.
18. Ibid:17.
19. Ibid:17.
20. Ibid:19.
21. Ibid:21. Also see Swimme and Tucker 2011a, b.
22. Ibid:31. Also, see pp. 90, 154–155, 193.
23. Ibid:24.
24. For example, Maathai 2010:50–53, 78, 85, 120–122. Also see Kalu 2001.
25. For example, see Maathai 2010:77–91.
26. Maathai 2010:59, 74.
27. Ibid:95–96. Also, see pp. 148–149, 164.
28. Ibid:113.
29. Ibid: 159–164, 171, 173–179, 183, 197–199.
30. Wangari Maathai Institute for Peace and the Environment 2010.
31. Mazur and Miles 2009:211.
32. Maathai 2010:190–191.

Chapter 17. Desert Spirituality, Burning Man

1. Gilmore 2010a:11. Gilmore has been a participant as well as an observer in the Burning Man festival for over a decade. This special vantage point facilitates her captivating description and interpretation of the complex meaning and significance of this unique phenomenon. The bibliography in Gilmore's book cites other useful publications on this subject. A documentary film by Gillman (2010b) is included with her book as a DVD. Documentary films by Rauner (2010) and Silverman (2005), among others, can be found at Amazon.com. Also, see the anthology by Gilmore and Van Proyen 2005.
2. Gilmore 2010a:20.
3. Rauner 2010.
4. Gilmore 2010a:1, 61–62, 66, 70–73, 82, 119, 167.
5. Ibid. 69, 101, 155.
6. See Chapter 2 titled "Spiritual, but Not Religious" in Gilmore 2010a.
7. Gilmore 2010a:1–5, 22.

8. Ibid. 13–14
9. Ibid. 69, 98, 162.
10. Silverman 2005. Another festival that is similar in some ways is the Rainbow Gathering (Timothy Miller 2005).
11. Gilmore 2010a:20.
12. Ibid.:48, 53–54, 68, 103, 126, 157.
13. Ibid.:113–117.
14. Ibid.:38–43, 104, 156, 165. Also see the "Survival Guide"on the website Burning Man 2011.
15. Gilmore 2010a:51–52, 66, 106, 154.
16. Ibid.:69.
17. Ibid.:95. See also Howard 2009.
18. Ibid.:104–105, 111–112, 143–145.
19. Silverman 2005.
20. Burning Man 2011. Also see Gilmore 2010a:78.
21. Gilmore 2010a:45, 123–125, 166–167.
22. Sapir 1924.
23. Gilmore 2010a:65. See Swimme and Tucker 2011a, b.
24. Ibid.:66–67. Also see Bowditch 2010, and Gilmore and Van Proyen 2005.
25. For other studies of desert spiritual ecology see Abbey 1968, Bratton 2009, Cowan 2004, Keller 2005, Lane 1998, Williams 1995, and Williams, et al., 1998.

Chapter 18. Avatar, Opening Pandora's Box, James Cameron

1. Cameron 2010c.
2. Cameron 2011.
3. For example, Mahoney 2010.
4. Taylor 2010c.
5. The spelling *unobtainium* is also used in the literature. See Mahoney 2010:26.
6. Hinnells 1995:58–59.
7. Lewis 2009.
8. Mahoney 2010:55–57.
9. Ibid.:2010:4, 27–29, 34–35, 71, 96–97, 130, and Campbell 1949.
10. Keegan 2010:231–255. Motion capture is described in great detail in the segment "Capturing Avatar" of the Three-Disc Extended Collector's Edition (Cameron 2010b) as well as in the book by Duncan and Fitzpatrick 2010.
11. Keegan 2010.

12. Mahoney 2010:61–62. Much of the extraordinary background research for the construction of the Na'vi society and landscape of Pandora is detailed in the DVD program *Capturing Avatar* (Cameron 2010b), a special manual (Wilhelm and Mathison 2009), and a chapter in a biography of Cameron (Keegan 2010:231–255). *Avatar: A Confidential Report on the Biological and Social History of Pandora* by Wilhem and Mathison is especially fascinating.
13. For example, Wilhelm and Mathison 2009:46–47. On the art of Avatar see Fitzpatrick, Jackson, and Landau 2009.
14. Barnhill 2010, Kline 2009, Mahoney 2010:118–119, and Wieland 2010.
15. See Bodley 1988, 2008a, and Churchill 1997.
16. Andreas 2004, Bullfrog Films 2010, Churchill 2003, Network of Concerned Anthropologists 2011, and Price 2011.
17. Mahoney 2010:118–119.
18. Ali 2003, Bullfrog Films 2006, Butler and Tompkins 2009, Christians for the Mountains 2006, Grinde and Johansen 1995, LaDuke 1999, McLeod 2002, 2012, Moody 2007, and Scott 2010.
19. Mahoney 2010:132.
20. Table 18.1 after Bennett 1976:139, Figure 8. For a similar but more detailed model of the attributes of ecologically sustainable and unsustainable societies see Metzner 1999:171–182.
21. Reichel-Dolmatoff 1971, 1976.
22. See Bodley 2005, 2008a, b, Merkel 2003, International Union for the Conservation of Nature and Natural Resources 1997, and Reichel-Dolmatoff 1971, 1976.
23. Sponsel 2005. See Bodley 1988, 2008a, Churchill 1997, Johnston 2011.
24. Sponsel 2001b.
25. Bodley 2008a, Churchill 1997.
26. For example, Wilhelm and Mathison 2009:25.
27. Ibid.:34.
28. Deravy 2009, Kinsley 1995, Posey, et al., 1999, and Reichel-Dolmatoff 1971, 1976.
29. Harvey 2006, and Sponsel 2006.
30. On Pantheism see Harrison 2004, and Russell 2008.
31. Lovelock 1979, 2006, 2009. Also, see Jensen 2004 and LaDuke 2005.
32. Wilhelm and Mathison 2009: xiv-xv.
33. Ibid.:186.
34. Ibid.:28–29. Also, see Mahoney 2010:66 and Sideris 2010.
35. cf. Taylor 2010a, b.
36. Louv 2005, cf. Shepard 1982.
37. Metzner 1999.

38. Frommer 2010.
39. Kellert and Wilson 1993, Tuan 1990, and Wilson 1984.
40. Keegan 2010:254.
41. Gould, et al., 2010, Justice 2010, Smith 1999, Sponsel 2001a, and Survival International 2010a, b.
42. Keegan 2010:8.
43. Ibid.:255.
44. Mahoney 2010:85, 133.
46. Barrionuevo 2010. Also, see AmazonWatch 2010, Cameron 2010c, Films Incorporated Video 1991, and Turner 2011.
47. Cameron 2010d.
48. Ibid.:2010e.
49. Keegan 2010:2.
50. Ibid.:2010:4, 9.
51. Ibid.:14, 254–255.
52. Ibid.:xiii.
53. Ibid.:257.
54. Ibid.:xiii.
55. See Anderson 2010, Holtmeier 2010, and also the remarkable Manifesto and other activities at Na'vi Movement 2010. For discussions by and about fans of the movie see avatar-forums.com 2010, naviblue.com 2010, and Istoft 2010. Also see Pitesa 2009, Resurgence 2010, and Taylor and Ivakhiv 2010.

Chapter 19. Atheist Spiritual Ecology, Donald A. Crosby

1. Limitations of space disallow any lengthy discussion of this and many closely related subjects, but sources have been liberally cited for those who may wish to pursue such matters further.
2. Crosby 2002:113–114.
3. Ibid.: 169. Also see Chickerneo 2008, Coleman 2006, Danaan 2009, Elgin 2009, Elkins 1998, Lake 2010, Lionberger 2007, Milton 2006, Moore 2010, Plotkin 2008, von Essen 2010, and Wallace 2005.
4. Crosby 2002:xi.
5. Ibid.: 5.
6. Ibid.: 6–7.
7. Ibid.: 10.
8. Ibid.: 21.
9. See, for example, Tucker and Berling 2003.

10. Ibid.: 45–48, 59.
11. Ibid.: 49. Also see Matthews, et al., 2002, Peters 2002, and Swimme and Tucker 2011a, b.
12. Crosby 2002:58.
13. Ibid.: 70, 72.
14. Bookchin 1995, Dawkins 2006, 2011a, b, Lett 1997, Nasr 1992, and Stenmark 1997.
15. Gottlieb 2006a:71.
16. Ibid.: 68, 104.
17. Clayton and Simpson 2006:4. Beyond the books by the New Atheists, see Atheism.about.com 2011. For the discussion and debate over the relationship between science and religion, see Barbour 2000, Beattie 2008, Birch 2008, Chopra and Mlodinow 2011, Clayton and Simpson 2006, Cohen 2011, Dixon 2008, Elgin 2009, Frank 2009, Hitchens 2007, Kauffman 2008, Kung 2007, Peacocke 2007, Raymo 2008, Rue 2005, Sheldrake 1994, Smith 2000, Stewart 2008, and Ward 2008. Clayton and Simpson 2006 include chapters on atheism and naturalism among many other pertinent topics. The faith of various scientists is discussed in Clayton and Schaal 2007 and in Frankenberry 2008. For one prominent scientist who comprehends the sacredness of nature see Suzuki 2003, 2006, 2010, 2011, Suzuki and Taylor 2009, and Suzuki, et al. 2007.
18. See Carroll and Warner 1998, Chapman, et al. 1999, Conroy and Petersen 2000, Kellert and Farnham 2002, Matthews, et al., 2002, Swimme and Berry 1992, and Swimme and Tucker 2011a, b.
19. This is a partial statement from "Preserving the Earth: An Appeal for Joint Commitment in Science and Religion" of the Global Forum, Moscow, January 1990. The full statement among others can be found on the website of the Forum of Religion and Ecology 2011. Also, see the Yale University Divinity School's "Initiative in Religion, Science, and Technology."
20. Gould 2002 and Sagan 2006.
21. Gottlieb 2006a:69. For other examples see Taylor 2010a.
22. Ibid.: 72.
23. Ibid.: 128.
24. Crosby 2002:118–121, 127–130. Also see Bratton 2002, Capra and Steindl-Rast 1991, Cohen 2011, de Quincey 2002. Goodall and Berman 1999, Goodenough 1998, Grassie 2010, Haught 2006, Smith 2000, Swenson 2009, Upton 2008, and von Essen 2010.
25. Crosby 2002:159–161, 163–164. Also see Coleman 2006, Riedelsheimer 2004, Swan 1990, 2000, and Swimme and Tucker 2011a, b.
26. Lovelock 1979, 2009.

27. Devereaux, et al., 1989, Harding 2006.
28. EcoBuddhism 2011, Garvey 2008, Gore 2006a, b, Gottlieb 2011, McFague 2008, Monaghan 2005, Nicholson and Rosen 1992, Northcott 2007, Ruether 1992, Skrimshire 2010, Stanley, et al., 2009, Taylor 2005, Tucker and Grim 2001, and Winter 1982.
29. Crosby 2002:156.
30. For a discussion of criticisms and their rebuttals see Gottlieb 2006:57–80, Hahn, et al., 2008, Haught 1990, Nasr 1992:94–96, and Taylor 2010a: 176–179. For scientific explorations of spirituality see Elahi 1997, Petrovic 2008, and Wolf 1999. On biological and other scientific analyses of religion and spirituality, some of them remarkably arrogant, myopic, ignorant, biased, dogmatic, fanatical, simplistic, and/or reductionistic, see Atran 2002, Beauregard and O'Leary 2007, Burkert 1996, Dawkins 2006, d'Aquili and Newberg 1999, Dennett 2006, Guthrie 1993, Hamer 2004, Harris 2004, Hitchens 2007, Horgan 2003, Morrison 1999, Peters 2002, Ray 2009, Rue 2005, Stenger 2007, Valliant 2008, Wade 2009, and Wilson 2002. Also see the websites for the Committee for the Scientific Examination of Religion 2011, Institute on Religion in an Age of Science, Inc. 2011, Metanexus Institute 2011, Mind and Life Institute 2011, Science and Religion Forum 2011, and Society for the Scientific Study of Religion 2011. For critiques of the so-called New Atheism see Beattie 2008, Cornwell 2007, Hahn and Wilker 2008, Haught 2008, Markham 2010, and Stewart 2008.
31. Frankenberry 2008:154.

Chapter 20. Natural Theology, Alister E. McGrath

1. McGrath 2002a:186.
2. Ibid.: xi, xvii-xviii.
3. See, for example, Swimme and Tucker 2011a, b.
4. For example, see Clayton and Schaal 2007, and Frankenberry 2008. Also see an intellectual biography by McDonald 2006 and McGrath 2006a, plus his website which includes his biography and bibliography at McGrath 2011.
5. McGarth 2002a:103.
6. Ibid.: v-xvi, 29–30, 77, 80–81.
7. Ibid.: 88–92.
8. Ibid.: 2–3, 67–72, 150–168.
9. Ibid.: 8, 68, 79.
10. Ibid.: 137. For counter examples see Taylor 2010a.
11. McGrath 2002:xiii-xiv, xvii, 146.

12. McGrath 2006b. Also see his books on Dawkins published in 2004 and 2007, on atheism in 2006, as well as Cornwell 2007, and Stewart 2008. For Dawkins and atheism see Dawkins 2011a, b, the American Humanist Association 2011, and the British Humanist Association 2011.
13. McGrath 2002a:138–143, 146.
14. Ibid.: 53–63.
15. Ibid.: 93–99, 101–103, 109–110.
16. Ibid.: 82–87.
17. Ibid.: 31–36, 184. See, for example, Bratton 2009, Cowan 2004, Keller 2005, and Lane 1998.
18. McGrath 2002a:11–21, 25.
19. Ibid.: 36–52.
20. Ibid.: 117, 129–137.
21. Ibid.: 6, 128.
22. Ibid.: 64, 115.
23. See McGrath 2006c.
24. See the Templeton Foundation 2011.
25. See Swimme and Tucker 2011a, b.
26. Nasr 1997:4. Also, see Nasr 1993, 1996, and the reference volume edited by Clayton and Simpson 2006.

Chapter 21. Secularization of the Sacred, His Holiness the 14th Dalai Lama of Tibet

1. Autobiographical accounts by His Holiness the 14th Dalai Lama of Tibet include his book in 1998 and another with Sofia Stril-Rever in 2010. Also see his website. Biographical accounts are by Chhaya 2007 and Iyer 2008 and in the film by Scorsese 1997. His Holiness the 14th Dalai Lama of Tibet is unusually broad minded, intensely interested in Western science. Among the more recent books on this are Harrington and Zajonc 2003, and Houshmand 2009. Also see the Mind and Life Institute 2011 and the documentary films by Darvich 2009a.b, and Ray 2006. His Holiness the 14th Dalai Lama of Tibet is also receptive to dialog with other religions as well as to identifying and exploring commonalities. See his 1999 and 2010 books. For Tibetan culture see Harrer 1982, Kapstein 2006, and Klieger 2007. On Tibetan Buddhism see His Holiness the 14th Dalai Lama of Tibet 1987, Powers 2007, and the website for Tibetan Buddhism 2011.

2. His Holiness the 14th Dalai Lama of Tibet, 1989 (December 11), Speech at the University of Aula, Oslo, Norway. His speech is available at Tibet Environmental Watch 2011.
3. Brauen 2004, Dodin and Rather 2001, and Lopez 1998.
4. On the environment and environmentalism in Tibet see Atisha 1991, Cantwell 2001, Conservation International 2008, Clarke 2001, Flemming, et al., 2007, Hakkenberg 2008, His Holiness the 14th Dalai Lama of Tibet and Stril-Rever 2010:218–255, Huber 1991, Norberg-Hodge 2001, Khoryug 2009, and Thurman 2008:209–220. Also see the websites EcoBuddhism 2011, Life on the Tibetan Plateau 2011, Tibet Environmental Watch 2011, and Tibet Environmental Network 2011. For the sacred landscape of Tibet see Pistono 2011, Thubron 2011, and Thurman and Wise 1999. Also see the documentary films by Wiese 2006 and Vendetti 2007.
5. Conservation International 2008.
6. Flemming, et al., 2007:101.
7. Atisha 1991, Huber 1991.
8. For the history of Tibet including the conflict with China see Bagdro 1998, Shakya 1999, and Smith 2008. Also see the websites of Free Tibet 2011, the International Campaign for Tibet 2011, and the Tibetan Government in Exile 2011 as well as the films by Annaud 2005, Bacon 2005, Dugdale 2008, and Rather 2008.
9. Beech 2011.
10. Flemming, et al., 2007.
11. See Elsass 1992 for attributes of cultures that promote survival.
12. See Tibet Environment Watch 2011, and Atisha 1991:14.

Epilogue

1. Leopold 1966:246. Also see The Aldo Leopold Foundation 2011 and Meine 1987.
2. Among places to continue this pilgrimage are the website of the Forum on Religion and Ecology 2011, Bauman, et al. 2011, Gottlieb 2006a, b, Kinsley 1995, Rockefeller and Elder 1991, Spring and Manousos 2007, Taylor 2005, 2010a, and Tucker and Berling 2003. Kumar 2009 and Tucker 2003 would be a fascinating place to begin. Kinsley provides the first textbook, although some critics view it as too sanguine. Forum on Religion and Ecology 2011, Gottlieb 2006b, and Taylor 2005, 2011 are most useful reference works. In addition, especially relevant are documentary films by

Ereira 1990; Herzog 2011; Lansing 1989; McLeod 2002, 2012; Moyers 1991; and Swimme and Tucker 2011.

3. Extracted from the discussion in Kinsley 1995:227–232. This list previously appeared in Sponsel 2007a. Numerous biologists, conservationists, ecologists, and environmentalists would resonate with many of these points.
4. Pedersen 1998 identifies a list of similar common principles. Also see the Earth Charter Initiative 2011.
5. For example, see Smith and Pulver 2009.
6. Havel 1998:30.
7. Earth Ministry 2011. Also see Roberts and Amidon 1991 and the video *Holocene* by Iver (2011). The website for the present book is http://spiritualecology.info. The author welcomes any comments from readers at les.sponsel@gmail.com.

APPENDIX: SELECTED LIST OF CONTRIBUTORS TO SPIRITUAL ECOLOGY

Edward Abbey
David Abram
Ansel Adams
Catherine L. Albanese
Eugene N. Anderson
Liberty Hyde Bailey
Ecumenical Patriarch Bartholomew II
Basho
Gregory Bateson
Marc Bekoff
Fikret Berkes
Edwin Bernbaum
Thomas Berry
Wendell Berry
Hildegard von Bingen
Sally G. Bingham
David Brower
Martin Buber
Leonard Buff
Black Elk
David Bohm
Buddha
J. Baird Callicott
Fritjof Capra
Rachel Carson
John B. Cobb, Jr.
Anna Botsford Comstock
Jacques Cousteau
The 14th Dalai Lama of Tibet
Wade Davis
K. Lauren de Boer
Vine DeLoria, Jr.
Bill Devall

Calvin DeWitt
Rene Dubos
Saint Francis of Assisi
Heather Eaton
Loren Eiseley
Ralph Waldo Emerson
Ronald Engel
Alan Ereira
Dave Foreman
Matthew Fox
Mahatma Gandhi
Gary T. Gardner
Clarence Glacken
Jane Goodall
Al Gore
Roger S. Gottlieb
John Grim
Thich Nhat Hahn
Thom Hartman
Graham Harvey
Dieter Hessel
Julia Butterfly Hill
Linda Hogan
J. Donald Hughes
John Robinson Jeffers
Carl Gustav Jung
Carl Jung
Stephanie Kaza
Petra Kelly
David Kinsley
Jiddu Krishnamurti
Satish Kumar
Dolores LaChapelle

Winona LaDuke
Beldon Lane
K. Lauren de Boer
Aldo Leopold
Barry Lopez
James Lovelock
David Loy
Oren Lyons
Wangari Maathai
Joanna Macy
Maimonides
Jerry Mander
George Perkins Marsh
Calvin Luther Martin
Peter Matthiessen
Jay McDaniel
Sallie McFague
Alister McGrath
Terence McKenna
Christopher McLeod
Thomas Merton
W. S. Merwin
Ralph Metzner
Kay Milton
John Muir
Arne Naess
Rodrick Nash
Seyyed Hossein Nasr
Richard Nelson
Julian of Norwich
Sigurd Olson
Martin Palmer
Roy A. Rappaport
Larry Rasmussen
Gerardo Reichel-Dolmatoff
Steven C. Rockefeller
Holmes Rolston III
Theodore Roszak
Jean-Jacques Rousseau

Rosemart Radford Ruether
E. F. Schumacher
Albert Schweitzer
John Seed
George Sessions
Rupert Sheldrake
Paul Shepard
Vandana Shiva
Peter Singer
Sulak Sivaraksa
Henryk Skolimowski
Gary Snyder
David Sopher
Baruch de Spinoza
Charlene Spretnak
Dorothy Stang
Starhawk
Rudolf Steiner
David Suzuki
James Swan
Emanuel Swedenborg
Brian Swimme
Rabindranath Tagore
Bron R. Taylor
Pierre Teilhard de Chardin
Henry David Thoreau
Yi-fu Tuan
Mary Evelyn Tucker
Stewart L. Udall
William Wadsworth
Paul Waldau
Alfred Russell Wallace
Alan Watts
Lynn White, Jr.
Walt Whitman
Ken Wilber
Terry Tempest Williams
Edward O. Wilson
Paul Winter

BIBLIOGRAPHY

Note: All websites were accessed on December 29, 2011.

Abbey, Edward. 1968. *Desert Solitaire.* New York, NY: McGraw-Hill.

Abram, David. 1996. *The Spell of the Sensuous: Perception and Language in a More-Than-Human World.* New York, NY: Random House/Vintage Books.

Abrams, Elliot M., AnnCorinne Freter, David J. Rue, and John D. Wingard. 1996. "The Role of Deforestation in the Collapse of the Late Classic Copan Maya State." In *Tropical Deforestation: The Human Dimension,* Leslie E. Sponsel, Thomas N. Headland, and Robert C. Bailey (eds.). New York, NY: Columbia University Press, pp. 55–75.

Adams, David. 2001. *Season of the Loon: One Man's Search for Wilderness in Increasingly Strange Times.* St. Cloud, MN: North Star Press of St. Cloud, Inc.

Adams, David. 2011. *Institute for Cultural Ecology.* http://www.cultural-ecology.com/.

Aitken, Robert. 1990. "Right Livedlihood for the Western Buddhist." In *Dharma Gaia: A Harvest of Essays in Buddhism and Ecology,* Alan Hunt Badiner (ed.). Berkeley, CA: Parallax Press, pp. 227–232.

Aitken, Robert, and Michael Toms. 1998. "Zen Ethics." In *Buddhism in the West: Spiritual Wisdom for the 21st Century.* Carlsbad, CA: Hay House, Inc., pp. 69–72.

Albanese, Catherine L. 1990. *Nature Religion in America: From the Algonkian Indians to the New Age.* Chicago, IL: University of Chicago Press.

Albanese, Catherine L. 2002. *Reconsidering Nature Religion,* Harrisburg. PA: Trinity Press International.

Albrecht, Glenn. 2006. "Solastalgia." *Alternatives Journal* 32(4/5):34–36.

Albrecht, Glenn, Gina-Maree Sartore, Linda Connor, Nch Higginbotham, Sonia Freeman, Brian Kelly, Helen Stain, Anne Tonna, and Georgia Pollard. 2007. "Solastalgia: The Distress Caused by Environmental Change." *Australasian Psychiatry* 15 Supplement:S95–S98.

Ali, Saleem H. 2003. *Mining, the Environment and Indigenous Development Conflicts.* Tucson, AZ: University of Arizona Press.

Alliance of Religions and Conservation. 2011. http://www.arcworld.org/.

Altman, Nathaniel. 1994. *Sacred Trees.* San Francisco, CA: Sierra Club Books.

Altman, Nathaniel. 2002. *Sacred Water: The Spiritual Source of Life.* Mahwah, NJ: Paulist Press/HiddenSpring.

Alvard, Michael S. 1993. "Testing the 'Ecologically Noble Savage' Hypothesis: Interspecific Prey Choice by Piro Hunters of Amazonian Peru." *Human Ecology* 21: 355–87.

Amazon Watch. 2010.http://amazonwatch.org/

American Academy of Poets. 2011. "W. S. Merwin." http://www.poets.org/poet .php/prmPID/123.

American Academy of Religion. 2011. Religion and Ecology Group. http:// www.aarweb.org.

American Humanist Association. 2011. http://www.americanhumanist.org.

American Public Media, 2010. Joanna Macy Radio Interview.

American Teilhard Association. 2011. http://teilharddechardin.org

American Transcendentalism Web, 2011. http://www.vcu.edu/engweb/ transcendentalism/.

Anderson, E. N. 1996. *Ecologies of the Heart: Emotion, Belief, and the Environment.* New York: Oxford University Press.

Anderson, E. N. 2010. *The Pursuit of Ecotopia: Lessons from Indigenius and Traditional Societies for the Human Ecology of Our Modern World.* Santa Barbara, CA: ABC-CLIO, LCC/Praeger.

Andreas, Joel. 2004. *Addicted to War: Why Can't the U.S. Kick Militarism.* Oakland, CA: AK Press. http://www.addictedtowar.com.

Annaud, Jean-Jacques. 2005. *Seven Years in Tibet.* Culver City, CA: Sony Pictures (DVD, 136 minutes).

Armstrong, Edward A. 1973. *Saint Francis: Nature Mystic: The Derivation and Significance of the Nature Stories in the Franciscan Legend.* Berkeley, CA: University of California Press.

Armstrong, Karen. 2001. *Buddha.* New York, NY: Penguin Group.

Arnz, William, and Betsy Chasse. 2004. *What the Bleep Do We Know?* Beverly Hills, CA: Twentieth Century Fox Home Entertainment, Inc. (108 minutes). http://www.whatthebleep.com.

Assisi Nature Council. 2011. Assisi, Italy. http://www.assisinc.ch/.

Association for Forests, Development, and Conservation. 2011. http://www.afdc .org.lb/home.php.

Association of Buddhists for the Environment (ABE). 2011. *Cambodia.* http:// www.arcworld.org/projects.asp?projectID=320.

Atheism.about.com. 2011. http://atheism.about.com.

Atisha, Tenzon P. 1991. "The Tibetan Approach to Ecology." *Tibetan Review* XXVI(2): 9–14.

Atran, Scott. 2002. *In Gods We Trust: The Evolutionary Landscape of Religion.* New York, NY: Oxford University Press.

Austin, A.T. 2004. "The Human Footprint in Ecology: Past, Present and Future." *New Phytologist* 164(3):419–22.

Avatar-forums.com. 2010. http://www.avatar-forums.com

Ayres, Ed. 1999. *God's Last Offer: Negotiating for a Sustainable Future.* New York, NY: Four Walls Eight Windows.

Bacon, William. 2005. *Tibet Hope.* Anchorage: William Bacon Productions and Swenson Media Group (DVD, 52 minutes).

Bade, William F. (ed.). 1916. *A Thousand-Mile Walk to the Gulf.* Boston, MA: Houghton Mifflin Company.

Bade, William F. (ed.). 1924. *The Life and Letters of John Muir.* Boston, MA: Houghton Mifflin Company, 2 volumes.

Badiner, Allan Hunt (ed.). 2002. *Mindfulness in the Market Place: Compassionate Responses to Consumerism.* Berkeley, CA: Parallax Press.

Bagdro, Venerable. 1998. *A Hell on Earth: A Brief Biography of a Tibetan Political Prisoner.* Dharamsala, India: Venerable Bagdro.

Bailey, Greg, and Ian Mabbett. 2003. *The Sociology of Early Buddhism.* Cambridge, UK: Cambridge University Press.

Balee, William. 1998. "Historical Ecology: Premises and Postulates." In *Advances in Historical Ecology.* William Balee (ed.). New York, NY: Columbia University Press, pp. 13–29.

Barbour, Ian G. (ed.). 1973. *Western Man and Environmental Ethics: Attitudes Toward Nature and Technology.* Reading, MA: Addison-Wesley Publishing Company.

Barbour, Ian G. 2000. *When Science Meets Religion: Enemies, Strangers, or Partners?* San Francisco, CA: HarperSanFrancisco.

Barker, Holy M. 2003. *Bravo for the Marshallese: Regaining Control in a Post-Nuclear, Post-Colonial World.* Beverly, MA: Wadsworth Publishing.

Barnard, Alan. 1999. "Images of Hunters and Gatherers in European Social Thought." In *The Cambridge Encyclopedia of Hunters and Gatherers.* Richard B. Lee and Richard H. Daly (eds.). New York, NY: Cambridge University Press, pp. 375–383.

Barnes, Michael H. 1990. *In the Presence of Mystery: An Introduction to the Story of Human Religiousness.* Mystic, CT: Twenty-Third Publications.

Barnhill, David Landis. 2005. "East Asian Buddhism and Nature." In *The Encyclopedia of Religion and Nature.* Bron Taylor (Editor-in-Chief). New York, NY: Thoemmes Continuum, 1, pp. 236–239.

Barnhill, David Landis 2010. "Spirituality and Resistance: Ursula Le Guin's The Word for World Is Forest and the Film *Avatar.*" *Journal for the Study of Religion, Nature and Culture* 4(4):478–498.

Barnhill, David Landis, and Roger S. Gottlieb (eds.). 2001. *Deep Ecology and World Religions: New Essays on Sacred Ground*. Albany, NY: State University of New York Press.

Barrionuevo, Alexei. 2010 (April 10). "Tribes of Amazon Find an Ally Out of 'Avatar.'" *New York Times*. http://www.nytimes.com/2010/04/11/world/americas/11brazil.html.

Barrows, Anita. 2007. "Joanna Macy: Empowerment Activist." In *Visionaries: The 20th Century's 100 Most Important Inspirational Leaders*. Satish Kumar and Freddie Whitefield (eds.). White River Junction, VT: Chelsea Green Publishing, pp. 212–213.

Bartholomew I, His All Holiness, Archbishop of Constantinople, New Rome and Ecumenical Patriarch, 2011. http://www.patriarchate.org.

Barton, Matthew (ed.). 2008. *Spiritual Ecology: Reading the Book of Nature and Reconnecting with the World*. Forest Row, UK: Rudolf Steiner Press.

Bassett, Libby, John T. Brinkman, and Kusumita P. Pedersen (eds.). 2000. *Earth and Faith: A Book of Reflection for Action*. New York, NY: United Nations Environment Programme Interfaith Partnership for the Environment.

Batchelor, Stephen. 1994. *The Awakening of the West: The Encounter of Buddhism and Western Culture*. Berkeley, CA: Parallax Press.

Bauman, Whitney A., Richard R. Bohannon II, and Kevin J. O'Brien (eds.). 2011. *Grounding Religion: A Field Guide to the Study of Religion and Ecology*. New York, NY: Routledge.

Beattie, Tina. 2008. *The New Atheists: The Twilight of Reason and the War on Religion*. Mahwah, NJ: Orbis Books.

Beauregard, Mario, and Denyse O'Leary. 2007. *The Spiritual Brain: A Neuroscientist's Case for the Existence of Soul*. New York, NY: HarperCollins Publishers.

Becher, Anne, et al. (eds.). 2000. *American Environmental Leaders from Colonial Times to the Present*. Santa Barbara, CA: ABC-CLIO, Inc.

Beck, Peggy V., Anna Lee Walters, and Nia Francisco. 1996. *The Sacred: Ways of Knowledge, Sources of Life*. Tsaile, AZ: Navajo Community College Press.

Beckwith, Martha Warren. 1981. *The Kumulipo: A Hawaiian Creation Chant*. Honolulu, HI: University of Hawai'i Press.

Beech, Hannah. 2011 (November 14). "Burning Desire for Freedom." *Time* 178 (19):46–51.

Bender, Lawrence, and Laurie David. 2006. *An Inconvenient Truth: A Global Warning* (with Al Gore). Hollywood, CA: Paramount (DVD, 96 minutes).

Bennett, David H. 1996. "Valuing a Tree: The Ethics of Environmental Evaluation." In *Tropical Rainforest Research—Current Issues*, D. S. Edwards, W. E. Booth, and S. C. Choy (eds.). Boston, MA: Kluwer Academic Publishers, pp. 467–475.

Bennett, John W. 1976. "The Ecological Transition: From Equilibrium to Disequilibrium." In *The Ecological Transition: Cultural Anthropology and Human* Adaptation. John W. Bennett. New York, NY: Pergamon Press, pp. 123–155.

Berkes, Fikret. 1999. Sacred *Ecology: Traditional Ecological Knowledge and Resource Management*. Philadelphia, PA: Taylor & Francis.

Berkhofer, Robert F., Jr. 1979. *The White Man's Indian: Images of the American Indian from Columbus to the Present*. New York, NY: Vintage Books.

Berkwitz, Stephen C. (ed.). 2006. *Buddhism in World Cultures: Comparative Perspectives*. Santa Barbara, CA: ABC-CLIO, Inc.

Berry, Thomas. 1999. *The Great Work: Our Way into the Future*. New York, NY: Bell Tower.

Berry, Thomas. 2006a. *Dream of the Earth*. San Francisc, CA: Sierra Club Books (2nd Edition).

Berry, Thomas. 2006b. *Evening Thoughts: Reflecting on Earth as Sacred Community*. Mary Evelyn Tucker (ed.). San Francisco, CA: Sierra Club Books.

Berry, Thomas. 2009. *The Sacred Universe: Earth, Spirituality, and Religion in the Twenty-first Century*. New York, NY: Columbia University Press.

Berry, Thomas. 2011. Homepage. http://www.thomasberry.org.

Berry, Thomas, and Thomas Clarke. 1991. *Befriending the Earth: A Theology of Reconciliation between Humans and the Earth*. Mystic, CT: Twenty-Third Publications.

Best, Steven, and Anthony J. Nocella II. (eds.). 2006. *Igniting a Revolution: Voices in Defense of the Earth*. Oakland, CA: AK Press.

Beyer, Stephan V., et al. 2012. "Special Ayahuasca Issue." *Anthropology of Consciousness* 23(1):1–109.

Bierhorst, John. 1994. *The Way of the Earth: Native America and the Environment*. New York, NY: William Morrow and Co.

Bilimoria, Purushottama. 2001. "Buddha, fifth century BCE." In *Fifty Key Thinkers on the Environment*. Joy A. Palmer (ed.). New York, NY: Routledge, pp. 1–7.

Birch, Charles. 2008. *Science and Soul*. Philadelphia, PA: Templeton Foundation Press.

Blackburn, T. C., and K. Anderson. 1993. *Before Wilderness: Environmental Management by Native Californians*. Menlo Park, CA: Ballena Press.

Blow, Richard. 1998. "The Great American Whale Hunt." *Mother Jones* 23 (5):49–53, 86–87.

Bobin, Christian. 1999. *The Secret of Francis of Assisi: A Meditation*. Boston, MA: Shambhala Publications, Inc.

Bodhi Tree Forest Monastery and Retreat Center. 2011. Tullera, Australia. http://www.buddhanet.net/bodhi-tree/.

Bodhi, Bhikkhu. 1987. "Foreword." In *Buddhist Perspectives on the Ecocrisis*. Klas Sandell (ed.). Kandy, Sri Lanka: Buddhist Publications Society, pp. v–viii.

Bodley, John H. (ed.). 1988. *Tribal Peoples and Development Issues: A Global Overview*. Mountain View, CA: Mayfield Publishing.

Bodley, John H. 2008a. *Victims of Progress*. Lanham, MD: AltaMira Press (5th Edition).

Bodley, John H. 2008b. *Anthropology and Contemporary Human Problems*. Lanham, MD: AltaMira Press (5th Edition).

Boff, Leonardo. 1997. "All the Cardinal Ecological Virtues: St. Francis of Assisi." In *Cry of the Earth, Cry of the Poor*. Leonardo Boff. Maryknoll, NY: Orbis Books, pp. 203–220.

Bookchin, Murray. 1995. *Re-Enchanting Humanity: A Defense of the Human Spirit against Anti-Humanism, Misanthropy, Mysticism and Primitivism*. London, UK: Cassell.

Boord, Martin. 1994. "Buddhism." In *Sacred Place*. Jean Holm and John Bowker (eds.). New York, NY: Pinter Publishers, pp. 8–32.

Booth, Annie L. 2003. "We Are the Land: Native American Views of Nature." In *Nature Across Cultures: Views of Nature and the Environment in Non-Western Cultures*. Helaine Selin (ed.). Boston, MA: Kluwer Academic Publishers, pp. 329–349.

Bourne, Edmund J. 2008. *Global Shift: How a New World View Is Transforming Humanity*. Oakland. CA: New Harbinger Publications, Inc.

Bowditch, Rachel. 2010. *On the Edge of Utopia: Performance and Ritual at Burning Man*. London, UK: Seagull.

Bratton, Susan Power. 1993. "A Cave outside the City (St. Francis)." In *Christianity, Wilderness and Wildlife: The Original Desert Solitaire*. Scranton, PA: University of Scranton Press, pp. 209–221.

Bratton, Susan Power. 2002. "Ecology and Religion: New Science, Old Relationships," In *The Oxford Handbook of Religion and Science*. Philip Clayton and Zachary Simpson (eds.). New York, NY: Oxford University Press, pp. 207–225.

Bratton, Susan Power. 2007. *Environmental Values in Christian Art*. Albany, NY: State University of New York Press.

Bratton, Susan Power. 2009. *Christianity, Wilderness and Wildlife*. Scranton, PA: University of Scranton Press.

Brauen, Martin. 2004. *Dream World Tibet: Western Illusions*. Turmbull, CT: Weatherhill, Inc.

Brent, Morgan. 2005. "Ayahuasca." In *The Encyclopedia of Religion and Nature*. Bron R. Taylor (Editor-in-Chief). New York, NY: Thoemmes Continuum, 1, pp. 141–143.

Brent, Morgan. 2011. *Tribes of Creation*. http://www.tribesofcreation.com/index.html.

Breton, Mary Joy. 1998. "Wangari Maathai (1940–): Recruits Army of Green Belt Foresters." In *Women Pioneers for the Environment*. Boston, MA: Northeastern University Press, pp. 11–18.

Breully, Elizabeth, and Martin Palmer. 1992. *Christianity and Ecology*. London, UK: Cassell

Brinkley, Douglas. 2009. *Theodore Roosevelt: The Wilderness Warrior and the Crusade for America*. New York, NY: Harper.

British Humanist Association. 2011. http://www.humanism.org.uk/home.

Brockelman, Norbert C. 1997. *Encyclopedia of Sacred Places*. Santa Barbara, CA: ABC-CLIO, Inc.

Browman, Barry, and William Warren. 2005. *Spiritual Abodes of Thailand*. Singapore: Marshall Cavendish.

Brown, Peter (ed.). 1988. *John Muir in His Own Words: A Book of Quotations*. Lafayette, CA: Great West Books.

Bryson, J. Scott. 2002. *Ecopoetry: A Critical Introduction*. Salt Lake City, UT: University of Utah Press.

Buber, Martin, 1923/1970. *I and Thou*. New York, NY: Charles Scribner's Sons (new translation by Walter Kaufmann).

Buber, Martin. 2011. Martin Buber Homepage. http://buber.de/en/.

Buddhadasa Bhikkhu. 1987. "A Notion of Buddhist Ecology." *Seeds of Peace* 3(2):22–27.

Buddhist Declaration on Climate Change. 2011. http://www.ecobuddhism.org/bcp/all_content/buddhist_declaration/.

Buddhist Institute. 1999. *Cry from the Forest: A Buddhism and Ecology Community Learning Tool*. Phnom Penh, Cambodia: Buddhist Institute.

Buddhist Peace Fellowship. 2011. http://www.bpf.org/.

Buege, Douglas J. 1996. "The Ecological Noble Savage Revisited." *Environmental Ethics* 18(1):71–88.

Bullfrog Films. 2006. Black Diamonds: Mountaintop Removal and the Fight for Coalfield Justice. Oley, PA: Bullfrog Films. http://www.bullfrogfilms.com.

Bullfrog Films. 2010. *Human Terrain: War Becomes Academic*. Oley, PA: Bullfrog Films (84 minutes). http://www.bullfrogfilms.com.

Burger, Edward A. 2007. *Amongst White Clouds: Buddhist Hermit Masters of China's Zhongnan Mountains*. Oakland, CA: Festival Media/International Buddhist Film Festival (DVD, 86 minutes).

Burkert, Walter. 1996. *Creation of the Sacred: Tracks of Biology in Early Religions.* Cambridge, MA: Harvard University Press.

Burney David A., and William Ki Pila Kikuchi. 2006. "A Millennium of Human Activity at Makauwahi Cave, Maha'ulepu, Kaua'i." *Human Ecology* 34 (2):219–247.

Burney, David A. 2010. *Back to the Future in the Caves of Kaua'i: A Scientists Adventures in the Dark.* New Haven, CT: Yale University Press.

Burning Man. 2011. http://www.burningman.org.

Burrell, David, and Elena Malits. 1997. *Original Peace: Restoring God's Creation.* Mahwah, NJ: Paulist Press.

Burton, Lloyd. 2002. *Worship and Wilderness: Culture, Religion, and Law in Public Lands Management.* Madison, WI: University of Wisconsin Press.

Butler, Tom, and Doug Tompkins. 2009. *Plundering Appalachia: The Tragedy of Mountain Top Removal Coal Mining.* San Rafael, CA: EarthAware Editions.

Buzzell, Linda, and Craig Chalquist (eds). 2009. *Ecotherapy: Healing with Nature in Mind.* San Francisco, CA: Sierra Club Books.

Cajete, Gregory. 1999. *Native Science: Natural Laws of Interdependence.* Santa Fe, NM: Clear Light Publishers.

Caldecott, Moyra. 1993. *Myths of the Sacred Tree.* Rochester, VT: Destiny Books.

Callicott, J. Baird, and Roger T. Ames. 1989. *Nature in Asian Traditions of Thought: Essays in Environmental Philosophy.* Albany, NY: State University of New York Press.

Callicott, J. Baird, and Michael P. Nelson (eds.). 1998. *The Great New Wilderness Debate.* Athens, GA: The University of Georgia Press.

Cameron, James. 2010a. *Avatar* (Three-Disc Extended Collector's Edition). Los Angeles, CA: Twentieth Century Fox Corporation. http://www .avatarmovie.com/.

Cameron, James. 2010b. "Capturing *Avatar.*" *Avatar* (Three-Disc Extended Collector's Edition). Los Angeles, CA: Twentieth Century Fox Corporation, Disc 3.

Cameron, James. 2010c. "A Message from Pandora." *Avatar* (Three-Disc Extended Collector's Edition). Los Angeles, CA: Twentieth Century Fox Corporation, Disc 2.

Cameron, James. 2010d. *Earth Day Rally, Washington, D.C.* (8 minutes). http:// www.youtube.com/watch?v=YDHkO5-Hf78.

Cameron, James. 2010e. *Avatar Home Tree Initiative,* Los Angeles, http://www .avatarmovie.com/hometree/.

Cameron, James. 2011. *James Cameron Online.* http://www.jamescamerononline .com/.

Cameron, Larry C., and John R. Carpenter. 1997. *Witness: The Ecological Poetry of W. S. Merwin*. New York, NY: Films for the Humanities and Sciences (56 minutes).

Campbell, Joseph. 1949. *The Hero with a Thousand Faces*. New York, NY: Pantheon Books.

Canadian Forum on Religion and Ecology. 2011. http://www.cfore.ca.

Cantwell, Cathy. 2001. "Reflections on Ecological Ethics and the Tibetan Ritual." *The Eastern Buddhist* n.s. 33(1):106–127.

Capra, Fritjof. 1982, *The Turning Point: Science, Society and the Rising Culture*. New York, NY: Simon and Schuster.

Capra, Fritjof, and David Steindl-Rast. 1991. *Belonging to the Universe: Explorations on the Frontiers of Science and Spirituality*. San Francisco, CA: HarperCollins.

Carrithers, Michael. 2001. *Buddha: A Very Short Introduction*. New York, NY: Oxford University Press.

Carroll, John E., and Keith Warner(eds.). 1998. *Ecology and Religion: Scientists Speak*. Quincy, IL: Franciscan Press.

Carspecken, Lucinda. 2012. *An Unreal Estate: Sustainability and Freedom in an Evolving Community*. Bloomington, IN: Indiana University Press.

Castro, Alfonso P. 1991. "Indigenous Kikuyu Agroforestry: A Case Study of Kirinyaga, Kenya." *Human Ecology* 19(1):1–18.

Cavani, Liliana. 2003. *Francesco*. North Hollywood, CA: Legacy Entertainment Inc. (DVD 115 minutes).

Center for Global Nonkilling. 2011. http://www.nonkilling.org.

Center for the Study of Religion and Culture. 2011. "Ecology and Spirituality in America: Exploring Possibilities for Cultural Transmission." Nashville, TN: Vanderbilt University Center for the Study of Religion and Culture. http://www.vanderbilt.edu/csrc/re.html.

Chalquist, Craig. 2007. *Terrapsychology: Reengaging the Soul of Place*. New Orleans, LA: Spring Journal Books.

Chandrakanth, M. G., and Jeff Romm. 1991. "Sacred Forests, Secular Forest Policies and People's Actions." *Natural Resources Journal* 31:741–756.

Chandrakanth, M. G., J. K. Gilless, V. Gowramma, and M. G. Nagaraja. 1990. "Temple Forests in India's Forest Development." *Agroforestry Systems* 11(3): 199–211.

Chang, Heewon V., and Drick Boyd. (eds.). 2011. *Spirituality in Higher Education: Autoethnographies*. Walnut Creek, CA: Left Coast Press, Inc.

Chapman, Audrey R., Rodney L. Petersen, and Barbara Smith-Morgan (eds.). 1999. *Consumption, Population and Sustainability: Perspectives from Religion and Science*.Washington, D.C.: Island Press.

Chapple, Christopher Key. 1996. *Nonviolence to Animals, Earth, and Self in Asian Traditions*. Albany, NY: State University of New York Press.

Chapple, Christopher Key. 1997. "Animals and Environment in the Buddhist Birth Stories." In *Buddhism and Ecology: The Interconnection of Dharma and Deeds*. Mary Evelyn Tucker and Duncan Ryuken Williams (eds.). Cambridge, MA: Harvard University Press, pp. 131–148.

Chapple, Christopher Key (ed.). 2002. *Jainism and Ecology: Nonviolence in the Web of Life*. Cambridge, MA: Harvard University Press/Harvard University Center for the Study of World Religions.

Chapple, Christopher Key, and Mary Evelyn Tucker (eds). 2000. *Hinduism and Ecology: The Intersection of Earth, Sky, and Water*. Cambridge, MA: Harvard University Press/Harvard University Center for the Study of World Religions.

Chase, Steven. 2011a. *Nature as Spiritual Practice*. Grand Rapids, MI: William Eerdmans Publishing Company.

Chase, Steven. 2011b. *A Field Guide to Nature as Spiritual Practice*. Grand Rapids, MI: William Eerdmans Publishing Company.

Chatenever, Rick, 2011 (February 20). "A Few Words with W.S. Merwin." Maui, HI: Maui News. http://www.mauinews.com/page/content.detail/id/546341/A-few-words-with-W-S—Merwin.html?nav=12.

Cherniack, David. 1999, "Fire on the Mountain: A Gathering of Shamans." New York, NY: Mystic Fire Video (DVD, 106 minutes).

Chhaya, Mayank. 2007. *Dalai Lama: Man, Monk, Mystic*. New York, NY: Doubleday Broadway Publishing Group.

Chicarelli, Charles F. 2004. *Buddhist Art: An Illustrated Introduction*. Chiang Mai, Thailand: Silkworm Books.

Chickerneo, Nancy Barrett. 2008. *Woman Spirit: Awakening in Nature, Growing into the Fullness of Who You Are*. Woodstock, VT: Skylight Paths Publishing.

Chimedsengee, Urantsatsral, et al. 2009. "Mongolian Buddhists Protecting Nature: A Handbook on Faiths, Environment and Development." Bath, UK: Alliance of Religions and Conservation. http://www.scribd.com/doc/38647651/Mongolian-Buddhist-Environment-Handbook.

Chopra, Deepak, and Leonard Mlodinow. 2011. *War of the Worldviews: Science vs. Spirituality*. New York, NY: Crown Publishing/Harmony Books.

Christhilf, Mark. 1986. *W. S. Merwin the Mythmaker*. Columbia, MO: University of Missouri Press.

Christians for the Mountains. 2006. *Mountain Mourning*. Lewisburg, VA: Patchwork Films and Christians for the Mountains (DVD, 73 minutes).

Christians for the Mountains. 2011, http://www.ChristiansForTheMountains.org.

Chryssavgis, John (ed.). 2003. *Cosmic Grace Humble Prayer: The Ecological Vision of the Green Patriarch Bartholomew I.* Grand Rapids, MI: William B. Eerdmans Publishing Company.

Chryssavgis, John. 2005. "Bartholomew, Ecumenical Patriarch (1940–)." In *The Encyclopedia of Religion and Nature.* Bron R. Taylor (Editor-in-Chief). New York, NY: Thoemmes Continuum, 1, pp. 158–159.

Chryssavgis, John. 2006. "The Earth as Sacrament: Insights from Orthodox Christian Theology and Spirituality." In *The Oxford Handbook of Religion and Ecology.* Roger S. Gottlieb (ed.). New York, NY: Oxford University Press, pp. 92–114.

Chryssavgis, John. 2007. "Ecumenical Patriarch Bartholomew: Insights into an Orthodox Christian worldview." *The International Journal of Environmental Studies* 64(1):9–18.

Chun, Allison A. 2002. *The Discourses (Re)constructing the Sacred Geography of Kaho'olawe Island, Hawai'i.* Manoa, HI: University of Hawai'i Manoa Doctoral Dissertation in Geography.

Churchill, Ward. 1997. *A Little Matter of Genocide: Holocaust and Denial in the Americas 1492 to the Present.* San Francisco, CA: City Lights Books.

Churchill, Ward. 2003. *On the Justice of Roosting Chickens: Reflections on the Consequences of U.S. Imperial Arrogance and Criminality.* Oakland, CA: AK Press.

Circle of Life Foundation, 2011. http://www.circleoflife.org, www.juliabutterfly.com.

Clark, Leslie, and Catherine Tatge. 2011. *John Muir in The New World.* West Long Branch, NJ: Kultur (DVD 85 minutes). http://www.kultur.com.

Clark, Mary E. 2002. *In Search of Human Nature.* New York, NY: Routledge.

Clarke, Graham E., 2001. "Tradition, Modernity, and Environmental Change in Tibet." In *Imagining Tibet: Perceptions, Projections, and Fantasies.* Thierry Dodin and Heinz Rather (eds.). Boston, MA: Wisdom Publications, pp. 339–356.

Clarke, John James. 1997. *Oriental Enlightenment: The Encounter Between Asian and Western Thought.* New York, NY: Routledge.

Clayton, Philip, and Jim Schaal. (eds.). 2007. *Practicing Science, Living Faith: Interviews with 12 Leading Scientists.* New York, NY: Columbia University Press.

Clayton, Philip, and Zachary Simpson, eds. 2006. *The Oxford Handbook of Religion and Science.* New York, NY: Oxford University Press.

Clippard, Seth Devere. 2011. "The Lorax Wears Saffron: Toward a Buddhist Environmentalism." *Journal of Buddhist Ethics* 18:212–248. http://blogs.dickinson.edu/buddhistethics/files/2011/06/Clippard1.pdf.

Coalition on the Environment and Jewish Life (COEJL). 2011. http://www
.coejl.org/index.php.

Coates, Peter. 1988. *Nature: Western Attitudes since Ancient Times*. Berkeley, CA:
University of California Press.

Cohen, Andrew. 2011. *Evolutionary Enlightenment: A New Path to Spiritual
Awakening*. New York, NY: SelectBooks, Inc.

Cohen, Michael J. 1997. *Reconnecting with Nature: Finding Wellness through
Restoring Your Bond with the Earth*. Corvallis, OR: Ecopress.

Cohen, Michael J. 1984. *The Pathless Way: John Muir and American Wilderness*.
Madison, WI: University of Wisconsin Press.

Cohen-Kiener, Andrea. 2009. *Claiming Earth as Common Ground: The Ecological
Crisis through the Lens of Faith*. Woodstock, VT: Skylight Paths Publishing.

Coleman, Mark. 2006. *Awake in the Wild: Mindfulness in Nature as a Path to Self-
Discovery*. Makawao, Maui, HI: Inner Ocean Publishing, Inc.

Coleman, Mark. 2011. *Awake in the Wild*. http://www.awakeinthewild.com.

Collett, Jonathan, and Stephen Karakashian (eds.). 1996. *Greening the College
Curriculum: A Guide to Environmental Teaching in the Liberal Arts*.
Washington, D.C.: Island Press.

Committee for the Scientific Examination of Religion. 2011. http://secularhum
anism.org/index.php?section=main&page=CSER.

Cone, Robert Temple Cole. 2005. *Ecological Revisions of the Romantic Nature
Lyric: Robinson Jeffers, Ted Hughes, and W. S. Merwin*. Madison, WI:
University of Wisconsin Doctoral Dissertation.

Conklin, Beth A., and Laura R. Graham. 1995. "The Shifting Middle Ground:
Amazonian Indians and Eco-Politics." *American Anthropologist* 97(4):695–710.

Conroy, Donald B., and Rodney Lawrence Petersen(eds.). 2000. *Earth at Risk:
An Environmental Dialogue between Religion and Science*. Amherst, NY:
Humanity Books.

Conservation International. 2008. "Biological Diversity in the Himalayas." In
Encyclopedia of Earth. Cutler J. Cleveland (ed.). Washington, D.C.:
Environmental Information Coalition, National Council for Science and
the Environment). http://www.eoearth.org/article/Biological_diversity
_in_the_Himalayas.

Cooper, David E., and Simon P. James. 2005. *Buddhism, Virtue and
Environment*. Burlington, VT: Ashgate Publishing Company.

Cooper, Laurence D. 1999. *Rousseau, Nature, and the Problem of the Good Life*.
University Park, PA: Pennsylvania State University Press.

Corcoran, Peter Blaze. 2001. "John Muir (1838–1914)." In *Fifty Key Thinkers on
the Environment*. Joy A. Palmer (ed.). New York, NY: Routledge,
pp. 131–136.

Cornwell, John. 2007. *Darwin's Angel: A Seraphic Response to The God Delusion.* London, UK: Profile Books Ltd.

Cote, Charlotte. 2010. *Spirits of Our Whaling Ancestors: Revitalizing Makah and Nuu-chah-nulth Traditions.* Seattle, WA: University of Washington Press.

Cowan, James. 2004. *Desert Father: A Journey in the Wilderness with Saint Anthony.* Boston, MA: Shambhala.

Cowell, E.B. (ed.). 1895–1905. *Jataka Stories.* London, UK: Pali Text Society, Volumes I–VI.

Crabtree, Maril. 2005. *Sacred Waters: Stories of Healing, Cleansing, and Renewal.* Avon, MA: Adams Media Corporation.

Cronon, William. 1983. *Changes in the Land: Indians, Colonists, and the Ecology of New England.* New York, NY: Hill and Wang.

Cronon, William (ed.). 1995. *Uncommon Ground: Toward Reinventing Nature.* New York, NY: W. W. Norton and Company.

Crosby, Donald A. 2002. *A Religion of Nature.* Albany, NY: State University of New York Press.

Culliney, John L. 2006. *Islands in a Far Sea: Nature and Man in Hawaii.* Honolulu, HI: University of Hawai'i Press.

Cunningham, Scott. 1994. *Hawaiian Religion and Magic.* St. Paul, MN: Llewellyn Publications.

Curry, Patrick. 2011. *Ecological Ethics: An Introduction.* Malden, MA: Polity Press (2nd Edition).

d'Aquili, Eugene, and Andrew B. Newberg. 1999. *The Mystical Mind: Probing the Biology of Religious Experience.* Minneapolis, MN: Fortress Press.

Dalai Lama of Tibet, His Holiness the 14th. 1987. *The Buddhism of Tibet.* Ithaca, NY: Snow Lion Publications.

Dalai Lama of Tibet, His Holiness the 14th. 1992. "A Tibetan Buddhist Perspective on Spirit in Nature." In *Spirit and Nature: Why the Environment Is a Religious Issue: An Interfaith Dialogue.* Steven C. Rockefeller and John C. Elder (eds.). Boston. MA: Beacon Press, pp. 109–123.

Dalai Lama of Tibet, His Holiness the 14th. 1998. *Freedom in Exile: The Autobiography of the Dalai Lama of Tibet.* London, UK: Little, Brown Book Group/Abacus.

Dalai Lama of Tibet, His Holiness the 14th. 1999. *Ethics for the New Millennium.* New York, NY: Berkeley Publishing Group/Riverhead Books.

Dalai Lama of Tibet, His Holiness the 14th. 2010. *Toward a True Kinship of Faiths: How the World's Religions Can Come Together.* New York, NY: Crown Publishing Group/Doubleday Religion.

Dalai Lama of Tibet, His Holiness the 14th. 2011. Homepage. http://www.dalailama.com.

Dalai Lama of Tibet, His Holiness the 14th, with Sofia Stril-Rever. 2010. *My Spiritual Journey.* New York, NY: HarperCollins Publishers.

Danaan, Clea. 2009. *Voices of the Earth: The Path of Green Spirituality.* Woodbury, MN: Llewellyn Publications.

Daneel, Inus. 2001. *African Earthkeepers—Wholistic Interfaith Mission.* New York, NY: Orbis Books.

Daneel, Inus. 2005. "African Earthkeeping Churches—Association of (Zimbbwe)." In *The Encyclopedia of Religion and Nature.* Bron R. Taylor (Editor-in-Chief). New York, NY: Thoemmes Continuum, 1, pp. 21–24.

Daneel, Inus. 2006. "African Initiated Churches as Vehicles of Earth-Care in Africa," *In The Oxford Handbook of Religion and Ecology.* Roger S. Gottlieb (ed.). New York, NY: Oxford University Press, pp. 535–567.

Darlington, Susan M. 1998. "The Ordination of a Tree: The Buddhist Ecology Movement in Thailand." *Ethnology* 37(1):1–15.

Darlington, Susan M. 2003. "The Spirits(s) of Conservation in Buddhist Thailand." In *Nature Across Cultures.* Helaine Selin (ed.). Dordrecht, The Netherlands: Kluwer Academic Publishers, pp. 129–145.

Darvich, Khashyar. 2009a. Dalai Lama Renaissance. (DVD, 82 minutes). http://www.DalaiLamaFilm.com.

Darvich, Khashyar. 2009b. Dalai Lama Renaissance Volume 2—A Revolution of Ideas. Wakan Films. (DVD, 100 minutes). http://www.DalaiLamaFilm.com.

Das, Lama Surya. 2000. *Natural Meditation.* Boulder, CO: Sounds True (VHS, 34 minutes).

Davis, Jordan, 2011 (May 16). "Talking with W. S. Merwin." *The Nation* 292 (20):20–23.

Dawkins, Richard. 2006. *The God Delusion.* Boston, MA: Houghton Mifflin Company.

Dawkins, Richard. 2011a. Homepage. http://www.RichardDawkins.net.

Dawkins, Richard. 2011b. Richard Dawkins Foundation. http://www.RichardDawkinsFoundation.org.

Dawson, Todd E. 1993. "Hydraulic Life and Water Use by Plants: Implications for Water Balance, Performance and Plant-plant Interactions." *Oecologia* 95:565–574.

de Angelis, Ly, Emma Restall Orr, and Thom van Dooren (eds.). 2005. *Pagan Visions for a Sustainable Future.* Woodbury, MN: Llewellyn Publications.

de Quincey, Christian. 2002. *Radical Nature: Rediscovering the Soul of Matter.* Montpelier, VT: Invisible Cities Press.

de Sercey, Patrick. 2007. *Spiritual Ecology: Evolution beyond Faith Based Culture.* Bloomington, IN: Xlibris Corporation.

de Steiguer, J.E. 2006. *The Origins of Modern Environmental Thought*. Tucson, AZ: University of Arizona Press.

Delio, Ilia, Keith Douglass Warner, and Pamela Wood. 2007. *Care for Creation: A Franciscan Spirituality of the Earth*. Cincinnati, OH: St. Anthony Messenger Press.

Deloria, Vine, Jr. 2000. "The Speculations of Kretch: A Review Article of Shepard Krech, *The Ecological Indian*, W. W. Norton and Company 1999." *Worldviews* 4:283–293.

Denevan, William M. 1992. "The Pristine Myth: The Landscape of the Americas in 1492." *Annals of the Association of American Geographers* 82(3): 369–385.

Denevan, William M. 1996. "Pristine Myth." In *Encyclopedia of Cultural Anthropology*. David Levinson and Melvin Ember (eds.). New York, NY: Henry Holt and Co. 3, pp. 1034–1036.

Dennett, Daniel C. 2006. *Breaking the Spell: Religion as a Natural Phenomenon*. New York, NY: Penguin Group (USA) Inc.

Deravy, Echan. 2009. *Earth Pilgrims*. Los Angeles, CA: Waling Stick Productions, Inc. (DVD, 90 minutes).

Descola, Philippe. 1993. *The Spears of Twilight: Life and Death in the Amazon*. New York, NY: The New York Press.

Devall, Bill. 1990. "Ecocentric Sangha." In *Dharma Gaia: A Harvest of Essays in Buddhism and Ecology*. Allan Hunt Badiner (ed.). Berkeley, CA: Parallax Press, pp. 155–164.

Devall, Bill, and George Sessions. 1985. *Deep Ecology: Living as if Nature Mattered*. Salt Lake City, UT: Gibbs M. Smith, Inc.

Devereaux, Paul, John Steel, and David Kubrin. 1989. *Earth-Mind: Communicating with the Living World of Gaia*. Rochester, VT: Destiny Books.

DeWitt, Calvin B. 2007. *Earth-Wise: A Biblical Response to Environmental Issues*. Grand Rapids, MI: Faith Alive Christian Resources.

Dharma Net International. 2011. *Engaged Projects in Asia*. http://www .dharmanet.org/engagedasia.htm.

Diamond, Jared. 1986 (November 6). "The Environmentalist Myth." *Nature* 324:19–20.

Diamond, Jared. 1992. "The Golden Age That Never Was." In his *The Third Chimpanzee*. New York, NY: Harper-Collins Publishers, pp. 317–338, 386–388.

Diamond, Stanley. 1974. *In Search of the Primitive: A Critique of Civilization*. New Brunswick, NJ: Transaction Publishers.

Dixon, Thomas. 2008. *Science and Religion: A Very Short Introduction*. New York, NY: Oxford University Press.

Doane, Molly. 2007. "The Political Ecology of the Ecological Native." *American Anthropologist* 109(3):452–462.

Dobson, Andrew (ed.). 1991. *The Green Reader: Essays Toward A Sustainable Society*. San Francisco, CA: Mercury House.

Dodin, Thierry, and Heinz Rather (eds.). 2001. *Imagining Tibet: Projections, Projections, and Fantasies*. Boston, MA: Wisdom Publications.

Donner, Florinda. 1982. *Shabono*. New York, NY: Dell Publishing Company, Inc.

Dorman, Robert L. 1998. A *Word for Nature: Four Pioneering Environmental Advocates, 1845–1913*. Durham, NC: Duke University Press.

Dove, Michael R., Percy E. Sajise, and Amity A. Doolittle (eds.). 2011. *Beyond the Sacred Forest: Complicating Conservation in Southeast Asia*. Durham, NC: Duke University Press.

Doyle, Arthur Conan. 1912/1959. *The Lost World*. New York, NY: Random House.

Drengson, Alan. 1983. *Shifting Paradigms: From Technocrat to Planetary Person*. Victoria, British Columbia, Canada: Lightstar Press.

Drengson, Alan, and Bill Devall. 2008. *The Ecology of Wisdom: Writings by Arne Naess*. Berkeley, CA: Counterpoint.

DuBois, Thomas A. 2009. *An Introduction to Shamanism*. New York, NY: Cambridge University Press.

Dudley, Michael Kioni. 1990. *Man, Gods, and Nature*. Honolulu, HI: Na Kane O Ka Malo Press.

Dudley, Nigel, Liza Higgins-Zogib, and Stephanie Mansourian. 2005. *Beyond Belief: Linking Faiths and Protected Areas to Support Biodiversity Conservation*. Gland: World Wide Fund for Nature (WWF) and Alliance of Religions and Conservation. http://www.panda.org.

Duffy, Kathleen. (ed.). 2010. *Rediscovering Teilhard's Fire*. Philadelphia, PA: Saint Joseph's University Press.

Dugdale, Joshua. 2008. *The Unwinking Gaze: The Inside Story of the Dalai Lama's Struggle for Tibet*. Easthampton, MA: MRW Connected LLC (DVD, 70 minutes).

Duncan, Dayton, and Ken Burns. 2009. *The National Parks: America's Best Idea*. Washington, D.C.: Public Broadcasting Service Home Video (DVD, 6 episodes, 750 minutes). http://www.pbs.org/nationalparks/.

Duncan, Dayton, and Ken Burns. 2011. *The National Parks: America's Best Idea*. New York, NY: Knopf.

Duncan, Jody, and Liza Fitzpatrick. 2010. *The Making of Avatar*. New York, NY: Abrams.

Earth Charter Initiative. 2011. *Earth Charter*. http://www.earthcharterinaction
.org/content/.

Earth Ministry. 2011. *A Prayer of Gratitude*. Seattle, WA. http://www.earthministry
.org.

Earth Sangha. 2011. *Earth Sangha*. Washington, D.C.: Earth Sangha. http://www
.earthsangha.org.

Eaton, Heather (Guest Editor). 2001. "The Great Work." *Worldviews:
Environment, Culture, Religion* 5(2–3):115–222.

Eckberg, Douglas Lee, and T. Jean Blocker. 1989. "Varieties of Religious
Involvement and Environmental Concerns: Testing the Lynn White
Thesis." *Journal for the Scientific Study of Religion* 28(4):509–517.

EcoBuddhism. 2011. http://www.ecobuddhism.org.

Ecological Buddhism: *A Buddhist Response to Global Warming*. 2010. http://www
.ecobuddhism.org/bcp/all_content/buddhist_declaration/.

Edgerton, Robert B. 1992. *Sick Societies: Challenging the Myth of Primitive
Harmony*. New York, NY: Free Press.

Edwards, Denis. 2006. *Ecology at the Heart of Faith: The Change of Heart That
Leads to a New Way of Living on Earth*. Maryknoll, NY: Orbis Books.

Edwards, Jo, and Martin Palmer (eds.). 1997. *Holy Ground: The Guide to Faith
and Ecology*. Northamptonshire, UK: Pilkington Press Ltd.

Egan, Michael, and Jeff Crane (eds.). 2009. *Natural Protest: Essays on the History
of American Environmentalism*. New York, NY: Routledge.

Ehrlich, Gretel. 2000. *John Muir: Nature's Visionary*. Washington, D.C.:
National Geographic Society.

Ehrlich, Paul, 2008. *Paul Ehrlich: The Dominant Animal: Human Evolution and
the Environment*. San Simeon, CA: San Simeon Films/Whole Earth Films
(DVD, 88 min).

Ehrlich, Paul, and Anne H. Ehrlich. 2008. *The Dominant Animal: Human
Evolution and the Environment*. Washington, D.C.: Island Press. http://
dominantanimal.org/.

Ekachai, Sanituda. 2001. *Keeping the Faith: Thai Buddhism at the Crossroads*.
Bangkok, Thailand: The Post Publishing Company Plc.

Elahi, Bahram. 1997. *Foundations of Natural Spirituality: A Scientific Approach to
the Nature of the Spiritual Self*. Rockport, MA: Element Books, Inc.

Elgin, Duane. 2009. *The Living Universe: Where Are We? Who Are We? Where Are
We Going?* San Francisco, CA: Berrett-Koehler Publishers, Inc.

Elkins, David N. 1998. *Beyond Religion: A Personal Program for Building a
Spiritual Life Outside the Walls of Traditional Religion*. Wheaton, IL: The
Thesophical Publishing House/Quest Books.

Ellen, Roy F. 1986. "What Black Elk Left Unsaid: On the Illusory Images of Green Primitivism." *Anthropology Today* 2(6):8–12.

Ellingson, Ter. 2001. *The Myth of the Noble Savage*. Berkeley, CA: University of California Press.

Ellwood, Robert. 2005. "Theosophy." In *The Encyclopedia of Religion and Nature*. Bron R. Taylor (Editor-in-Chief). New York, NY: Thoemmes Continuum, 2, pp. 1632–1633.

Elon, Ari, Naomi Mara Hyman, and Arthur Waskow. 2000. *Trees, Earth and Torah*. Philadelphia, PA: Jewish Publication Society.

Elsass, Peter. 1992. *Strategies for Survival: The Psychology of Cultural Resilience in Ethnic Minorities*. New York: New York University Press.

Emerson, R. W. 1849. *On Nature*. Boston, MA: James Munroe & Company (New Edition of original 1836).

Englebert, Omer. 1965. *St. Francis of Assisi: A Biography*. Ann Arbor, MI: Servant Books.

English, Tom, and Frederick Krueger (eds.). 2010. *Witness for the Earth: Coalescing the Religious Environmental Movement*. Santa Rosa, CA: The National Religious Coalition on Creation Care.

Erdosy, George. 1998. "Deforestation in Pre- and Protohistoric South Asia." In *Nature and the Orient: The Environmental History of South and Southeast Asia*. Richard H. Grove, Vinita Damodaran, and Satpal Sangwan (eds.). Delhi, India: Oxford University Press, pp. 51–69.

Ereira, Alan. 1990. *From the Heart of the World: Elder Brother's Warning*. New York, NY: Mystic Fire Video (VHS 90 minutes).

Ereira, Alan. 1993. *The Elder Brothers: A Lost South American People and Their Wisdom*. New York, NY: Vintage.

Ereira, Alan. 2001. "Back to the Heart of Lightness." *The Ecologist* 31(6):34–38.

Ereira, Alan. 2009. *The Elder Brothers' Warning*. London, UK: Tairona Heritage Trust.

Escobin, Kim. 2011. *The 99,999 Trees Project*. (15 minutes). http://www.youtube.com/watch?v=SgupUHakXjA.

European Forum for the Study of Religion and Environment. 2011. http://www.hf.ntnu.no/relnateur.

Fairchild, Hoxie N. 1928/1961. *The Noble Savage: A Study in Romantic Naturalism*. New York, NY: Russell and Russell.

Felstiner, John. 2009. *Can Poetry Save the Earth? A Field Guide to Nature Poems*. New Haven, CT: Yale University Press.

Films Incorporated Video. 1991. *The Kayapo: Out of the Forest*. Chicago, IL: Films Incorporated Video.

Fink, Daniel B. 2010. "Judaism and Ecology: A Theology of Creation." Forum on Religion and Ecology. New Haven, CT: Yale University School of Forestry and Environmental Studies. http://fore.research.yale.edu/religion/judaism/.

Fitzpatrick, Lisa, James Cameron, Peter Jackson, and Jon Landau. 2009. *The Art of Avatar: James Cameron's Epic Adventure.* New York, NY: Abrams.

Flannery, T.F. 1995. *Future Eaters: An Ecological History of the Australasian Lands and People.* New York, NY: George Braziller.

Flemming, R.L., Jr., Dorje Tsering, and Liu Wulin. 2007. *Across the Tibetan Plateau: Ecosystems, Wildlife, and Conservation.* New York, NY: W.W. Norton.

Foley, Leonard, Jovian Weigel, and Patti Normile. 2000. *To Live As Francis Lived: A Guide for Secular Franciscans.* Cincinnati, OH: St. Anthony Messenger Press.

Foltz, Richard C., ed. 2003. *Worldviews, Religion, and the Environment: A Global Anthology.* Belmont, CA: Wadsworth/Thomson Learning.

Foltz, Richard C. 2006. "Islam." In *The Oxford Handbook of Religion and Ecology.* Roger S. Gottlieb (ed). New York, NY: Oxford University Press, pp. 207–219.

Foltz, Richard C., Frederick M. Denny, and Azizan Baharuddin (eds.). 2003. *Islam and Ecology: A Bestowed Trust.* Cambridge, MA: Harvard University Press/Harvard Divinity School Center for the Study of World Religions.

Forum on Religion and Ecology. 2004. "Jewish Engaged Projects: The Redwood Rabbis." New Haven, CT:Yale University School of Forestry and Environmental Studies. http://fore.research.yale.edu/religion/judaism/projects/redwood_rabbis.html.

Forum on Religion and Ecology. 2011. Forum on Religion and Ecology (FORE). New Haven, CT: Yale University. http://fore.research.yale.edu/.

Foster, John Bellamy, Brett Clark, and Richard York. 2010. *The Ecological Rift: Capitalism's War on the Earth.* New York, NY: Monthly Review Press.

Fox, Matthew. 1988. *The Coming of the Cosmic Christ: The Healing of Mother Earth and the Birth of a Global Renaissance.* San Francisco, CA: HarperOne.

Fox, Matthew. 2000. "Toward a Family Tree of Creation-Centered Spirituality." In *Original Blessing: A Primer in Creation Spirituality.* New York, NY: Jeremy P. Tarcher/Putnam, pp. 307–315.

Fox, Matthew. 2002. *Illuminations of Hildegard of Bingen.* Rochester. VT: Bear & Company.

Fox, Stephen. 1981. *John Muir and His Legacy: The American Conservation Movement.* Boston, MA: Little and Brown.

Frank, Adam. 2009. *The Constant Fire: Beyond the Science vs. Religion Debate.* Berkeley, CA: University of California Press.

Franke, Linda Bird. 2005. *On the Road with Francis of Assisi: A Timeless Journey Through Umbria and Tuscany, and Beyond.* New York, NY: Random House, Inc.

Frankenberry, Nancy K. (ed.). 2008. *The Faith of Scientists in Their Own Words.* Princeton, NJ: Princeton University Press.

Frazier, Jane. 1999. *From Origin to Ecology: Nature and the Poetry of W. S. Merwin.* Cranbury, NJ: Farleigh Dickinson University Press.

Free Tibet. 2011. http://www.freetibet.org.

French, William. 2005. "Rousseau, Jean-Jacques (1712–1778)." In *Encyclopedia of Religion and Nature.* Bron R. Taylor. (Editor-in-Chief). New York, NY: Thoemmes Continuum, 2, pp. 1428–1429.

Frommer, Paul. 2010. *Professor Paul Frommer Discusses the Na'vi language.* (5 minutes) http://www.youtube.com/watch?v=-AgnLH7Dw3w.

Fung, Cadi. 2011. *Human Ecology, Anthropocene Geography and Spiritual Ecology: A Case Study of Metta Forest Buddhist Monastery.* Flagstaff, AZ: Northern Arizona University M.S. Thesis in Applied Geospatial Sciences.

Gadgil, Madhav, and Ramachandra Guha. 1992. *This Fissured Land: An Ecological History of India.* Berkeley, CA: University of California Press.

Galvin, Kathleen A. 2001. "Hunter-Gatherer Societies, Ecological Impact." In *Encyclopedia of Biodiversity.* Simon Asher Levin (Editor-in-Chief). San Diego, CA: Academic Press, 3, pp. 411–415.

Gardner, Gary T. 2002. *Invoking the Spirit: Religion and Spirituality in the Quest for a Sustainable World.* Washington, D.C.: Worldwatch Institute Worldwatch Paper 164.

Gardner, Gary T. 2006. *Inspiring Progress: Religion's Contributions to Sustainable Development.* New York, NY: W. W. Norton & Company/Worldwatch Institute.

Gardner, Gary T. 2010a. "Engaging Religions to Shape Worldviews." In *2010 State of the World: Transforming Cultures From Consumerism to Sustainability.* Linda Starke and Lisa Mastny (eds.). NY: W. W. Norton & Company/Worldwatch Institute, pp. 23–29.

Gardner, Gary T. 2010b. "Ritual and Taboo as Ecological Guardians." In *2010 State of the World: Transforming Cultures from Consumerism to Sustainability.* Linda Starke and Lisa Mastny (eds.). New York, NY: W W. Norton & Company/Worldwatch Institute, pp. 30–40.

Garvey, James. 2008. *The Ethics of Climate Change: Right and Wrong in a Warming World.* London, UK: Continuum International Publishing Group.

Gatta, John. 2004. "Rare and Delectable Places: Thoreau's Imagination of Sacred Space at Walden." In *Making Nature Sacred: Literature, Religion, and Environment in America from the Puritans to the Present*. New York, NY: Oxford University Press, pp. 127–142.

Gellman, Jerome (Yehudah). 2002. "Early Hasidism and the Natural World." In *Judaism and Ecology: Created World and Revealed Word*. Hava Tirosh-Samuelson (ed.). Cambridge, MA: Harvard University Press/Harvard Divinity School Center for the Study of World Religions, pp. 36–388.

General Anthroposophy Society. 2011. http://www.anthroposophy.org

Gibson, James William. 2009. *A Reenchanted World: The Quest for a New Kinship with Nature*. New York, NY: Henry Holt and Company.

Gilmore, Lee. 2010a. *Theater in a Crowded Fire: Ritual and Spirituality at Burning Man*. Berkeley, CA: University of California Press.

Gilmore, Lee. 2010b. *Theater in a Crowded Fire: Ritual and Spiritual at Burning Man*. Berkeley, CA: University of California Press (DVD, 60 minutes).

Gilmore, Lee, and Mark Van Proyen, eds. 2005. *AfterBurn: Reflections on Burning Man*. Albuquerque, NM: University of New Mexico Press.

Girardot, N.J., James Miller, and Liu Xiaogan (eds). 2001. *Daoism and Ecology: Ways Within a Cosmic Landscape*. Cambridge, MA: Harvard University Press/Harvard Divinity University Center for the Study of World Religions.

Gisel, Bonnie. 2008. *Nature's Beloved Son: Rediscovering John Muir's Botanical Legacy*. Berkeley, CA: Heyday Books.

Gitau, Samson. 2000. *The Environmental Crisis: A Challenge for African Christianity*. Nairobi, Kenya: Acton Publishers.

Gitau, Samson. 2005. "Christian Environmentalism in Kenya." In *The Encyclopedia of Religion and Nature*. Bron R. Taylor (Editor-in-Chief). New York, NY: Thoemmes Continuum, 1, pp. 305–306.

Global Forum. 1990. "Preserving and Cherishing the Earth: An Appeal for Joint Commitment in Science and Religion." Forum of Religion and Ecology at Yale University. http://fore.research.yale.edu/publications/statements/ preserve.html).

Goldsworthy, Andy. 2004. *Andy Goldsworthy Rivers and Tides Working with Time*. New York, NY: New Video Group, Inc. (90 minutes). http://www .newvideo.com.

Goodall, Jane, and Phillip Berman. 1999. *Reason for Hope: A Spiritual Journey*. New York, NY: Warner Books, Inc.

Goodenough, Ursula. 1998. *The Sacred Depths of Nature*. New York, NY: Oxford University Press.

Gore, Al. 1993. *Earth in Balance: Ecology and the Human Spirit*. New York, NY: Penguin Books USA Inc.

Gore, Al. 2006a. *An Inconvenient Truth: The Planetary Emergency Of Global Warming and What We Can Do About It*. New York, NY: Rodale.

Gore, Al. 2006b. *An Inconvenient Truth: A Global Warning*. Hollywood, CA: Paramount. (DVD, 96 minutes) http://www.climatecrisis.net.

Goswami, Amit. 1995. *The Self-Aware Universe*. New York, NY: Tarcher/Putnam.

Gottlieb, Roger S. (ed.). 1996. *This Sacred Earth: Religion, Nature, Environment*. New York, NY: Routledge.

Gottlieb, Roger S. (ed.). 2004a. *This Sacred Earth: Religion, Nature, Environment*. New York, NY: Routledge (2nd Edition).

Gottlieb, Roger S. 2004b. "Earth 101." *Worldviews: Environment, Culture, Religion* 8(2–3):377–393.

Gottlieb, Roger S. 2006a. *A Greener Faith: Religious Environmentalism and our Planet's Future*. New York, NY: Oxford University Press.

Gottlieb, Roger S. 2006b. *Oxford Handbook of Religion and Ecology*. New York, NY: Oxford University Press.

Gottlieb, Roger S. 2007a. "Religious Environmentalism," Vanderbilt University guest lecture (November 15, 2007, 95 minutes). http://www.youtube.com/watch?v=BVpxdd1Oosg.

Gottlieb, Roger S. 2007b, "Religious Environmentalism: What It Is, Where It's Heading and Why We Should be Going in the Same Direction." *Journal for the Study of Religion, Nature and Culture* 1(1):81–91.

Gottlieb, Roger S. (ed.). 2010. *Religion and the Environment*. New York, NY: Routledge, Volumes 1–4.

Gottlieb, Roger S. 2011. *Engaging Voices: Tales of Morality and Meaning in an Age of Global Warming*. Waco, TX: Baylor University Press.

Gottlieb, Roger S. 2011. Homepage. http://users.wpi.edu/~gottlieb/index.html.

Gottlieb, Roger S. 2012. *Spirituality: What Is It and Why Does It Matter*. New York, NY: Oxford University Press (in press).

Gould, Rachelle K., Nicole M. Ardoin, Jennifer Kamakanipakolonahe'okekai Hashimoto. 2010. "'Malama the Aina, Malama the People on the Aina:' The Reaction to *Avatar* in Hawai'i." *Journal for the Study of Religion, Nature and Culture* 4(4):425–456.

Gould, Rebecca Kneale. 2005a. "Thoreau, Henry David (1817–1862)." In *The Encyclopedia of Religion and Nature*. Bron Taylor (Editor-in-Chief). London, UK: Thoemmes Continuum, 2, pp. 1634–1636.

Gould, Rebecca Kneale. 2005b. *At Home in Nature: Modern Homesteading and Spiritual Practice in America*. Berkeley, CA: University of California Press.

Gould, Stephen J. 2002. *Rock of Ages: Science and Religion in the Fullness of Life.* New York, NY: Ballantine Publishing Group.

Graeber, David. 2004. *Fragments of an Anarchist Anthropology.* Chicago, IL: Prickly Paradigm Press.

Graham, Mark, and Philip Round. 1994. *Thailand's Vanishing Flora and Fauna.* Bangkok, Thailand: Finance Once Public Co., Ltd.

Grande, John. 2003. *Balance: Art and Nature.* Montreal, Quebec, Canada: Black Rose Books (Revised Edition).

Grande, Sandy Marie Anglas. 1999. "Beyond the Ecologically Noble Savage: Deconstructing the White Man's Indian." *Environmental Ethics* 21 (3):307–320.

Grassie, William. 2010. *The New Science of Religion: Exploring Spirituality from the Outside In and Bottom Up.* New York, NY: Palgrave Macmillan.

Green Belt Movement. 2010. http://greenbeltmovement.org/index.php.

Green Museum. 2011. *The Green Museum.* http://www.GreenMuseum.org.

Grim, John A. (ed.). 2001. *Indigenous Traditions and Ecology: The Interbeing of Cosmology and Community.* Cambridge, MA: Harvard University Press/ Harvard University Center for the Study of World Religions.

Grim, John A., and Mary Evelyn Tucker. 2011. "Intellectual and Organizational Foundations of Religion and Ecology." In *Grounding Religion: A Field Guide to the Study of Religion and Ecology.* Whitney Bauman, Richard R. Bohannon II, and Kevin J. O'Brien (eds.). New York, NY: Routledge, pp. 81–95.

Grimsley, Ronald. 1968. *Rousseau and the Religious Quest.* Oxford, UK: Clarendon Press.

Grimsley, Ronald. 1970. *Religious Writings of Rousseau.* London, UK: Clarendon Press.

Grinde, Donald A., and Bruce E. Johansen. 1995. *Ecocide of Native America: Environmental Destruction of Indian Lands and Peoples.* Santa Fe, NM: Clear Light Publishers.

Grubin, David. 2010. *The Buddha: The Story of Siddartha.* Arlington, VA: Public Broadcasting Service (DVD, 2 hours).

Gudmundsson, B.J. 2006. *Mountain Mourning.* Lewisburg, VA: Patchwork Films/Christians for the Mountains (DVD, 78 minutes). http://www .PatchworkFilms.com and http://www.ChristiansfortheMountains.org.

Guha, Gita. 1995 (January–February). "A Culture of Trees." *Resurgence* 168:31–35.

Guthrie, Stewart. 1993. *Faces in the Clouds: A New Theory of Religion.* New York, NY: Oxford University Press.

Hackenberg, Robert A. 1974. "Ecosystemic Channeling: Cultural Ecology from the Viewpoint of Aerial Photography." In *Aerial Photography in*

Anthropological Field Research. Evon Z. Vogt (ed.). Cambridge, MA: Harvard University Press, pp. 28–39.

Hagan, William T. 1980. "Justifying Dispossession of the Indian: The Land Utilization Agrument." In *American Indian Environments: Ecological Issues in Native American History*. Christopher Vecsey and Robert W. Venables (eds.). Syracuse, NY: Syracuse University Press, pp. 65–80.

Hageneder, Fred. 2000. *The Spirit of Trees: Science, Symbiosis, and Inspiration*. New York, NY: Continuum International Publishing Group, Inc.

Hahn, Scott, and Benjamin Wilker. 2008. *Answering the New Atheism: Dismantling Dawkins' Case Against God*. Steubenville, OH: Emmaus Road Publishing.

Hakkenberg, Christopher. 2008. "Biodiversity and Sacred Sites: Vernacular Conservation Practices in Northwest Yunnan, China." *Worldviews: Global Religions, Culture, Ecology* 12(1):74–90.

Hall, Bert S. 1988. "Lynn White, Jr., April 1907–March 1987. *ISIS* 79(3): 478–481.

Hamer, Dean. 2004. *The God Gene. How Faith Is Hardwired into Our Genes*. New York, NY: Doubleday.

Hames, Raymond B. 1991. "Wildlife Conservation in Tribal Societies." In *Biodiversity: Culture, Conservation, and Ecodevelopment*. Margery L. Oldfield and Janis B. Alcorn (eds.). Boulder, CO: Westview Press, pp. 172–199.

Hames, Raymond B. 2007. "The Ecologically Noble Savage Debate." *Annual Review of Anthropology* 36:177–190.

Hamilton, Roy W., et al. 2003. *The Art of Rice: Spirit and Sustenance*. Los Angeles, CA: UCLA Fowler Museum of Cultural History.

Hamlin, Christopher, and David M. Lodge. 2006. "Beyond Lynn White: Religion, the Contexts of Ecology, and the Flux of Nature." In *Religion and the New Ecology: Environmental Responsibility in a World in Flux*. David M. Lodge and Christopher. Hamlin (eds.). Notre Dame, IN: University of Notre Dame Press, pp. 1–25.

Happynook, Tom Mexsis. 2000. "Indigenous Whalers and Traditional Resource Management Knowledge" *Indigenous Affairs* 2:64–71.

Harding, Stephan. 2006. *Animate Earth: Science, Intuition and Gaia*. White River Junction, VT: Chelsea Green Publishing Company.

Hareuveni, Nogah, and Helen Frenkley. 1984. *Trees and Shrubs in our Biblical Heritage*. Modi'in, Israel: Neot Kedumim: The Biblical Landscape Reserve in Israel.

Hargrove, Eugene C. (ed.). 1986. *Religion and Environmental Crisis*. Athens, GA: University of Georgia Press.

Harkin, Michael E., and David Rich Lewis (eds.). 2007. *Native Americans and the Environment: Perspectives on the Ecological Indian*. Lincoln, NE: University of Nebraska Press.

Harnden, Philip. 2003. *Journeys of Simplicity: Traveling Light*. Woodstock, VT: Skylight Paths Publishing.

Harner, Michael. 2011. *The Foundation for Shamanic Studies*. http://www.shamanism.org.

Harrer, Heinrich. 1982. *Seven Years in Tibet*. New York, NY: Penguin Putnam Inc./Jeremy P. Tarcher/Punam.

Harrington, Anne, and Arthur Zajonc. 2003. *The Dalai Lama at MIT*. Cambridge, MA: Harvard University Press.

Harris, Ian. 1991. "How Environmentalist Is Buddhism?" *Religion* 21:101–114.

Harris, Ian. 1994. "Buddhism," In *Attitudes to Nature. Jean Holm and John Bowker* (eds.). New York, NY: Pinter Publishers, pp. 8–27.

Harris, Ian. 1995a. "Buddhist Environmental Ethics and Detraditionalization: The Case of EcoBuddhism." *Religion* 25:199–211.

Harris, Ian. 1995b. "Getting to Grips with Buddhist Environmentalism: A Provisional Typology." *Journal of Buddhist Ethics* 2:173–190.

Harris, Ian. 1995c. "An American Appropriation of Buddhism." In *Buddhist Forum 4*, Tadeusz Skorupski (ed.). Tring, UK: Institute of Buddhist Studies, pp. 43–59.

Harris, Ian 1997. "Buddhism and the Discourse of Environmental Concern: Some Methodological Problems." In *Buddhism and Ecology: The Interconnection of Dharma and Deeds*. Mary Evelyn Tucker and Duncan Ryuken Williams. (eds.). Cambridge, MA: Harvard University Press, pp. 377–402.

Harris, Sam. 2004. *The End of Faith: Relgion, Terror, and the Future of Reason*. New York, NY: W. W. Norton & Co.

Harrison, Paul. 2004. *Elements of Pantheism: Religious Reverence of Nature and the Universe*. Coral Springs, FL: Llumina Press.

Hart, John. 2004. *What Are They Saying about Environmental Theology?* Mahwah, NJ: Paulist Press.

Hart, Keith, and Conrad Kottak. 1999. "Roy A. 'Skip' Rappaport (1926–1997)." *American Anthropologist* 101(1):159–161.

Hartman, Thom. 1999. *The Last Hours of Ancient Sunlight: Waking Up to Personal and Global Transformation*. New York, NY: Three Rivers Press.

Harvey, Graham. 1997. *Contemporary Paganism: Listening People, Speaking Earth*. Washington Square, NY: New York University Press.

Harvey, Graham (ed.). 2003. *Shamanism: A Reader*. New York, NY: Routledge.

Harvey, Graham. 2006. *Animism: Respecting the Living World*. New York, NY: Columbia University Press. http://www.grahamharvey.org.

Harvey, Nelson. 2006 (April 19). "Interview with Roger S. Gottlieb." *The American Prospect* http://www.prospect.org/cs/articles?articleId=11430.

Harvey, Peter. 1998. "Buddhist Attitudes to and Treatment of Non-Human Nature." *Ecotheology* 4:35–50.

Harvey, Peter. 2000. "Attitude to and Treatment of the Natural World." In *An Introduction to Buddhist Ethics*. Peter Harvey. New York, NY: Cambridge University Press, pp. 150–186.

Haught, John F. 1990. *What Is Religion? An Introduction*. Mahwah, NJ: Paulist Press.

Haught, John F. 2006. *Is Nature Enough? Meaning and Truth in the Age of Science*. New York, NY: Cambridge University Press.

Haught, John F. 2008. *God and the New Atheism: A Critical Response to Dawkins, Harris, and Hitchens*. Louisville, KY: Westminster John Knox Press.

Havel, Vaclav. 1998 (November–December). "Spirit of the Earth." *Resurgence* 191:30.

Hawken, Paul. 2007. *Blessed Unrest: How the Largest Movement in the World Came into Being and Why No One Saw It Coming*. New York, NY: Viking.

HDH Communications. 2006. *The Holy Cities: Assisi*. Milano, Italy: HDH Communications/Danae Film Production (DVD, 60 minutes).

Headland, Thomas N. (ed.). 1992. *The Tasaday Controversy: Assessing the Evidence*. Washington, D.C.: American Anthropological Association Special Publication.

Headland, Thomas N. 1997. "Revisionism in Ecological Anthropology." *Current Anthropology* 38(4):605–630.

Henning, Daniel H. 2001. *Tree Talk and Tales*. Bloomington, IN: Xlibris Corporation.

Henning, Daniel H. 2002a. *Buddhism and Deep Ecology*. Bloomington, IN: 1stBooks.

Henning, Daniel H. 2002b. *A Manual for Buddhism and Deep Ecology*. Buddha Dharma Educational Association, Inc., http://www.buddhanet.net/pdf _file/deep_ecology.pdf.

Herzog, Werner. 2011. *Cave of Forgotten Dreams*. Orland Park, Il: MPI Home Video.

Hessel, Dieter T., and Rosemary Radford Ruether (eds.). 2000. *Christianity and Ecology: Seeking the Well-Being of Earth and Humans*. Cambridge, MA: Harvard University Press/Harvard University Center for the Study of World Religions.

Higginbotham, Joyce, and River Higginbotham. 2010. *Paganism: An Introduction to Earth-Centered Religions*. Woodbury, MN: Llewellyn Publications.

Highland, John. (ed.). 2001. *Meditations of John Muir: Nature's Temple*. Berkeley, CA: Wilderness Press.

Highland, John. 2008. "John Muir: The Wild Gospel of Nature." [reading from Highland's book Meditations of John Muir: Nature's Temple] http://www.naturetemple.net, http://www.youtube.com/watch?v=Ygw1cmEYlHg.

Highwater, Jamake. 1981. *The Primal Mind: Vision and Reality in Indian America.* New York, NY: New American Library.

Hill, Julia Butterfly. 2000. *The Legacy of Luna: The Story of a Tree, a Woman, and the Struggle to Save the Redwoods.* San Francisco, CA: HarperSanFrancisco.

Hill, Julia Butterfly. 2011. Homepage. http://www.juliabutterfly.com.

Hill, Julia Butterfly, and Jessica Hurley. 2002. *One Makes the Difference: Inspiring Actions That Change the World.* San Francisco, CA: HarperOne.

Hindes, Daniel. 2010. *Defending Steiner.* http://www.defendingsteiner.com.

Hinnells, John R. 1995. *The Penguin Dictionary of Religions.* New York, NY: Penguin Books (2nd Edition).

Hitchens, Christopher. 2007. *God Is Not Great: How Religion Poisons Everything.* New York, NY: Hachette Book Group USA.

Hix, H.L. 1997. *Understanding W. S. Merwin.* Columbia, SC: University of South Carolina Press.

Hollister, C. Warren. 1998. *Medieval Europe: A Short History.* New York, NY: McGraw-Hill Companies, Inc. (8th ed.).

Holm, Jean, and John Bowker. (eds.) 1994a. *Attitudes to Nature.* New York, NY: Pinter Publishers.

Holm, Jean, and John Bowker. (eds.) 1994b. *Sacred Places.* New York, NY: Pinter Publishers.

Holmes, Steven J. 1999. *The Young John Muir: An Environmental Biography.* Madison, WI: University of Wisconsin Press.

Holmes, Steven J. 2005. "Muir, John (1838–1914)." In *The Encyclopedia of Religion and Nature.* Bron Taylor. (Editor-in-Chief). New York, NY: Thoemmes Continuum, 2, pp. 1126–1127.

Holt, Lawrence, Diane Garvey, and Ken Chowder. 2008. *The Wilderness Idea.* Santa Monica, CA: Floretine Films (DVD, 58 minutes).

Holtmeier, Matthew Alan. 2010. "Post-Pandoran Depression or Na'vi Sympathy: *Avatar,* Affect, and Audience Reception." *Journal for the Study of Religion, Nature and Culture* 4(4):414–424.

Hook, Harry. 2004. *The Last of His Tribe.* Home Box Office Pictures (Original 1992) (90 minutes).

Hopcke, Robert H., and Paul A. Scwartz. 2006. *Little Flowers of Francis of Assisi.* Boston, MA: New Seeds.

Horgan, John. 2003. *Rational Mysticism: Spirituality Meets Science in the Search for Enlightenment.* Boston, MA: Houghton Mifflin Company/Mariner Book.

Hosenfeld, Charlene. 2009. *Ecofaith: Creating and Sustaining Green Congregations*. Cleveland, OH: The Pilgrim Press.

Houge, Michael S. 2010. *The Promise of Religious Naturalism*. Lanham, MD: Rowman and Littlefield Publishers, Inc.

House, Adrian. 2000. *Francis of Assisi: A Revolutionary Life*. Mahwah, NJ: Paulist Press/HiddenSpring.

Houshmand, Zara (ed.). 2009. *Mind and Life: Discussions with the Dalai Lama on the Nature of Reality*. New York, NY: Columbia University Press.

Hout Bay Theravada Centre. 2011. *Climate Change and Buddhism*. Hout Bay, South Africa: Hout Bay Theravada Centre. http://www.theravada.org.za/environment.asp.

Howard, Michael. 2009. *Modern Wicca: A History from Gerald Gardner to the Present*. Woodbury, MN: Llewellyn Publications.

Huber, Toni, 1991 (Autumn), "Traditional Environmental Protectionism in Tibet Reconsidered." *The Tibet Journal* XVI(3):63–77.

Hudson, William H. 1916. *Green Mansions: A Romance of the Tropical Forest*. New York, NY: A. A. Knopf.

Hughes, J. Donald. 1975. *Ecology in Ancient Civilizations*. Albuquerque, NM: University of New Mexico Press.

Hughes, J. Donald. 1983. *American Indian Ecology*. El Paso, TX: Texas Western Press.

Ingram, David. 2004. *Green Screen: Environmentalism and Hollywood Cinema*. Exeter, UK: University of Exeter Press.

Institute for Contemporary Franciscan Life [Franciscan Studies distance learning program] Saint Francis University, Loretto, PA. http://www.francis.edu/ICFLHome.htm.

Institute of Noetic Sciences. 2010. Petaluna, CA. http://www.noetic.org.

Institute on Religion in an Age of Science, Inc. 2011. http://www.iras.org/home.htm/.

Interfaith Power and Light. 2007. *Renewal: Stories from America's Religious-Environmental Movement*. (DVD, 90 minutes). http://www.renewalproject.net.

Interfaith Power and Light. 2011. *Interfaith Power and Light*. http://www.theregenerationproject.org.

Intergovernmental Panel on Climate Change. 2011. *Intergovernmental Panel on Climate Change*. Geneva, Switzerland: World Meteorological Organization. http://www.ipcc.ch/.

International Campaign for Tibet. 2011. http://www.savetibet.org.

International Network of Engaged Buddhists. 2011. http://www.inebnetwork.org/.

International Society for the Study of Religion, Nature and Culture. 2011. http://www.religionandnature.com.

International Union for Conservation of Nature and Natural Resources (IUCN). 1997. *Indigenous Peoples and Sustainability: Cases and Actions*. Utrecht, The Netherlands: International Books.

Istoft, Britt. 2010. "*Avatar* Fandom as Nature-Religious Expression?" *Journal for the Study of Religion, Nature and Culture* 4(4):394–413.

I-Thou, 2011. http://www.ithou.org/.

Iver, Bon. 2011. *Holocene*. http://www.youtube.com/watch?v=TWcyIpul80E.

Iyer, Pico. 2008. *The Open Road: The Global Journey of the Fourteenth Dalai Lama*. New York, NY: Alfred A. Knopf.

Jacobs, Mark X. 2002. "Jewish Environmentalism: Past Accomplishments and Future Challenges." In *Judaism and Ecology: Created World and Revealed Word*. Hava Tirosh-Samuelson (ed.). Cambridge, MA: Harvard University Press/Harvard Divinity School Center for the Study of World Religions, pp. 449–477.

Jacobs, Mark X. 2011. *Judaism and Ecology Bibliography. Forum on Religion and Ecology*. New Haven, CT: Yale University. http://fore.research.yale.edu/religion/judaism/judaism.pdf.

Jahoda, Gustav. 1999. *Images of Savages: Ancient Roots of Modern Prejudice in Western Culture*. New York, NY: Routledge.

James, William. 1902. *The Varieties of Religious Experience*. New York, NY: Longmans, Green.

Jenkins, Willis. 2009a (March). "Religion and Ecology: A Review Essay on the Field." *Journal of the American Academy of Religion* 77(1):183–186.

Jenkins, Willis. 2009b. "After Lynn White: Religious Ethics and Environmental Problems." *Journal of Religious Ethics* 37(2):283–309.

Jensen, Derrick. 2004. *A Language Older Than Words*. White River Junction, VT: Chelsea Green Publishing Company.

Jensen, Derrick, and Aric McBay. 2009. *What We Leave Behind*. New York, NY: Seven Stories Press.

John Muir Association. 2011. http://www.johnmuirassociation.org/php/links.php.

John Muir College. 2011. University of California, San Diego, CA. http://muir.ucsd.edu.

John Muir Global Network. 2011. http://www.johnmuir.org.

John Muir Institute of the Environment at University of California Davis, 2011. http://johnmuir.ucdavis.edu/.

Johnson, Allen. 1989. "How the Machigenga Manage Resources: Conservation or Exploitation of Nature?" *Advances in Economic Botany* 7:213–222.

Johnson, Greg, 2005. "Romanticism and Indigenous Peoples." *Encyclopedia of Religion and Nature*. Bron R. Taylor (Editor-in-Chief). New York, NY: Thoemmes Continuum, 2, pp. 1418–1419.

Johnson, William Ted. 2006. "The Lives of Great Environmentalists: John Muir." *Electronic Green Journal* 1(24, Article 5):1–7.

Johnston, Barbara Rose (ed.). 2007. *Half-Lives and Half-Truths: Confronting the Radioactive Legacies of the Cold War*. Santa Fe, NM: New School for Advanced Research Press.

Johnston, Barbara Rose (ed.). 2011. *Life and Death Matters: Human Rights, Environment, Social Justice*. Walnut Creek, CA: Left Coast Press (2nd Edition).

Johnston, Barbara Rose, and Holly M. Barker. 2008. *Consequential Damages of Nuclear War: The Rongelap Report*. Walnut Creek, CA: Left Coast Press.

Johnston, Lucas. 2006. "The 'Nature' of Buddhism: A Survey of Relevant Literature and Themes." *Worldviews: Environment, Culture, Religion* 10 (1):69–99.

Jones, Holway R. 1965. *John Muir and the Sierra Club: The Battle for Yosemite*. San Francisco, CA: Sierra Club Books.

Jones, Owain, and Paul Cloke. 2002. *Tree Cultures: The Place of Trees and Trees in Their Place*. New York, NY: Berg.

Journal for the Study of Religion, Nature and Culture, 2011. http://www.religionandnature.com/journal/index.htm.

Justice, Daniel Heath. 2010 (January 20). "Daniel Heath Justice on Avatar." *First Peoples: New Directions in Indigenous Studies*. http://firstpeoplesnewdirections.org/blog/index.php?search=true&s=avatar&terms=avatar&t=b.

Kabilsingh, Chatsumarn. 1987. *A Cry from the Forest: Buddhist Perception of Nature, A New Perspective for Conservation Education*. Bangkok, Thailand: Wildlife Fund Thailand.

Kabilsingh, Chatsumarn. 1997. "Green Dharma: Buddhism and Ecological Activism in Thailand." In *Ecological Responsibility: A Dialogue With Buddhism*. Julia Martin (ed.). Delhi, India: Tibet House, pp. 127–137.

Kabilsingh, Chatsumarn. 1998. *Buddhism and Nature Conservation*. Bangkok, Thailand: Thammasat University Press.

Kahn, Roshi Paul Genki. 2011 (Spring). "Remembering Aitken Roshi." *Tricycle: The Buddhist Review*, 21(2):34–37.

Kalland, Arne. 1993 (December). "Whale Politics and Green Legitimacy: A Critique of the Anti-Whaling Campaign." *Anthropology Today* 9(6): 3–7.

Kalland, Arne. 2003. "Environmentalism and Images of the Other." In *Nature Across Cultures: Views of Nature and the Environment in Non-Western*

Cultures. Helaine Selin (ed.). Boston, MA: Kluwer Academic Publishers, pp. 1–17.

Kalu, Ogbu U. 2001. "The Sacred Egg: Worldview, Ecology, and Development in West Africa." In *Indigenous Traditions and Ecology: The Interbeing of Cosmology and Community*. John A. Grim (ed.). Cambridge, MA: Harvard University Press/Harvard Divinity School Center for the Study of World Religions, pp. 225–248.

Kapstein, Matthew T. 2006. *The Tibetans*. Malden, MA: Blackwell Publishing.

Karmapa, His Holiness the 17th, Ogyen Trinley Dorje. 2011. "Enlightened Activity." http://www.khoryug.com/blog/karmapa-launches-a-new-website-for-environmental-protection/, http://www.khoryug.com/vision/.

Kauffman, Stuart A. 2008. *Reinventing the Sacred: A New View of Science, Reason, and Religion*. New York, NY: Perseus Books Group/Basic Books.

Kawagley, A. Oscar. 1995. *A Yupiaq Worldview: A Pathway to Ecology and Spirit*. Prospect Heights, IL: Waveland Press, Inc.

Kaza, Stephanie. 1996. *The Attentive Heart: Conversations with Trees*. Boston, MA: Shambhala Press.

Kaza, Stephanie. 1997. "American Buddhist Response to the Land: Ecological Practices at Two West Coast Retreat Centers." In *Buddhism and Ecology: The Interconnection of Dharma and Deeds*. Mary Evelyn Tucker and Duncan Ryuken Williams (eds.). Cambridge, MA: Harvard University Press, pp. 219–248.

Kaza, Stephanie. 2000. "To Save All Beings: Buddhist Environmental Activism." In *Engaged Buddhism in the West*. Christopher S. Queen (ed.). Boston, MA: Wisdom Publications, pp. 159–183.

Kaza, Stephanie (ed.). 2005. *Hooked! Buddhist Writings on Greed, Desire, and the Urge to Consume*. Boston, MA: Shambhala Publications, Inc.

Kaza, Stephanie. 2006. "The Greening of Buddhism: Promise and Perils." In *Oxford Handbook of Religion and Ecology*. Roger S. Gottlieb (ed.). New York, NY: Oxford University Press, pp.184–206.

Kaza, Stephanie. 2008. *Mindfully Green: A Personal and Spiritual Guide to Whole Earth Thinking*. Boston, MA: Shambhala.

Kaza, Stephanie, and Kenneth Kraft (eds.). 2000. *Dharma Rain: Sources of Buddhist Environmentalism*. Boston, MA: Shambhala Publications, Inc.Kearns, Laurel, and Catherine Keller. 2007. *Ecospirit: Religions and Philosophies of the Earth*. Bronx, NY: Fordham University Press.

Keegan, Rebecca. 2010. *The Futurist: The Life and Films of James Cameron*. New York, NY: Three Rivers Press.

Kehoe, Alice Beck. 2000. *Shamans and Religion: An Anthropological Exploration in Critical Thinking*. Prospect Heights, IL: Waveland Press, Inc.

Keller, David G.R. 2005. *Oasis of Wisdom: The Worlds of the Desert Fathers and Mothers*. Collegeville, MN: Liturgical Press.

Keller, Robert H., and Michael F. Turek. 1998. *American Indians and National Parks*. Tucson, AZ: University of Arizona Press.

Kellert, Stephen R. 1995. "Concepts of Nature East and West." In *Reinventing Nature? Responses to Postmodern Deconstruction*. Michael Soule and Gary Lease (eds.) Washington, D.C.: Island Press, pp. 103–121.

Kellert, Stephen R. 2005. "Biophilia." In *Encyclopedia of Religion and Nature*. Bron Taylor (Editor-in-Chief). New York, NY: Thoemmes Continuum, 1, pp. 183–188.

Kellert, Stephen R. 2007. "The Biophilia Hypothesis." *Journal for the Study of Religion, Nature and Culture* 1(1):25–37.

Kellert, Stephen R., and Edward O. Wilson. (eds.). 1993. *The Biophilia Hypothesis*. Washington, D.C.: Island Press.

Kellert, Stephen R., and Timothy J. Farnham(eds.). 2002. *The Good in Nature and Humanity: Connecting Science, Religion, and Spirituality with the Natural World*. Washington, D.C.: Island Press.

Keown, Damien. 2000. *Buddhism: A Very Short Introduction*. New York, NY: Oxford University Press.

Keown, Damien. 2005. *Buddhist Ethics: A Very Short Introduction*. New York, NY: Oxford University Press.

Khalid, Fazlun, and Joanne O'Brien. 1992. *Islam and Ecology*. London, UK: Cassell.

Khoryug. 2009. http://www.khoryug.com/blog/karmapa-launches-a-new -website-for-environmental-protection/.

Kibbutz Lotan: 2005. Center for Creative Ecology. Kibbutz Lotan, Israel. http:// www.kibbutzlotan.com/community/friendsLotan/tuBshvat.html.

Kienzle, Beverly. 2006. "The Bestiary of Heretics: Imagining Medieval Christian Heresy with Insects and Animals." In *A Communion of Subjects: Animals in Religion, Science & Ethics*. Paul Waldau and Kimberley Patton (eds.). New York, NY: Columbia University Press, pp. 103–116.

Kimball, Charles. 2002. *When Religion Becomes Evil*. San Francisco, CA: HarperSanFrancisco.

King, Sallie B. 1991. *Buddha Nature*. Albany, NY: State University of New York Press.

King, Ursula. 2011. *Teilhard de Chardin and Eastern Religions: Spirituality and Mysticism in an Evolutionary World*. Mahwah, NJ: Paulist Press.

Kinsley, David. 1995. *Ecology and Religion: Ecological Spirituality in Cross-Cultural Perspective*. Englewood Cliffs, NJ: Prentice-Hall, Inc.

Klein, Kerwin Lee. 1997. *Frontiers of the Historical Imagination: Narrating the European Conquest of Native America, 1890–1990*. Berkeley, CA: University of California Press.

Klieger, P. Christiaan. 2007. "The People of Tibet." In *Disappearing Peoples? Indigenous Groups and Ethnic Minorities in South and Central Asia*. Barbara A. Brower and Barbara Rose Johnston (eds.). Walnut Creek, CA: Left Coast Press, Inc., pp. 221–241.

Kline, Phill. 2009 (December 25). "*Avatar* the Movie: The Religion of the Left." *Renew America*. http://www.renewamerica.com/columns/kline/091225.

Koizumi, Tetsunori. 2010. "The Noble Eightfold Path as a Prescription for Sustainable Living." In *How Much Is Enough? Buddhism, Consumerism, and the Human Environment*. Richard K. Payne (ed.). Boston, MA: Wisdom Publications, pp. 133–145.

Korten, David C. 2006. *The Great Turning: From Empire to Earth Community*. San Francisco, CA: Berrett-Koehler. http://www.davidkorten.org. http://thegreatturning.net.

Kozak, David. 2000. "Shamanism: Past and Present." In *Religion and Culture: An Anthropological Focus*. Raymond Scupin (ed.). Upper Saddle River, NJ: Prentice Hall, pp. 106–121.

Kozlovsky, Daniel G. 1974. *An Ecological and Evolutionary Ethic*. Englewood Cliffs, NJ: Prentice-Hall.

Kraft, Kenneth. 1997. "Nuclear Ecology and Engaged Buddhism." In *Buddhism and Ecology: The Interconnection of Dharma and Deeds*. Mary Evelyn Tucker and Duncan Ryuken Williams (eds.). Cambridge, MA: Harvard University Press/Harvard University Center for the Study of World Religions, pp. 269–290.

Kraus, James. 2005. "Merwin, W. S. (William Stanley)(1927–)." In *The Encyclopedia of Religion and Nature*. Bron Taylor (Editor-in-Chief). New York, NY: Thoemmes Continuum, 2, p. 1084.

Krech, Shepard. 1999. *The Ecological Indian: Myth and History*. New York: W W. Norton.

Krech, Shepard. 2005a. "American Indians as First Ecologists." In *Encyclopedia of Religion and Nature*. Bron R. Taylor (Editor-in-Chief). New York, NY: Thoemmes Continuum, 1, pp. 42–45.

Krech, Shepard. 2005b. "Reflections on Conservation, Sustainability, and Environmentalism in Indigenous North America." *American Anthropologist* 107(1):78–86.

Kroeber, Theodora. 1961. *Ishi in Two Worlds: A Biography of the Last Wild Indian in North America*. Berkeley, CA: University of California Press.

Kubota, Gary T. 2010 (September 26). "Expression through Poems and Palms." Honolulu, HI: Honolulu Star Advertiser, G1, G10.

Kull, Kalevi, Toomas Kukk, and Aleksei Lotman. 2003. "When Culture Supports Biodiversity: The Case of the Wooded Meadow." In *Imagining Nature: Practices of Cosmology and Identity*. Andraes Roepstorff, Nils Burbandt, and Kalevi Kull (eds.). Aarhus, Denmark: Aarhus University Press, pp. 76–96.

Kumar, Satish, and Freddie Whitefield. 2006. *Visionaries: The 20th Century's 100 Most Inspirational Leaders*. White River Junction, VT: Chelsea Publishing.

Kung, Hans. 2007. *The Beginnings of All Things: Science and Religion*. Grand Rapids, MI: William B. Eerdmans Publishing Company.

Kunnie, Julian E., and Nomalungelo I. Goduka (eds.). 2004. *Indigenous People's Wisdom and Power: Affirming Our Knowledge Through Narratives*. Aldershot, UK: Ashgate Publishing Limited.

Kupihea, Moke. 2001. *Kahuna of Light: The World of Hawaiian Spirituality*. Rochester, VT: Inner Traditions International.

Kvaloy, Sigmund. 1987. "Norwegian Ecophilosophy and Ecopolitics and Their Influence from Buddhism." In *Buddhist Perspectives on the Ecocrisis*. Klas Sandell, ed. Kandy, Sri Lanka: Buddhist Publication Society/The Wheel Publication No. 346/348, pp. 49–72.

Kynes, Sandra. 2006. *Whispers from the Woods: The Lore and Magic of Trees*. Woodbury, MN: Llewellyn Publications.

LaDuke, Winona. 1999. *All Our Relations: Native Struggles for Land and Life*. Cambridge, MA: South End Press.

LaDuke, Winona. 2005. *Recovering the Sacred: The Power of Naming and Claiming*. Cambridge, MA: South End Press.

LaFleur, William R. 2000. "Enlightenment for Plants and Trees." In *Dharma Rain: Sources of Buddhist Environmentalism*. Stephanie Kaza and Kenneth Kraft (eds.). Boston, MA: Shambhala Publications, pp. 109–116.

Lake, Osprey Orielle. 2010. *Uprisings for the Earth: Reconnecting Culture with Nature*. Ashland, OR: White Cloud Press.

Lane, Belden C. 1998. *The Solace of Fierce Landscapes: Exploring Desert and Mountain Spirituality*. New York, NY: Oxford University Press.

Lansing, J. Stephen. 1989. *The Goddess and the Computer*. London, UK: Royal Anthropological Institute of Great Britain and Ireland (VHS, 54 minutes).

Laszlo, Ervin, and Allan Combs (eds.). 2011. *Thomas Berry, Dreamer of the Earth: The Spiritual Ecology of the Father of Environmentalism*. Rochester, VT: Inner Traditions.

Le Goff, Jacques. 2004. *Saint Francis of Assisi*. London, UK: Routledge.

Le Guin, Ursula. 1972. *The Word for World Is Forest*. New York, NY: Berkley Publishing Corporation.

Leonard, Patrick. 2008 (October 29). "Meditation: A Walk through the Sierras." YouTube.com. http://www.youtube.com/watch?v=rAs0hZb-DNs&feature =related.

Leopold, Aldo. 1966 [1949]. *A Sand County Almanac with Essays on Conservation from Round River*. New York, NY: Oxford University Press, Inc.

Lerner, Michael. 2000. *Spirit Matters*. Charlottesville, VA: Hampton Road Publishing Company, Inc.

Lerner, Steve. 1998. *Eco-Pioneers: Practical Visionaries Solving Today's Environmental Problems*. Cambridge, MA: MIT Press.

Leslie, John. 1996. *The End of the World: The Science and Ethics of Human Extinction*. New York, NY: Routledge.

Lett, James. 1997. "Science, Religion, and Anthropology." In *Anthropology of Religion: A Handbook*. Stephen D. Glazier (ed.). Westport, CT: Praeger, pp. 103–120.

Levitt, Tom. 2010 (December 10). "Torbay in Groundbreakng Move to Start Valuing Trees." *The Ecologist*. http://www.theecologist.org/News/news _round_up/692058/torbay_in_groundbreaking_move_to_start_valuing_its _trees.html.

Lewis, Leona. 2009. "I See You" [*Avatar* movie theme song, 4 minutes] http:// www.youtube.com/watch?v=3YDz-ftqr1g.

Life on the Tibetan Plateau. 2011. http://kekexili.typepad.com.

Linkola, Pentti. 2009. *Can Life Prevail? A Radical Approach to the Environmental Crisis*. London, UK: Integral Tradition Publishing.

Linzey, Andrew, and Ara Barsam. 2001. "Saint Francis of Assisi 1181/2–1226." In *Fifty Key Thinkers on the Environment*. Joy A. Palmer (ed.). New York, NY: Routledge, pp. 22–27.

Lionberger, John. 2007. *Renewal in the Wilderness: A Spiritual Guide to Connecting with God in the Natural World*. Woodstock, VT: Skylight Paths Publishing.

Lohmann, Larry. 1993. "Green Orientalism." *The Ecologist* 23(6):202–204.

Loori, John Daido. 2000. *Mountains and Rivers: Mystical Realism of Zen Master Dogen*. Mount Tremper, NY: Dharma Communications (VHS, 45 minutes).

Lopez, Jr., Donald S. 1998. *Prisoners of Shangri-La: Tibetan Buddhism and the West*. Chicago, IL: University of Chicago Press.

Louv, Richard. 2005. *Last Child in the Woods: Saving Our Children from Nature-Deficit Disorder*. Chapel Hill, NC: Algonquin Books of Chapel Hill.

Lovejoy, Arthur O., and George Boas. 1935/1997. *Primitivism and Related Ideas in Antiquity*. Baltimore, MD: Johns Hopkins University Press.

Lovelock, James E. 1979. *Gaia: A New Look at Life on Earth*. New York, NY: Oxford University Press.

Lovelock, James E. 2006. *The Revenge of Gaia: Earth's Climate in Crisis and the Fate of Humanity*. New York, NY: Basic Books.

Lovelock, James E. 2009. *The Vanishing Face of Gaia: A Final Warning*. New York, NY: Basic Books.

Lumbini Crane Conservation Center. 2011. *Buddhism and Nature*. Kathmandu, Nepal: Lumbini Crane Conservation Center. http://www.lumbinicrane .org/index.php?f=Buddhism_Nature#dname.

Lund, Elizabeth. 2003 (April 24). "A Master Gardener of Verse," *Christian Science Monitor*. http://www.csmonitor.com/2003/0424/p15s02-bogn .html.

Luskin, Ryan. 2011.http://www.thesailingmovie.com, http://www.youtube.com/ watch?v=TMXhokbhZX8.

Lynn, David, and David Baker. 2010 (Fall). *A Conversation with Poet Laureate W. S. Merwin*. (35 minutes). http://www.kenyonreview.org/conversation/ w-s-merwin/.

Maathai, Wangari. 2004. *The Green Belt Movement: Sharing the Approach and the Experience*. New York, NY: Lantern Books.

Maathai, Wangari. 2006. *Unbowed: A Memoir*. New York, NY: Alfred A. Knopf.

Maathai, Wangari. 2010. *Replenishing the Earth: Spiritual Values for Healing Ourselves and the World*. New York, NY: Doubleday.

MacDonald, Mia. 2006. "Wangari Maathai: Mother of the Trees." In *Visionaries: The 20th Century's 100 Most Important Inspirational Leaders*. Satish Kumar and Freddie Whitefield (eds.). White River Junction, VT: Chelsea Green Publishing, pp. 86–87.

Mackenzie, Vicki. 1998. *Cave in the Snow: A Western Woman's Quest for Enlightenment*. New York, NY: Bloomsbury Publishing.

Macy, Joanna. 1983. *Despair and Personal Power in the Nuclear Age*. Gabriola Island, British Columbia, Canada: New Society Publishers.

Macy, Joanna. 1988. "Taking Heart: Spiritual Exercises for Social Activists." In *The Path of Compassion: Writings on Socially Engaged Buddhism*. Fred Eppsteiner (ed.). Berkeley, CA: Parallax Press, pp. 203–213.

Macy, Joanna. 1991a. *Mutual Causality in Buddhism and General Systems Theory: The Dharma of Natural Systems*. Albany, NY: State University of New York Press.

Macy, Joanna. 1991b. *World As Lover, World As Self*. Berkeley, CA: Parallax Press.

Macy, Joanna. 2006. *Joanna Macy: The Work That Reconnects*. Gabriola Island, British Columbia, Canada: New Society Publishers (DVD, 4 hours 21 minutes). http://www.newsociety.com.

Macy, Joanna. 2007. *Widening Circles: A Memoir*. Gabriola Island, British Columbia, Canada: New Catalyst Books.

Macy, Joanna. 2010 (September 16). *A Wild Love for the World* [interview by Krista Tippett]. Minneapolis, MN: Minnesota Public Radio/American Public Media. http://being.publicradio.org/programs/2010/wild-love-for-world/.

Macy, Joanna. 2011. Joanna Macy. http://www.joannamacy.net.

Macy, Joanna, and Chris Johnstone. 2012. *Active Hope: How to Face the Mess We're in without Going Crazy Novato*, CA: New World Library.

Macy, Joanna, and Molly Young Brown. 1998. *Coming Back to Life: Practices to Reconnect Our Lives, Our World*. Gabriola Island, British Columbia, Canada: New Society Publishers.

Mahoney, Kevin Patrick. 2010. *The Ultimate Fan's Guide to Avatar: James Cameron's Epic Movie*. London, UK: Punked Books.

Makrides, Vasilios N. 2005. "Christianity—Eastern versus Western." In *The Encyclopedia of Religion and Nature*. Bron R. Taylor (Editor-in-Chief). New York, NY: Thoemmes Continuum, 1, pp. 314–316.

Malkin, John. 2007. "Revolution!" [Interview with Joanna Macy]. Montreal, Quebec, Canada: Ascent Magazine. http://www.ascentmagazine.com/articles.aspx?articleID=283&issueID=38.

Malone, Patrick. 2002. *A Celebration of Creation: The Blessings of the Animals at New York's The Cathedral of Saint John the Divine*. Mississauga, Ontario, Canada: South Bay Productions Ltd. (DVD, 59 minutes).

Mander, Jerry. 1991. *In the Absence of the Sacred: The Failure of Technology and the Survival of the Indian Nations*. San Francisco, CA: Sierra Club Books.

Mann, Charles C. 2002 (March). "1491." *The Atlantic Monthly* 289(3):41–53.

Mann, Charles C. 2005. *1491: New Revelations of the Americas Before Columbus*. New York, NY: Knopf.

Marchand, Peter J. 2000. "Holey Waters." *Natural History* 109(7)12–13.

Margulies, Hune. 2008. The Martin Buber Institute for Dialogical Ecology. http://www.martinbuberinstitute.org/.

Markham, Ian S. 2010. *Against Atheism: Why Dawkins, Hitchens, and Harris Are Fundamentally Wrong*. Malden, MA: Wiley-Blackwell.

Marsh, G. P., 1864/1965. *Man and Nature*. David Lowenthal (ed.). Cambridge: The Harvard University Press/Belknap Press.

Marten, Gerald G. 2003. *Human Ecology: Basic Concepts for Sustainable Development*. Sterling, VA: Earthscan Publications, Ltd. http://gerryma rten.com/human-ecology/tableofcontents.html.

Marten, Gerald G. 2011. *Ecotipping Points*. http://www.ecotippingpoints.org.

Martin Buber Institute. 2011. http://www.martinbuberinstitute.org/.

Martin, Calvin. 1978. *Keepers of the Game: Indian-Animal Relationships and the Fur Trade*. Berkeley, CA: University of California Press.

Martin, Julia (ed.). 1997. *Ecological Responsibility: A Dialogue with Buddhism*. Delhi, India: Tibet House.

Matthews, Charles, et al. 2009 (March). "Roundtable: *The Encyclopedia of Religion and Nature*." *Journal of the American Acadmy of Religion* 77(1): 55–119.

Matthews, Clifford N., Mary Evelyn Tucker, and Philip Hefner (eds.). 2002. *When Worlds Converge: What Science and Religion Tell Us about the Story of the Universe and Our Place in It*. LaSalle, IL: Open Court Publishing Company.

Matthiessen, Peter. 1984. *Indian Country*. New York, NY: Penguin Books USA Inc.

Maudlin, Michael G., et al. (eds.). 2008. *The Green Bible*. New York, NY : HarperCollins Publishers.

Mazur, Laura, and Louella Miles. 2009. "Professor Wangari Maathai." In *Conversations with Green Gurus: The Collective Wisdom of Environmental Movers and Shakers*. Chichester, West Sussex, UK: John Wiley & Sons, Ltd., pp. 209–224.

Mburu, Gathuru. 2005. "Kenya Green Belt Movement." In *The Encyclopedia of Religion and Nature*. Bron R. Taylor (Editor-in-Chief). New York, NY: Thoemmes Continuum, 2, pp. 957–961.

McDonald, Levy S. 2006. *The Merging of Theology and Spirituality: An Examination of the Life and Work of Alister E. McGrath*. Lanham, MD: University Press of America.

McFadden, Steven. 1991. *Profiles in Wisdom: Native Elders Speak About the Earth*. Santa Fe, NM: Bear & Co.

McFague, Sallie. 2008. *A New Climate for Theology: God, the World, and Global Warming*. Minneapolis, MN: Fortress Press.

McGee, R. John. 1990. *Life, Ritual and Religion among the Lacandon Maya*. Belmont, CA: Wadsworth.

McGrath, Alister E. 1998. *Science and Religion: An Introduction*. Oxford, UK: Wiley-Blackwell.

McGrath, Alister E. 2001. *Scientific Theology: Nature*. Edinburgh, Scotland: T. & T. Clark.

McGrath, Alister E. 2002a. *The Reenchantment of Nature: The Denial of Religion and the Ecological Crisis*. New York, NY: Doubleday/Galilee.

McGrath, Alister E. 2002b. *Scientific Theology: Reality*, Edinburgh. Scotland: T. & T. Clark.

McGrath, Alister E. 2003. *Scientific Theology: Theory*. Edinburgh, Scotland: T. & T. Clark.

McGrath, Alister E. 2004a. *Dawkins' God: Genes, Memes, and the Meaning of Life*. Oxford, UK: Wiley-Blackwell.

McGrath, Alister E. 2004b. *The Science of God: An Introduction to Scientific Theology*. London, UK: Continuum.

McGrath, Alister E. 2006a. *Thomas F. Torrance: An Intellectual Biography*. Edinburgh, Scotland: T. and T. Clark Publishers.

McGrath, Alister E. 2006b. *The Twilight of Atheism: The Rise and Fall of Disbelief in the Modern World*. New York, NY: Doubleday.

McGrath, Alister E. 2006c. "Darwinism." In *The Oxford Handbook of Religion and Science*. Philip Clayton and Zachary Simpson (eds.). New York, NY: Oxford University Press, pp. 681–696.

McGrath, Alister E. 2008. *The Open Secret: Renewing the Vision of Natural Theology*. Oxford, UK: Wiley-Blackwell.

McGrath, Alister E. 2009. *A Fine-Tuned Universe: The Quest for God in Science and Theology*. Louisville, KY: Westminister John Knox Press.

McGrath, Alister E. 2011. Homepage. http://users.ox.ac.uk/~mcgrath.

McGrath, Alister E., and Joanna Collicutt McGrath. 2007. *The Dawkins Delusion? Atheist Fundamentalism and the Denial of the Divine*. London, UK: SPCK.

McKay, Alex. 2006. "Kailas: The Making of a Sacred Mountain." *The Middle Way* 81(2):91–103.

McKibben, Bill. 2006. *The End of Nature*. New York, NY: Random House.

McKibben, Bill (ed.). 2008. *American Earth: Environmental Writings Since Thoreau*. New York, NY: Library of America. http://www.americanearth .org.

McKibben, Bill. 2010. *Eaarth: Making a Life on a Tough New Planet*. New York, NY: Henry Holt and Company.

McLeod, Christopher. 2002. *In Light of Reverence*. Oley, PA: Bullfrog Films (DVD 77 minutes). http://www.sacredland.org.

McLeod, Christopher. 2011. *Sacred Land Film Project*. www.sacredland.org.

McLeod, Christopher. 2012. *Standing on Sacred Ground*. Berkeley, CA: Earth Island Institute/Sacred Land Film Project (DVD, Parts 1–4). http://www .sacredland.org.

McClosky, J.M., and H. Spalding. 1989. "A Reconnaissance-level Inventory of the Amount of Wilderness Remaining in the World." *Ambio* 18:221–227.

McNeely, Jeffrey A.(ed.). 1995. *Expanding Partnerships in Conservation.* Washington, D.C.: Island Press.

McNeley, James K. 1997. *Holy Wind in Navajo Philosophy.* Tucson, AZ: University of Arizona Press.

McPherson, Robert S. 1992. *Sacred Land, Sacred View: Navajo Perception of the Four Corners Region.* Salt Lake City, UT: Bringham Young University Press.

Meadows, D., D. Meadows, and J. Randers. 1993. *Beyond the Limits: Confronting Global Collapse, Envisioning a Sustainable Future.* Post Mills, VT: Chelsea Green.

Meine, Curt. 1987. Aldo Leopold: His Life and Work. Madison, WI: University of Wisconsin Press.

Meissonnier, Martin. 2003. *Life of the Buddha: The True Story of The Man Who Changed The World.* Chicago, IL: Facets Multi-Media (DVD, 90 minutes).

Merchant, Carolyn. 2005. *Radical Ecology: The Search for a Sustainable World* (2nd Edition). New York, NY: Routledge.

Merkel, Jim. 2003. *Radical Simplicity: Small Footprints on a Finite Earth.* Gabriola Island, British Columbia, Canada: New Society Publishers.

Merkel, Jim. 2011. *Global Living Project.* http://radicalsimplicity.org.

Merkel, Jim, and Jan Cannon. 2005. *Radically Simple.* Oley, PA: Bullfrog Films (DVD, 35 minutes).

Merton, Lisa, and Alan Dater. 2008. *Taking Root: The Vision of Wangari Maathi.* Marlboro, VT: Marlboro Productions (DVD, 80 minutes). http://takingrootfilm.com/.

Merwin Conservancy. 2011. *A Walk through the Palms with W. S. Merwin.* Haiuku, Maui, HI: Merwin Conservancy http://www.merwinconservancy.org/.

Merwin, W. S. 1971 (June 3). "On Being Awarded the Pulitzer Prize." *The New York Review of Books.* http://www.nybooks.com/articles/archives/1971/jun/03/on-being-awarded-the-pulitzer-prize/.

Merwin, W. S. 1988. *The Rain in the Trees,* New York, NY: Alfred A. Knopf.

Merwin, W. S. 1991. *W. S.Merwin: The Rain in the Trees.* New York, NY:Atlas Video, Inc. (VHS, 30 minutes).

Merwin, W. S. 2011 (Winter). "The House and the Garden: The Emergence of a Dream." *The Kenyon Review* IV(1):10–24. http://www.merwinconservancy.org/about-the-conservancy/writing-about-the-land/.

Messer, Ellen, and Michael Lambek (eds.). 2001. *Ecology and the Sacred: Engaging the Anthropology of Roy A. Rappaport.* Ann Arbor, MI: University of Michigan Press.

Metanexus Institute, 2011. http://www.metanexus.net/.

Metzner, Ralph. 1999. *Green Psychology: Transforming Our Relationship to the Earth*. Rochester, VT: Park Street Press.

Meyer, John M. 1997. "Gifford Pinchot, John Muir, and the Boundaries of Politics in American Thought." *Polity* 30(2):267–284.

Miller, Char. 2001. *Gifford Pinchot and the Making of Modern Environmentalism*. Washington, D.C.: Island Press.

Miller, R. 2005. *John Muir: Magnificent Tramp*. New York, NY: Tom Doherty Associates.

Miller, Sally M. (ed.). 1995. *John Muir: Life and Work*. Albuquerque, NM: University of New Mexico Press.

Miller, Sally R. (ed.). 1999. *John Muir in Historical Perspective*. New York, NY: Peter Land Publishing Inc.

Miller, Timothy. 2005. "Rainbow Family." In *The Encyclopedia of Religion and Nature*. Bron R. Taylor. (Editor-in-Chief). New York, NY: Thoemmes Continuum, 2, pp. 1335–1336.

Milton, John P. 2006. *Sky Above, Earth Below: Spiritual Practice in Nature*. Boulder, CO: Sentient Publications, LLC.

Milton, Kay. 2002. *Loving Nature: Towards an Ecology of Emotion*. New York, NY: Routledge.

Mind and Life Institute. 2011. http://www.mindandlife.org.

Mitchell, Donald W., and William Skudlarek (eds.). 2010. *Green Monasticism: A Buddhist-Catholic Response to an Environmental Calamity*. Brooklyn, NY: Lantern Books. http://www.urbandharma.org/G3/index.html.

Mizzoni, John. 2008 (Spring). "Franciscan Biocentrism and the Franciscan Tradition." *Environment & Ethics* 13(1):121–134.

Monaghan, Patricia. 2005. "Gaia." In *The Encyclopedia of Religion and Nature*. Bron R. Tayor (Editor-in-Chief). New York, NY: Thoemmes Continuum, 1, pp. 679–680.

Monserud, Bruce. 2002. "Religion and Ecology: Visions for an Emerging Academic Field Consultation Report." *Worldviews: Environment, Culture, Religion* 6(1): 81–93.

Montejo, Victor D. 2001. "The Road to Heaven: Jakaltek Maya Beliefs, Religion, and Ecology." In *Indigenous Traditions and Ecology: The Interbeing of Cosmology and Community*. John A. Grim (ed.). Cambridge: Harvard University Press, pp. 175–195.

Montgomery, Pam. 1997. *Partner Earth: A Spiritual Ecology*. Rochester, VT: Destiny Books.

Moody, Roger. 2007. *Rocks and Hard Places: The Globalization of Mining*. London, UK: Zed Books.

Moon, Warren. 2011. Wilderness Awareness School. Duvall, WA. http://www
.wildernessawareness.org/index.html.

Moore, Kathleen Dean. 2010. *Wild Comfort: The Solace of Nature*. Boston, MA:
Shambhala Publications, Inc./Trumpeter Books.

Moore, Kathleen Dean, and Michael P. Nelson (eds.). 2010. *Moral Ground:
Ethical Action for a Planet in Peril*. San Antonio, TX: Trinity University
Press.

Morrell, Rima A. 2005. *The Sacred Power of Huna: Spirituality and Shamanism in
Hawai'i*. Rochester, VT: Inner Traditions.

Morris, Brian. 2000. *Animals and Ancestors: An Ethnography*. New York, NY:
Berg.

Morrison, Reg. 1999. *The Spirit in the Gene. Humanity's Proud Illusion and the
Laws of Nature*. Ithaca, NY: Cornell University Press.

Motovalli, Jim. 2002 (October 31). "Steward of the Earth: The Growing
Religious Mission to Protect the Environment." *Environmental Magazine*
16(6):2–16. http://www.emagazine.com/archive/924.

Moyers, Bill. 1991. *Spirit & Nature*. New York, NY: Mystic Fire Video (VHS
88 minutes).

Moyers, Bill. 2006. "Bill Moyers On America: Is God Green?" Arlington, VA:
Public Broadcasting Service. http://www.pbs.org/moyers/moyersonamerica/
green/index.html.

Moyers, Bill. 2009 (June 26). "W. S. Merwin." Arlington, VA: Public
Broadcasting Service Bill Moyers Journal. http://www.pbs.org/moyers/
journal/06262009/watch.html.

Mueller, Roger C. 1977 (Winter). "A Significant Buddhist Translation by
Thoreau." *The Thoreau Society Bulletin* 1–2.

Muir Woods National Monument. 2011. http://www.nps.gov/muwo/.

Muir, John. 1896 (January). "The National Parks and Forest Reservations." *Sierra
Club Bulletin* 1(7):271–284.

Muir, John. 2011. Online text versions of works. San Francisco, CA: Sierra Club.
http://www.sierraclub.org/john%5Fmuir%5Fexhibit/.

Muir, John. 1997 [1916]. "Cedar Keys." In *Muir: Nature Writings*. William
Cronon (ed.). New York, NY: The Library of America, pp. 818–827.

Mukonyora, Isabel. 2005. "Masowe Wilderness Apostles." In *The Encyclopedia of
Religion and Nature*. Bron R. Taylor (Editor-in-Chief). New York, NY:
Thoemmes Continuum, 2, pp. 1054–1056.

Murtagh, Thomas. 2002. "St. Francis and Ecology." In *Franciscan Theology of the
Environment: An Introductory Reader*. Dawn M. Nothwehr (ed.). Quincy,
IL: Quincy University Franciscan Press, pp. 143–154.

Myerhoff, Barbara G. 1974. *Peyote Hunt: The Sacred Journey of the Huichol Indians.* Ithaca, NY: Cornell University Press.

Myerson, Joel (ed.). 1984. *Transcendentalism: A Reader.* Oxford, UK: Oxford University Press.

Nabhan, Gary Paul. 1995. "Cultural Parallax in Viewing North American Habitats." In *Reinventing Nature? Responses to Postmodern Deconstruction.* Michael Soule and Gary Lease (eds.). Washington, D.C.: Island Press, pp. 87–101.

Na'vi Movement. 2010. http://navimovement.com.

Nabokov, Peter. 2006. *Where the Lightening Strikes: The Lives of American Indian Sacred Places.* New York, NY: Penguin Group (USA) Inc.

Nadasdy, Paul. 2005. "Transcending the Debate over the Ecologically Noble Indian: Indigenous Peoples and Environmentalism." *Ethnohistory* 52 (2):291–331.

Nadkarni, Nalini M. 2008. *Between Earth and Sky: Our Intimate Connections to Trees.* Berkeley, CA: University of California Press.

Naess, Arne. 1989. *Ecology, Community and Lifestyle.* Cambridge, UK: Cambridge University Press (David Rothenberg, translator and editor).

Naess, Arne. 2002. *Life's Philosophy: Reason and Feeling in a Deeper World.* Athens, GA: University of Georgia Press.

Namgyal Rinpoche, Venerable Lungrig. 1986. "Buddhist Declaration of Nature." In *The Assisi Declarations: Messages on Man and Nature from Buddhism, Christianity, Hinduism, Islam and Judaism.* Assisi, Italy: Basilica di S. Francesco, World Wildlife Fund 25th Anniversary Interfaith Meeting (September 29, 1986), pp. 3–7.

Narby, Jeremy, and Francis Huxley (eds.). 2001. *Shamans through Time: 500 Years on the Path to Knowledge.* New York, NY: Jeremy P. Tarcher/Putnam.

Nash, James A. 1991. *Loving Nature: Ecological Integrity and Christian Responsibility.* Nashville, TN: Abingdon Press.

Nash, Roderick Frazier, 1989. *The Rights of Nature: A History of Environmental Ethics.* Madison, WI: University of Wisconsin Press.

Nash, Roderick Frazier. 2001. *Wilderness and the American Mind.* Roderick Frazier Nash. New Haven, CT: Yale University Press (4th Edition).

Nasr, Seyyed Hossein. 1992. "Islam and the Environmental Crisis." In *Spirit and Nature: Why the Environment Is a Religious Issue: An Interfaith Dialogue.* Steven C. Rockefeller and John C. Elder. (eds.). Boston, MA: Beacon Press, pp. 83–108.

Nasr, Seyyed Hossein. 1993. *The Need for a Sacred Science.* Albany, NY: State University of New York Press.

Nasr, Seyyed Hossein. 1996. *Religion and the Order of Nature*. New York, NY: Oxford University Press.

Nasr, Seyyed Hossein. 1997. *Man and Nature: The Spiritual Crisis of Modern Man*. Chicago, IL: ABC International Group, Inc.

National Park Service. 2011. http://www.nps.gov/muwo/.

National Religious Partnership for the Environment. 2011. http://www.nrpe.org.

Naviblue.com. 2010. http://www.naviblue.com.

Nelson, Richard K. 1982. "A Conservation Ethic and Environment: The Koyukon of Alaska." In *Resource Managers: North American and Australian Hunter-Gatherers*. Nancy M. Williams and Eugene S. Hunn (eds.). Boulder, CO: Westview Press, pp. 211–228.

Nelson, Richard K. 1983. *Make Prayers to the Raven: A Koyukon View of the Northern Forest*. Chicago, IL: University of Illinois Press.

Network of Concerned Anthropologists. 2009. *The Counterinsurgency Manual: Or, Notes on Demilitarizing American Society*. Chicago, IL: Prickly Paradigm Press.

Nhat Hanh, Thich. 2004. *Touching the Earth: Intimate Conversations with the Buddha*. Berkeley, CA: Parallax Press.

Nhat Hanh, Thich. 2008. *The World We Have: A Buddhist Approach to Peace and Ecology*. Berkeley, CA: Parallax Press.

Nicholson, Shirely, and Brenda Rosen. 1992. *Gaia's Hidden Life: The Unseen Intelligence of Nature*. Wheaton, IL: Quest Books.

Nollman, Jim. 1990. *Spiritual Ecology: A Guide to Reconnecting with Nature*. New York, NY: Bantam Books.

Norberg-Hodge, Helena. 2001. "Tibetan Culture as a Model of Ecological Sustainability." In *Imagining Tibet: Perceptions, Projections, and Fantasies*. Thierry Dodin and Heinz Rather (eds.). Boston, MA: Wisdom Publications, pp. 331–338.

Northcott, Michael S. 2007. *A Moral Climate: The Ethics of Global Warming*. Maryknoll, NY: Orbis Books.

Nothwehr, Dawn M. (ed.). 2002. *Franciscan Theology of the Environment: An Introductory Reader*. Quincy, IL: Quincy University Franciscan Press.

Nyamweru, Celia. 2005. "Sacred Groves of Africa." In *The Encyclopedia of Religion and Nature*. Bron R. Taylor (Editor-in-Chief). New York, NY: Thoemmes Continuum, 2, pp. 1451–1456.

Oelschlaeger, Max. 1991. *The Idea of Wilderness: From Prehistory to the Age of Ecology*. New Haven, CT: Yale University Press.

Oliver, Paul. 2009. *Mysticism: A Guide for the Perplexed*. New York, NY: Continuum International Publishing Group.

Olupona, Jacob K. (ed.). 2004. *Beyond Primitivism: Indigenous Religious Traditions and Modernity*. New York, NY: Routledge.

Ono, Sokyo. 1962. *Shinto: The Kami Way*. Rutland, VT: Tuttle Publishing.

Ostrow, Marty, and Terry Kay Rockefeller. 2007. *Renewal: Stories from America's Religious-Environmental Movement*. Takoma Park, WA: Fine Cut Productions, LLC (DVD, 90 minutes). http://www.renewalproject.net.

Pakenham, Thomas. 2004. *The Remarkable Baobab*. London, UK: Weidenfeld & Nicolson.

Palmer, Joy A. (ed.) 2001. *Fifty Key Thinkers on the Environment*. New York, NY: Routledge.

Palmer, Martin. 1996. *Travels Through Sacred China*. San Francisco, CA: HarperCollins Publishers/Thorsons.

Palmer, Martin, and Esther Bisset. 1985. *Worlds of Differences*. Walton-on-Thames, Surrey: Thomas Nelson and Sons, Ltd.

Palmer, Martin, and Victoria Finlay. 2003. *Faith in Conservation: New Approaches to Religions and Environment*. Washington, D.C.: World Bank Publications.

Palmer, Martin, and Nigel Palmer. 1997. *Sacred Britain: A Guide to the Sacred Sites and Pilgrim Routes of England, Scotland, and Wales*. London, UK: Judy Piatkus (Publishers) Ltd.

Pandian, Jacob. 1985. "The Mythology of the Savage Other in the Western Traditions," in his *Anthropology and the Western Tradition: Toward an Authentic Anthropology*. Prospect Heights, IL: Waveland Press, Inc., pp. 62–69.

Panorama International Productions. 1990. *John Muir: The Man, The Poet, The Legacy*. Beverly Hills, CA: Panorama International Productions (VHS 60 minutes).

Parachin, Janet W. 1999. "Joanna Macy: At One with the Natural World." In *Engaged Spirituality: Ten Lives of Contemplation and Action*. St. Louis, MO: Chalice Press, pp. 113–128.

Parker, Eugene. 1992. "Forest Islands and Kayapo Resource Management in Amazonia: A Reappraisal of the Apete." *American Anthropologist* 94: 406–428.

Parker, Eugene. 1993. "Fact and Fiction in Amazonia: The Case of Apete." *American Anthropologist* 95:715–723.

Paterson, Jacqueline Memory. 1996. *Tree Wisdom*. London, UK: HarperCollinsPublishers Limited.

Pauling, Chris. 1990 (February–April). "A Buddhist Life Is a Green Life." *Golden Drum: A Magazine for Western Buddhists*, pp. 5–7.

Payne, Richard K. (ed.). 2010. How *Much Is Enough? Buddhism, Consumerism, and the Human Environment.* Somerville, MA: Wisdom Publications.

Payne, Richard K. "Buddhism and the Environment." New York, NY: Oxford University Press/Oxford Bibliographies Online. http://www.oup.com.

Peacocke, Arthur. 2007. *All That Is: A Naturalistic Faith for the Twenty-First Century.* Minneapolis, MN: Fortress Press.

Pearson, Joanne (ed.). 1998. *Nature Religion Today: Paganism in the Modern World.* Edinburgh, UK: Edinburgh University Press.

Pedersen, Kusumita P. 1998. "Environmental Ethics in Interreligious Perspective," In *Global Ethics: Comparative Religious Ethics and Interreligious Dialogue.* Sumner B. Twiss and Bruce Grelle (eds.). Boulder, CO: Westview Press, pp. 253–290.

Pei, Shengji, 1993, "Managing for Biodiversity Conservation in Temple Yards and Holy Hills: The Traditional Practices of the Xishuangbanna Dai Community, Southwest China." In *Ethics, Religion and Biodiversity: Relations between Conservation and Cultural Values.* Lawrence S. Hamilton (ed.). Cambridge, UK: The White Horse Press. pp. 118–132.

Pennybacker, Mindy. 2000 (February 7). "The First Environmentalists." *The Nation* 270(5):29–31.

Pepper, David. 1996. *Modern Environmentalism: An Introduction.* New York, NY: Routledge.

Perkins, John, and Shakaim Mariano Shakai Ijisam Chumpi. 2001. *Spirit of the Shuar: Wisdom from the Last Unconquered People of the Amazon.* Rochester, VT: Destiny Books.

Perlman, Michael. 1994. *The Power of Trees: The Reforesting of the Soul.* Dallas. TX: Spring Publications.

Peters, Karl E. 2002. *Dancing with the Sacred: Evolution, Ecology, and God.* Harrisburg, PA: Trinity Press International.

Petri, Hans, and Ferene van Damme. 2003. *Hildegard von Bingen In Portrait.* West Long Beach, NJ: Kultur (DVD, 239 minutes).

Petrovic, John J. 2008. *The First Principles: A Scientist's Guide to the Spiritual.* Los Alamos, NM: John Joseph Petrovic.

Philpot, J.H. 2004. *The Sacred Tree in Religion and Myth.* Mineola, NY: Dover Publications, Inc. (Original edition 1897).

Pick, Philip L. 1992. "Tu Bi Shevat: A Happy New Year to All Trees!" In *Judaism and Ecology.* Aubrey Rose (ed.). London, UK: Cassell Publishers Limited, pp. 67–73.

Pistono, Matteo. 2011. *In the Shadow of the Buddha: Secret Journeys, Sacred Histories, and Spiritual Discovery in Tibet.* New York, NY: Penguin Group (USA) Inc./Dutton.

Pitesa, Nicole. 2009. *James Cameron's Avatar: The Na'vi Quest*. New York, NY: HarperFestival.

Plotkin, Bill. 2008. *Nature and the Human Soul: Cultivating Wholeness and Community in a Fragmented World*. Novato, CA: New World Library. http://www.natureandthehumansoul.com.

Plum Village. 2011. http://www.plumvillage.org/.

Poetry Foundation. 2011. http://www.poetryfoundation.org.

Poets Against the War. 2011. *Poets against the War*. http://www.poetsagainstwar .ca/ http://www.poetsagainstthewar.org/.

Posey, Darrell A. 1982. "Keepers of the Forest." *Garden* 6:18–24.

Posey, Darrell A. 1985. "Indigenous Management of Tropical Forest Ecosystems: The Case of the Kayapo Indians of the Brazilian Amazon." *Agroforestry Systems* 3:139–158.

Posey, Darrell A. 1989. "Alternatives to Forest Destruction: Lessons from the Mebengokre Indians." *Ecologist* 19(6):241–244.

Posey, Darrell A. 1992. "Reply to Parker." *American Anthropologist* 94:406–428.

Posey, Darrell A., et al. (eds.). 1999. *Cultural and Spiritual Values of Biodiversity*. London, UK: Intermediate Technology Publications/United Nations Environmental Programme (UNEP).

Posey, Darrell A., and W. Balee (eds.). 1989. "Resource Management in Amazonia: Indigenous and Folk Strategies." Advances in Economic Botany Volume 7.

Powers, John. 2007. *Introduction to Tibetan Buddhism*. Ithaca, NY: Snow Lion Publications (Revised Edition).

Preston, Christopher J., 2009. *Saving Creation: Nature and Faith in the Life of Holmes Rolston III*. San Antonio, TX: Trinity University Press.

Price, David H. 2011. *Weaponizing Anthropology: Social Science in Service of the Militarized State*. Petrolia, CA: CounterPunch and Oakland, CA: Ak Press.

Prince, Ranchor. 1992. *Hinduism and Ecology*. London, UK: Cassell.

Protect Kaho'olawe 'Ohana. 2011, http://www.kahoolawe.org.

Queen, Christopher S. (ed.). 2000. *Engaged Buddhism in the West*. Boston, MA: Wisdom Publications.

Queen, Christopher S., and Sallie B. King (eds.). 1996. *Engaged Buddhism: Buddhist Liberation Movements in Asia*. Albany, NY: State University of New York Press.

Rajotte, Freda. 1998. *First Nations Faith and Ecology*. London, UK: Cassell.

Ramakrishnan, P. S., K. G. Saxena, and U. M. Chandrashekara (eds.). 1998. *Conserving the Sacred for Biodiversity Management*. Enfield, NH: Science Publishers, Inc.

Rambo, A. Terry. 1985. *Primitive Polluters: Semang Impact on the Malaysian Tropical Rain Forest System*. Ann Arbor, MI: University of Michigan Anthropological Papers.

Rampell, Ed. 2010 (November). "W. S. Merwin." *The Progressive* 74(11):35–39.

Ranger, Terence. 2005. "Zimbabwe's Matopo Hills." In *The Encyclopedia of Religion and Nature*. Bron R. Taylor (Editor-in-Chief). New York, NY: Thoemmes Continuum, 2, pp. 1807–1810.

Rappaport, Roy A. 1967. "Ritual Regulation of Environmental Relations among a New Guinea People." *Ethnology* 6:17–30.

Rappaport, Roy A. 1967/1984. *Pigs for the Ancestors: Ritual in the Ecology of a New Guinea People*. New Haven, CT: Yale University Press (2nd Edition).

Rappaport, Roy A. 1979. *Ecology, Meaning, and Religion*. Richmond, CA: North Atlantic Press.

Rappaport, Roy A. 1999. *Ritual and Religion in the Making of Humanity*. New York, NY: Cambridge University Press.

Rather, Dan. 2008. *One Man vs. China*. Dallas, TX: HDNet Dan Rather Reports Episode 234 (DVD, 60 minutes).

Rauner, Michael. 2010. How to Survive the Apocalypse: A Burning Opera. http://www.burningopera.com/home.

Ray, Darrel W. 2009. *The God Virus: How Religion Infects Our Lives and Culture*. Bonner Springs, KS: IPC Press.

Ray, Rick. 2006. *10 Questions for the Dalai Lama: One Man's Journey through the Northern Himalayas*. Thousand Oaks, CA: Monterey Media Inc. (DVD, 85 minutes).

Raymo, Chet. 2008. *When God Is Gone Everything Is Holy: The Making of a Religious Naturalist*. Notre Dame, IN: Sorin Books.

Redford, Kent H. 1990. "The Ecological Noble Savage." *Orion Nature Quarterly* 9(3):25–29.

Redford, Kent H. 1992. "The Empty Forest." *BioScience* 42(6):412–22.

Redford, Kent H., K. H., and Allyn M. Stearman. 1993. "Forest-dwelling Native Amazonians and the Conservation of Biodiversity: Interests in Common or in Collision?" *Conservation Biology* 7(2):248–255.

Redman, Charles L. 1999. *Human Impact on Ancient Environments*. Tucson, AZ: University of Arizona Press.

Rees, William E. and Mathis Wackernagel. 1998. *Our Ecological Footprint: Reducing Human Impact on the Earth*. Gabriola Island, British Columbia, Canada: New Society Publishers.

Reichel-Dolmatoff, Gerardo. 1971. *Amazonian Cosmos: The Sexual and Religious Symbolism of the Tukano Indians*. Chicago: University of Chicago Press.

Reichel-Dolmatoff, Gerardo. 1976. "Cosmology as Ecological Analysis: A View from the Rainforest." *Man* 11(3):307–318.

Reichel-Dolmatoff, Gerardo. 1990. *Sacred Mountain of Colombia's Kogi Indians.* New York, NY: E. J. Brill.

Reichel-Dolmatoff, Gerardo. 1999. "A View from the Headwaters." *The Ecologist* 29(4):276–280.

Religion and Ethics News Weekly, 2011. Public Broadcasting Service (PBS). http://www.pbs.org/wnet/religionandethics/.

Religion, Science and Environment Symposia. 2011. http://www.rsesymposia .org/.

Restore Hetch Hetchy. 2009. http://www.hetchhetchy.org.

Resurgence. 2010. "Avatar: Sowing the Seeds of Respect for a Truly Global Community." Resurgence ebook. http://www.resurgence.org/education/ resources.html.

Reynolds, Frank E. and Jason A. Carbine (eds.). 2000,. *The Life of Buddhism.* Berkeley, CA: University of California Press.

Riedelsheimer, Thomas. 2004. *Andy Goldsworthy Rivers and Tides Working with Time.* New York, NY: Mediopolis, Art and Design/New Video (DVD, 90 minutes).

Rifkin, Ira. 2008. *Spiritual Leaders Who Changed the World.* Woodstock, VT: Skylight Paths Publishing.

Rival, Laura (ed.). 1998. *The Social Life of Trees: Anthropological Perspectives on Tree Symbolism.* New York, NY: Berg.

Roads, Michael J. 1987. *Talking with Nature.* Tiburon, CA: H. J. Kramer, Inc.

Roberts, Elizabeth, and Elias Amidon (eds.). 1991. *Earth Prayers from Around the World.* New York, NY: HarperCollins Publishers, Inc.

Robinson, Kim Stanley (ed.). 1994. *Future Primitive: The New Ecotopias.* New York, NY: Tom Doherty Associates, Inc.

Robson, Michael J. P. 2011. *The Cambridge Companion to Francis of Assisi.* New York, NY: Cambridge University Press.

Rockefeller, Steven C. 1996. "Religion." In *Greening the College Curriculum: A Guide to Environmental Teaching in the Liberal Arts.* Jonathan Collett and Stephen Karakashian (eds.). Washington, D.C.: Island Press, pp. 268–308.

Rockefeller, Steven C., and John C. Elder, eds. 1992. *Spirit and Nature: Why the Environment Is a Religious Issue.* Boston, MA: Beacon Press. [Available at Google books].

Rockefeller, Steven C., and John C. Elder. 1991 (Winter). "Spirit and Nature: Visions of Interdependence." *Orion Nature Quarterly* 10(1):42–48.

Rose, Aubrey (ed.). 1992. *Judaism and Ecology: Created World and Revealed World.* London, UK: Cassell Publishers Limited.

Rose, Deborah B. 1992. *Dingo Makes Us Human: Life and Land in an Australian Aboriginal Culture.* New York, NY: Cambridge University Press.

Rossellini, Roberto. 2003. *The Flowers of St. Francis.* New York, NY: Criterion (DVD, 87 minutes).

Roszak, Theodore. 1978. *Person/Planet: The Creative Disintegration of Industrial Society.* Garden City, NY: Anchor/Doubleday.

Roszak, Theodore. 1992. *The Voice of the Earth: An Exploration of Ecopsychology.* New York, NY: Simon & Schuster/Touchstone Book.

Roszak, Theodore, Mary E. Gomes, and Allen D. Kanner (eds.). 1995. *Ecopsychology: Restoring the Earth Healing the Mind.* San Francisco, CA: Sierra Club Books.

Roszak, T. S. Conn, and C. Anthony. 1995. *Ecopsychology: Restoring the Earth, Healing the Self.* Palo Alto: Foundation for Global Community (VHS, 26 minutes). http://www.globalcommunity.org.

Rothenberg, David. 1996 (Winter). "Will the Real Chief Seattle Please Speak Up: An Interview with Ted Perry." *Terra Nova* 1(1):68–82.

Rousseau, Jean-Jacques. 1762/1979. "Profession of Faith of the Savoyard Vicar." In *Emile or On Education.* New York, NY: Basic Books.

Rousseau, Jean-Jacques. 1782/1979. *Reveries of the Solitary Walker.* New York, NY: Penguin Books.

Rudolf Steiner Archive, 2011. http://www.rsarchive.org.

Rue, Loyal. 2005. *Religion Is Not About God: How Spiritual Traditions Nurture Our Biological Nature And What To Expect When They Fail.* New Brunswick, NJ: Rutgers University Press.

Ruether, Rosemary Radford. 1992. *Gaia and God: An Ecofeminist Theory of Earth Healing.* San Francisco, CA: HarperSanFrancisco.

Russell, Sharman Apt. 2008. *Standing in the Light: My Life as a Pantheist.* New York, NY: Basic Books/Perseus Books.

Ryan, P.D. 1998. *Buddhism and the Natural World.* Birmingham, UK: Windhorse Publications.

Sackman, Douglas Cazaux, 2011. *Wild Men: Ishi and Kroeber in the Wilderness of Modern America.* New York, NY: Oxford University Press.

Sagan, Carl. 2006. *The Varieties of Scientific Experience: A Personal View of the Search for God.* New York, NY: Penguin Books.

Sahni, Pragati. 2008. "Environmental Ethics in the Jatakas." In *Environmental Ethics in Buddhism: A Virtues Approach.* New York, NY Routledge, pp. 144–163.

Saint-Laurent, George E. 2000. *Spirituality and World Religions: An Introduction*. Mountain View, CA: Mayfield Publishing Company.

Sale, Kirkpatrick. 2000 (June). "Again, the Savage Indian." *The Ecologist* 30(4): 52.

Santikaro Bhikkhu. 2000. "Dhamma Walk around Songkhla Lake." In *Dharma Rain: Sources of Buddhist Environmentalism*. Stephanie Kaza and Kenneth Kraft (eds.). Boston, MA: Shambhala Publications, Inc., pp. 206–215.

Santmire, H. Paul. 1970. *Brother Earth. Nature, God and Ecology in Times of Crisis*. New York, NY: Thomas Nelson Inc.

Sapir, Edward. 1924. "Culture, Genuine and Spurious." *American Journal of Sociology* XXIX: 401–429.

Sbicca, Arturo. 2005. *Francis of Assisi*. Beverly Hills, CA: Twentieth Century Fox Film Corporation. (DVD, 105 minutes).

Scharper, Stephen Bede, and Hilary Cunningham. 2002. *The Green Bible*. New York, NY: Lantern Books.

Schefold, Reimar. 1988. "The Mentawai Equilibrium and the Modern World." In *The Real and the Imagined Role of Culture in Development: Case Studies from Indonesia*. Michael R. Dove (ed.). Honolulu, HI: University of Hawai'i Press, pp. 201–215.

Schelgel, Stuart A. 1998. *Wisdom from a Rainforest: The Spiritual Journey of an Anthropologist*. Athens, GA: University of Georgia Press.

Schmithausen, Lambert. 1991a. *The Problem of the Sentience of Plants in Earliest Buddhism*. Tokyo, Japan: The International Institute for Buddhist Studies.

Schmithausen, Lambert. 1991b. *Buddhism and Nature*. Tokyo, Japan: The International Institute for Buddhist Studies.

Schmithausen, Lambert. 1997. "The Early Buddhist Tradition and Ecological Ethics." *Journal of Buddhist Ethics* 4: 1–74.

Schmithausen, Lambert. 2000. "Buddhism and the Ethics of Nature-Some Remarks." *The Eastern Buddhist* 32 (2):26–78.

Schumacher, E. F. 1973. *Small Is Beautiful: Economics as if People Mattered*. New York, NY: Harper & Row, Publishers, Inc.

Schwartzschild, Steven S. 1984. "The Unnatural Jew." *Environmental Ethics* 6(4):347–362.

Science and Religion Forum. 2011. http://www.srforum.org.

Science and Spirit. 2011. http://www.science-spirit.org.

Scorsese, Martin. 1997. *Kundun*. Burbank, CA: Touchstone Pictures (DVD, 135 minutes).

Scott, Rebecca R. 2010. *Removing Mountains: Extracting Nature and Identity in the Appalachian Coalfields*. Minneapolis, MN: University of Minnesota Press.

Scupin, Raymond. 2000. "Aboriginal Religions." In *Religion and Culture: An Anthropological Focus*. Raymond Scupin (ed.). Upper Saddle River, NJ: Prentice Hall, pp. 145–177.

Seamans, Joseph. 1996. *Keeping the Earth: Religious and Scientific Perspectives on the Environment*. Cambridge, MA: Union of Concerned Scientists (VHS, 27 minutes).

Seed, John, Joanna Macy, Pat Flemming, and Arne Naess. 1988/2007. *Thinking Like a Mountain: Toward a Council of All Beings*. Gabriola Island, British Columbia, Canada: New Catalyst Books.

Seeger, Anthony. 1981. *Nature and Society in Central Brazil: The Suya Indians of Mato Grosso*. Cambridge, MA: Harvard University Press.

Selin, Helaine (ed.) 2003. *Nature Across Cultures: Views of Nature and the Environment in Non-Western Cultures*. Boston, MA: Kluwer Academic Publishers.

Senior, John. 2005. "Noble Savage." In *The Encyclopedia of Religion and Nature*. Bron R. Taylor (Editor-in-Chief). New York, NY: Continuum, 2, pp. 1208–1209.

Sessions, George (ed). 1995. *Deep Ecology for the 21st Century*. Boston, MA: Shambhala Publications, Inc.

Severson, Lucky. 2010 (January 15). *Forest Monks*. Arlington, VA: PBS Religion & Ethics News Weekly (8 minutes). http://www.pbs.org/wnet/religionan dethics/episodes/january-15-2010/forest-monks/5472/.

Shakya, Tsering. 1999. *The Dragon in the Land of Snows: A History of Modern Tibet since 1947*. New York, NY: Penguin Group (USA) Inc.

Shalom Center. 2010. http://www.shalomctr.org.

Sheldrake, Rupert. 1994. *The Rebirth of Nature: The Greening of Science and God*. Rochester, VT: Park Street Press.

Shepard, Paul. 1973. *The Tender Carnivore and the Sacred Game*. New York, NY: Scribner.

Shepard, Paul. 1982. *Nature and Madness*. San Francisco, CA: Sierra Club Books.

Sheridan, Michael J., and Celia Nyamweru (eds.). 2008. *African Sacred Groves: Ecological Dynamics and Social Change*. Athens, OH: Ohio University Press.

Shiva, Vandana. 1993. *Monocultures of the Mind: Perspectives on Biodiversity and Biotechnology*. Atlantic Highlands, NJ: Zed Books.

Shore, Dick. 2009. *John Muir Stories*. http://www.youtube.com/watch ?v=uSBAikiFAgM.

Shrader-Frechette, K.S. 1981. *Environmental Ethics*. Pacific Grove, CA: Boxwood Press.

Shyam, Bhajju, Durga Bai, and Ram Singh Urveti. 2010. *The Night Life of Trees*. Chennai, India: Tara Books.

Sideris, Lisa Hatton. 2006. "Religion, Environmentalism, and the Meaning of Ecology." In *The Oxford Handbook of Religion and Ecology*. Roger S. Gottlieb (ed.) New York, NY: Oxford University Press, pp. 446–464.

Sideris, Lisa Hatton. 2010. "I See You: Interspecies Empathy and 'Avatar.'" *Journal for the Study of Religion, Nature and Culture* 4(4):457–477.

Sierra Club. 2011. *John Muir Exhibit*. http://www.sierraclub.org/.

Silverman, David. 2005. *Confessions of a Burning Man: Experience the Journey*. San Francisco, CA: Windline Films, LLC (DVD, 87 minutes). http://www.burningmanconfessions.com.

Sivaraksa, Sulak. 1993 (Winter). "On the Passing of Buddhadassa." *Tricycle*: The Budhdist Review 3(2):82–83.

Sivaraksa, Sulak. 2009. *The Wisdom of Sustainability: Buddhist Economics for the 21st Century*. Kihei, HI: Koa Books.

Sivaraksa, Sulak. 2011. Homepage. http://www.sulak-sivaraksa.org.

Skolimowski, Henryk. 1993. *A Sacred Place to Dwell: Living with Reverence Upon the Earth*. Rockport, MA: Element Books Limited.

Skrimshire, Stefan (ed.). 2010. *Future Ethics: Climate Change and Apocalyptic Imagination*. London, UK: Continuum International Publishing Group.

Slater, Candace. 2002. *Entangled Edens: Visions of the Amazon*. Berkeley: University of California Press.

Smith, Angela M., and Simone Pulver. 2009. "Ethics-Based Environmentalism in Practice: Religious-Environmental Organizations in the United States." *Worldviews: Global Religions, Culture and Ecology* 13(2):145–179.

Smith, Eric Alden, and Mark Wishnie. 2000. "Conservation and Subsistence in Small-Scale Societies." *Annual Review of Anthropology* 29:493–524.

Smith, Huston. 2000. *Why Religion Matters: The Fate of the Human Spirit in an Age of Disbelief*. San Francisco, CA: HarperSanFrancisco.

Smith, Jr., Warren W. 2008. *China's Tibet? Autonomy or Assimilation*. New York, NY: Rowman & Littlefield Publishers, Inc.

Smith, Linda Tuhiwai. 1999. *Decolonizing Methodologies: Research and Indigenous Peoples*. New York, NY: Zed Books.

Smith, Michael B. 1998 (June). "The Value of a Tree: Public Debates of John Muir and Gifford Pinchot." *The Historian* 60(4):757–778.

Smith, Nigel J. H. 1996. *The Enchanted Amazon Rain Forest: Stories from a Vanishing World*. Gainesville: University of Florida Press.

Society for the Anthropology of Consciousness. 2010. http://www.sacaaa.org/.

Society for the Scientific Study of Religion. 2011. http://www.sssrweb.org.

Solecki, Ralph S. 1971. *Shanidar, the First Flower People*. New York, NY: Knopf.

Solecki, Ralph S. 1975. "Shanidar IV, a Neanderthal Flower Burial in Northern Iraq." *Science* 190(4217):880–881.

Solomon, Norman. 1992. "Judaism and the Environment: Created World and Revealed World." In *Judaism and Ecology*. Aubrey Rose (ed.). London, UK: Cassell Publishers Limited, pp. 19–53.

Sorrell, Roger D. 1988. *St. Francis of Assisi and Nature: Tradition and Innovation in Western Christian Attitudes toward the Environment*. New York, NY: Oxford University Press.

Soule, Michael, and Gary Lease. (eds.). 1995. *Reinventing Nature? Responses to Postmodern Deconstruction*. Washington, D.C.: Island Press.

Spence, Mark David. 1999. *Dispossessing the Wilderness: Indian Removal and the Making of National Parks*. New York, NY: Oxford University Press.

Speth, James Gustave. 2008. *The Bridge at the Edge of the World: Capitalism, the Environment, and Crossing from Crisis to Sustainability*. New Haven, CT: Yale University Press.

Splain, Thomas. 2005. "Roman Catholic Religious Orders." In *The Encyclopedia of Religion and Nature*. Bron R. Taylor, Editor-in-Chief. London, UK: Thoemmes Continuum, 2, pp. 1403–1409.

Sponsel, Leslie E. 1986. "Amazon Ecology and Adaptation." *Annual Review of Anthropology* 15:67–97.

Sponsel, Leslie E. 1992a. "Our Fascination with the Tasaday: Anthropological Images and Images of Anthropology." In *The Tasaday Controversy: Assessing the Evidence*. Thomas N. Headland (ed.). Washington, D.C.: American Anthropological Association Special Publication, pp. 200–212.

Sponsel, Leslie E. 1992b. "The Environmental History of Amazonia: Natural and Human Disturbances, and the Ecological Transition." In *Changing Tropical Forests: Historical Perspectives on Today's Challenges in Central and South America*. Harold K. Steen and Richard P. Tucker (eds.). Durham, NC: Forest History Society, pp. 233–251.

Sponsel, Leslie E. 1998. "The Historical Ecology of Thailand: Increasing Thresholds of Human Environmental Impact from Prehistory to the Present." In *Advances in Historical Ecology*, William A. Balee (ed.). New York, NY: Columbia University Press, pp. 376–404.

Sponsel, Leslie E. 2001a. "Do Anthropologists Need Religion, and Vice Versa? Adventures and Dangers in Spiritual Ecology." In *New Directions in Anthropology and Environment: Intersections*. Carole L. Crumley (ed.). Walnut Creek, CA: AltaMira Press, pp. 177–200.

Sponsel, Leslie E. 2001b. "Human Impact on Biodiversity, Overview." In *Encyclopedia of Biodiversity*. Simon Asher Levin (Editor-in-Chief). San Diego, CA: Academic Press, 3, pp. 395–409.

Sponsel, Leslie E. 2001c. "Is Indigenous Spiritual Ecology a New Fad?: Reflections from the Historical and Spiritual Ecology of Hawai'i." In

Indigenous Traditions and Ecology: The Interbeing of Cosmology and Community. John Grim (ed.). Cambridge, MA: Harvard University Center for the Study of World Religions, pp. 159–174.

Sponsel, Leslie E. 2005a. "Animism." In *Encyclopedia of Anthropology*. H. James Birx (ed.). Walnut Creek, CA: AltaMira Press, 1, pp. 80–81.

Sponsel, Leslie E. 2005b. "Trees, Sacred." In *Encyclopedia of Religion and Nature*. Bron R. Taylor, Editor-in-Chief. London, UK: Thoemmes Continuum, 2, pp. 1661–1663.

Sponsel, Leslie E. 2005c. "Noble Savage and the Ecologically Noble Savage." In *The Encyclopedia of Religion and Nature*. Bron R. Taylor (Editor-in-Chief). London & New York: Continuum, 2, pp. 1210–1212.

Sponsel, Leslie E. 2006."Yanomamo." In *Encyclopedia of Anthropology*. H. James Birx (ed.). Thousand Oaks, CA: Sage Publications, 5, pp. 2347–2351.

Sponsel, Leslie E. 2007a."Religion, Nature and Environment." published online in *Encyclopedia of Earth*, Cultler J. Cleveland, et al. (eds.). Washington, D.C.: National Council for Science and the Environment, Environmental Information Coalition. http://www.eoearth.org.

Sponsel, Leslie E. 2007b. "Sacred Places and Biodiversity Conservation." published online in *Encyclopedia of Earth*, Cultler J. Cleveland, et al. (eds.). Washington, D.C.: National Council for Science and the Environment, Environmental Information Coalition. http://www.eoearth.org.

Sponsel, Leslie E. 2007c. "The Spiritual Lives of Great Environmentalists." *Electronic Green Journal* 25:1–9. http://escholarship.org/uc/item/6jq2x4wh?query=sponsel#page-1.

Sponsel, Leslie E. 2007d. "Spiritual Ecology: One Anthropologist's Reflections." *Journal for the Study of Religion, Nature, and Culture* 1(3):340–350.

Sponsel, Leslie E. 2007e. "Human Nature." In *Encyclopedia of Environment and Society*. Paul Robbins (General Editor) Thousand Oaks, CA: Sage Publications, 3, pp. 886–889.

Sponsel, Leslie E. 2008. "Amazon: Environment and Nature." In *Encyclopedia of the History of Science, Technology, and Medicine in Non-Western Cultures*. Helaine Selin (ed.). The Netherlands: Springer (2nd Edition), 1, pp. 557–562.

Sponsel, Leslie E. 2010a. "Religion and Environment: Exploring Spiritual Ecology." In *Religion and Society: Advances in Research*. Simon Coleman and Ramon Sarro (eds.) New York, NY: Berghahn Books, 1, pp. 131–145.

Sponsel, Leslie E. 2010b. "Into the Heart of Darkness: Rethinking the Canonical Ethnography on the Yanomamo," in *Nonkilling Societies*. Joam Evans Pim (ed.). Honolulu: Center for Global Nonkilling, pp. 197–242. http://www.nonkilling.org/pdf/nksocieties.pdf.

Sponsel, Leslie E. 2011a. "The Religion and Environment Interface: Spiritual Ecology in Ecological Anthropology," In *Environmental Anthropology Today*,.Helen Kopnina and Elle Ouimet (eds.). Abingdon, UK: Taylor & Francis Group/Routledge, pp. 37–55.

Sponsel, Leslie E. 2011b. Homepage. http://www.soc.hawaii.edu/Sponsel.

Sponsel, Leslie E., Thomas N. Headland, and Robert C. Bailey (eds.). 1996. *Tropical Deforestation: The Human Dimension*. New York, NY: Columbia University Press.

Sponsel, Leslie E., and Poranee Natadecha-Sponsel. 1997. "A Theoretical Analysis of the Potential Contribution of the Monastic Community in Promoting a Green Society in Thailand." In *Buddhism and Ecology: The Interconnection of Dharma and Deeds*. Mary Evelyn Tucker and Duncan Ryuken Williams (eds.). Cambridge, MA: Harvard University Press, pp. 41–68.

Sponsel, Leslie E., and Poranee Natadecha-Sponsel. 2001."Why a Tree Is More than a Tree: Reflections on the Spiritual Ecology of Sacred Trees in Thailand." In *Santi Pracha Dhamma*. Sulak Sivaraksa, et al.(eds.). Bangkok, Thailand: Santi Pracha Dhamma Institute, pp. 364–373.

Sponsel, Leslie E., and Poranee Natadecha-Sponsel. 2003. "Buddhist Views of Nature and the Environment." In *Nature Across Cultures: Views of Nature and the Environment in Non-Western Cultures*. Helaine Selin (ed.). Boston, MA: Kluwer Academic Publishers, pp. 351–371.

Sponsel, Leslie E., and Poranee Natadecha-Sponsel. 2004. "Illuminating Darkness: The Monk-Cave-Bat-Ecosystem Complex in Thailand." In *This Sacred Earth: Religion, Nature, Environment*. Roger S. Gottlieb (ed.). New York, NY: Routledge, pp. 134–144.

Sponsel, Leslie E., and Poranee Natadecha-Sponsel. 2008. "Buddhism: Environment and Nature." In *Encyclopedia of the History of Science, Technology, and Medicine in Non-Western Cultures*. Helaine Selin (ed.). The Netherlands: Springer (2nd Edition), 1, pp. 768–776.

Sponsel, Leslie E., and Poranee Natadecha-Sponsel. 2010 (July). "Enhancing Awareness: Buddhist Solutions for a Future World." *Patheos*. http://www.patheos.com/Resources/Additional-Resources/Enhancing-Awareness-Buddhist-Solutions-for-a-Future-World?offset=0&max=1.

Sponsel, Leslie E., Poranee Natadecha-Sponsel, Nukul Ruttanadakul, and Somporn Juntadach. 1998. "Sacred and/or Secular Approaches to Biodiversity Conservation in Thailand." *Worldviews: Environment, Culture, Religion* 2(2):155–167.

Spoto, Donald. 2002. *Reluctant Saint: The Life of Francis of Assisi*. New York, NY: Penguin Group (USA) Inc.

Spring Hill College. 2011. Theology Library. Mobile, AL. http://www.shc.edu/theolibrary/environ.htm.

Spring, Cindy, and Anthony Manousos (eds.). 2007. *EarthLight: Spiritual Wisdom for an Ecological Age*. San Francisco, CA: Friends Bulletin. http://www.earthlight.org.

Spring, David, and Eileen Spring (eds.). 1974. *Ecology and Religion in History*. New York, NY: Harper & Row, Publishers.

Stanley, John, David R. Loy, and Gyurme Dorje (eds.). 2009. *A Buddhist Response to the Climate Emergency*. Somerville, MA: Wisdom Publications.

Starke, Linda, and Lisa Mastny (eds.). 2010. *State of the World: Transforming Cultures From Consumerism to Sustainability*. New York, NY: W. W. Norton & Company/Worldwatch Institute.

Starkman, Michael. 2011. "Sacred Grove." *Reclaiming Quarterly* 102:46–51. http://reclaimingquarterly.org/102/RQ102-46-SacredGrove.pdf.

Stearman, Allyn M. 1992. "Commercial Hunting by Subsistence Hunters: Siriono Indians and Paraguayan Caiman in Lowland Bolivia." *Human Organization* 51(3):235–244.

Stearman, Allyn M. 1994. "Only Slaves Climb Trees—Revisiting the Myth of the Ecologically Noble Savage in Amazonia." *Human Nature* 5(4):339–357.

Steiner, Achim. 2007. *Art in Action: Nature, Creativity, and Our Collective Future*. San Francisco, CA: EarthAware Editions.

Steiner, Rudolf. 1999. *Autobiography, Chapters in the Course of My Life, 1861–1917*. Hudson, NY: Anthroposophic Society.

Steiner, Rudolf. 2011. Homepage. http://www.rudolfsteinerweb.com.

Stenger, Victor J. 2007. *God: The Failed Hypothesis: How Science Shows That God Does Not Exist*. Amherst, NY: Prometheus Books.

Stenmark, Mikael. 1997. "What Is Scientism?" *Religious Studies* 33(1):15–23.

Stevens, Stan (ed.). 1997. *Conservation through Cultural Survival: Indigenous Peoples and Protected Areas*. Washington, D.C.: Island Press.

Stewart, Robert B. 2008. *The Future of Atheism: Alister McGraith and Daniel Dennett in Dialogue*. Minneapolis, MN: Fortress Press.

Stoll, Steven. 2007. *U.S. Environmentalism since 1945: A Brief History with Documents*. Boston, MA: Bedford/St. Martin's.

Stone, Jerome Arthur. 2009. *Religious Naturalism Today: The Rebirth of a Forgotten Alternative*. Albany, NY: State University of New York Press.

Stone, Robert. 2010. *Earth Days*. Washington, D.C.: Public Broadcasting System American Experience (DVD, 102 minutes).

Strobel, Craig S. 2005. "Macy, Joanna (1929–)." In *The Encyclopedia of Religion and Nature*. Bron R. Taylor (Editor-in-Chief). New York, NY: Thoemmes Continuum, 2, pp. 1019–1020.

Suan Mokkh. 2011. http://www.suanmokkh.org/.

Sullivan, Franklin Stemple. 1972. *Spiritual Ecology*. Lakemont, GA: Tarnhelm Press.

Sullivan, Lawrence E. 1988. *Icanchu's Drum: An Orientation to Meanings in South American Religions*. New York: Macmillan.

Survival International. 2010a (January 25). *Avatar Is Real, Say Tribal People*. http://www.survivalinternational.org/news/5466.

Survival International. 2010b (August 24). *David v. Goliath: Indian Tribe in 'Stunning' Victory over Mining Giant*. http://www.survivalinternational.org/news/6385.

Suzuki, David. 2003. *The Sacred Balance with David Suzuki*. Toronto, Ontario, Canada: Title House e-Distribution (2 DVDs, 216 minutes). http://www.davidsuzuki.org.

Suzuki, David. 2006. *David Suzuki: The Autobiography*. Berkeley, CA: Greystone Books.

Suzuki, David. 2010. *The Legacy: An Elder's Vision for Our Sustainable Future*. Berkeley, CA: Greystone Books.

Suzuki, David. 2011. *The David Suzuki Foundation*. Vancouver, British Columbia, Canada. http://www.davidsuzuki.org.

Suzuki, David, and Wayne Grady. 2004. *Tree: A Life Story*. Vancouver, British Columbia, Canada: Greystone Books.

Suzuki, David, Amanda McConnell, and Adrienne Mason. 2007. *The Sacred Balance: Rediscovering Our Place in Nature*. Berkeley, CA: Greystone Books.

Suzuki, David, and Dave Robert Taylor. 2009. *The Big Picture: Reflections on Science, Humanity, and a Quickly Changing Planet*. Berkeley, CA: Greystone Books.

Swan, James A. 1990. *Sacred Places: How the Living Earth Seeks Our Friendship*. Santa Fe, NM: Bear & Company Publishing.

Swan, James A. 2000. *Nature as Teacher and Healer: How to Reawaken Your Connection with Nature*. Lincoln, NE: iUniverse.com, Inc.

Swearer, Donald K. 1997. "The Hermeneutics of Buddhist Ecology in Contemporary Thailand: Buddhadasa and Dhammapitaka." In *Buddhism and Ecology: The Interconnection of Dharma and Deeds*. Mary Evelyn Tucker and Duncan Ryuken Williams (eds.). Cambridge, MA: Harvard University Press, pp. 21–44.

Swearer, Donald K. 2003. "Sulak Sivaraksa: Engaged Buddhist Activist and Environmentalist." In *Socially Engaged Spirituality: Essays in Honor of Sulak Sivaraksa on His 70th Birthday*. David W. Chappell (ed.). Bangkok, Thailand: Sathirakoses-Nagapradipa Foundation, pp. 645–648.

Swearer, Donald K. 2005. "An Assessment of Buddhist Eco-Philosophy." Harvard University Center for the Study of World Religions-Dongguk Symposium on Buddhism and Ecology (December 9–10, 2005). http://www.hds.harvard.edu/cswr/resources/print/dongguk/swearer.pdf.

Swearer, Donald K. (ed.). 2009. *Ecology and the Environment: Perspectives from the Humanities.* Cambridge, MA: Harvard Divinity School Center for the Study of World Religions/Harvard University Press.

Swenson, Donald S. 2009. *Society, Spirituality, and the Sacred: A Social Scientific Introduction.* Toronto, Ontario, Canada: University of Toronto Press.

Swimme, Brian, and Thomas Berry. 1992. *The Universe Story: From the Primordial Flaring Forth to the Ecozoic Era: A Celebration of the Unfolding of the Cosmos.* San Francisco, CA: HarperCollins. http://www.emergingearth community.org.

Swimme, Brian Thomas, and Mary Evelyn Tucker. 2011a. *Journey of the Universe: The Epic Story of Cosmic, Earth and Human Transformation.* New Haven, CT: Brian Tomas Swimme and Mary Evelyn Tucker (58 minutes). http://www.JourneyoftheUniverse.org.

Swimme, Brian Thomas, and Mary Evelyn Tucker. 2011b. *Journey of the Universe: The Epic Story of Cosmic, Earth and Human Transformation.* New Haven, CT: Yale University Press.

Tairona Heritage Trust. 2011. *Tairona Heritage Trust.* http://www.taironatrust.org.

Takacs, David. 1996. *The Idea of Biodiversity: Philosophies of Paradise.* Baltimore, MD: Johns Hopkins University Press.

Tangvisutijit, N. 1989. "The Forest Monastery of Suan Mohk." *Seeds of Peace* 5 (3):32–33.

Tanner, Adrian. 1979. *Bringing Home Animals: Religious Ideology and Mode of Production of the Mistassini Cree Hunters.* St. John's, Newfoundland: Memorial University of Newfoundland Institute for Social and Economic Research.

Taylor, Bron (ed.). 1995. *Ecological Resistance Movements: The Global Emergence of Radical and Popular Environmentalism.* Albany, NY: State University of New York Press.

Taylor, Bron. 2001a. "Earth and Nature-Based Spirituality (Part I): From Deep Ecology to Radical Environmentalism." *Religion* 31(2):175–193.

Taylor, Bron. 2001b. "Earth and Nature-Based Spirituality (Part II): From Earth First! and Bioregionalism to Scientific Paganism and the New Age." *Religion* 31(3):225–245.

Taylor, Bron. 2004. "A Green Future for Religion." *Futures Journal* 36(9): 991–1008.

Taylor, Bron R. (Editor-in-Chief). 2005. *The Encyclopedia of Religion and Ecology*. New York, NY: Thoemmes Continuum, vols 1–2. http://www .religionandnature.com/ern/.

Taylor, Bron. 2006. "Religion and Environmentalism in America and Beyond." In *The Oxford Handbook of Religion and Ecology*. Roger S. Gottlieb (ed.). New York, NY: Oxford University Press, pp. 588–612.

Taylor, Bron. 2007a. "Surfing into Spirituality and a New Aquatic Nature Religion." *Journal of the American Academy of Religion* 75(4):923–951.

Taylor, Bron. 2007b. "Exploring Religion, Nature and Culture—Introducing the Journal for the Study of Religion, Nature and Culture." *Journal for the Study of Religion, Nature and Culture* 1(1):5–24. http://www.religionandnature .com/journal/sample/Taylor—JSRNC(1-1).pdf.

Taylor, Bron. 2009. "From the Ground Up: Dark Green Religion and the Environmental Future." In *Ecology and the Environment: Perspectives from the Humanities*. Donald K. Swearer (ed.). Cambridge, MA: Harvard Divinity School Center for the Study of World Religions/Harvard University Press, pp. 89–107.

Taylor, Bron. 2010a. *Dark Green Religion: Nature Spirituality and the Planetary Future*. Berkeley, CA: University of California Press.

Taylor, Bron. 2010b (July 1). *Statement on Religion, Nature, Culture and Environmental Values*" Global Risk Forum Davos (YouTube, 6 minutes). http://www.youtube.com/watch?v=uxIvBZEBS1M.

Taylor, Bron. 2010c. "Avatar as Rorschach." *Journal for the Study of Religion, Nature and Culture* 4(4):381–383.

Taylor, Bron. 2011. "Toward a Robust Scientific Investigation of the 'Religion' Variable in the Quest for Sustainability." *Journal for the Study of Religion, Nature and Culture* 5(3):253–262.

Taylor, Bron. 2012. *On Sacred Ground: Earth First! and Environmental Ethics*. Washington, D.C.: Island Press (in preparation).

Taylor, Bron. 2012. Bron Taylor Homepage. http://www.brontaylor.com.

Taylor, Bron, et al. 2006. "Abstract Book: Exploring Religion, Nature and Culture." The Inaugural Conference of the International Society for the Study of Religion, Nature and Culture. Gainesville, FL: University of Florida (April 6–9, 2006).

Taylor, Bron, et al. 2009 (March). "Roundtable: The Encyclopedia of Religion and Nature." *Journal of the American Academy of Religion* 77(1):55–80.

Taylor, Bron, and Adrian Ivakhiv. 2010. "Opening Pandora's Film." *Journal for the Study of Religion, Nature and Culture* 4(4):384–393.

Taylor, Sarah McFarland. 2005. "Gaian Mass." In *The Encyclopedia of Religion and Nature*. Bron R. Taylor (Editor-in-Chief). New York, NY: Thoemmes Continuum, 1, pp. 682–683.

Taylor, Sarah McFarland. 2007. *Green Sisters: A Spiritual Ecology*. Cambridge, MA: Harvard University Press.

Teilhard de Chardin, Pierre. 1959. *The Phenomenon of Man*. New York, NY: Harper.

Templeton Foundation. 2011. http://www.templeton.org.

Thakur, Vijay Kumar. 2004. "Buddhist Response to Ecological Changes in Early India." In *Buddhism and Ecology*. S. K. Pathak (ed.). New Delih, India: Om Publications, pp. 41–50.

Thanissaro Bhikkhu. 1994. *The Buddhist Monastic Code*. Valley Center, CA: Metta Forest Monastery.

The Aldo Leopold Foundation. 2011. *Green Fire: Aldo Leopold and a Land Ethic for Our Time*. Barbaoo, WI: The Aldo Leopold Foundation (DVD, 73 minutes). http://www.GreenFireMovie.com.

The Great Turning Times. 2010. http://www.greatturningtimes.org.

The Journal of Ecocriticism. 2011. http://ojs.unbc.ca/index.php/joe.

The Thoreau Reader. 2011. http://eserver.org/Thoreau.

The Thoreau Society. 2011. http://www.thoreausociety.org.

Thirgood, J. V. 1981. *Man and the Mediterranean Forest: A History of Resource Depletion*. New York. NY: Academic Press.

Thomas, Keith. 1983. *Man and the Natural World: A History of the Modern Sensibility*. New York, NY: Pantheon Books.

Thomas, N.C. 2005. "Steiner, Rudolf (1861–1925)—and Anthroposophy." In *The Encyclopedia of Religion and Nature*. Bron R. Taylor (Editor-in-Chief). New York, NY: Thoemmes Continuum, 2, pp. 1596–1597.

Thomas, Peter. 2000. *Trees: Their Natural History*. New York, NY: Cambridge University Press.

Thoreau Institute at Walden Woods. 2011. http://www.walden.org/Institute.

Thoreau, Henry David. 1854/1973. *Walden; or, Life in the Woods*. Garden City, NY: Anchor/Doubleday.

Thoreau, Henry David. 1862. "Walking." In *The Portable Thoreau*. Carl Bode (ed.). New York, NY: The Viking Press, pp. 592–630.

Thurbron, Colin. 2011. *To a Mountain In Tibet*. New York, NY: HarperCollinsPublishers.

Thurman, Robert A. F. 2008. *Why the Dalai Lama Matters: His Act of Truth as the Solution for China, Tibet, and the World*. New York, NY: Atria Books.

Thurman, Robert A. F., and Tad Wise. 2000. *Circling the Sacred Mountain: A Spiritual Adventure through the Himalayas*. NY: Bantam Books.

Thurman, Wilkins. 1995. *John Muir: Apostle of Nature*. Norman, OK: University of Oklahoma Press.

Tibet Environmental Watch. 2011. http://tew.org.

Tibetan Buddhism. 2011. http://www.tibetan-buddhist.org.

Tibetan Environmental Network. 2011. http://www.Tibet.net/en/diir/enviro/.

Tibetan Government in Exile. 2011. http://www.tibet.com and http://www .tibet.net.

Tiedje, Kristina, and Jeffrey G. Snodgrass (eds.). 2008. "Indigenous Religions and Environments: Intersections of Animism and Nature Conservation." *Journal for the Study of Religion, Nature and Culture* 2(1):5–158.

Timmerman, Peter. 1992. "It Is Dark Outside: Western Buddhism from the Enlightenment to the Global Crisis." In *Buddhism and Ecology*. Martine Batchelor and Kerry Brown (eds.). New York: Cassell Publications Limited, pp. 65–76.

Tippet, Krista. 2010 (September 16). *A Wild Love of the World* [interview with Joanna Macy]. Being/American Public Media. http://being.publicradio .org/programs/2010/wild-love-for-world/.

Tirosh-Samuelson, Hava. (ed.). 2002. *Judaism and Ecology: Created World and Revealed Word*. Cambridge, MA: Harvard University Press/Harvard University Center for the Study of World Religions.

Tirosh-Samuelson, Hava. 2006. "Judaism." In *The Oxford Handbook of Religion and Ecology*. Roger S. Gottlieb (ed.). New York, NY: Oxford University Press, pp. 25–64.

Titubarua. 2010. *Buddhism and Ecology* (13 minutes). http://www.youtube.com/ watch?v=Na3tFKacWYg.

Tiyavanich, Kamala. 2003. *The Buddha in the Jungle*. Chiang Mai, Thailand: Silkworm Books and Seattle, WA: University of Washington Press.

Tobias, Michael (ed.). 1988. *Deep Ecology*. San Marcos, CA: Avant Books.

Tobias, Michael, and Georgianne Cowan. 1996. *The Soul of Nature: Celebrating the Spirit of the Earth*. New York, NY: Penguin Group/Plume.

Tongphanna. 2008. *Monks and Community Forestry* [Parts 1–4, 18 min.]. http://www.youtube.com/results?search_query=communiy+forestry%2C +buddhism+and+cambodian+heritage.

Townsend, Joan B. 1999. "Shamanism." In *Anthropology of Religion: A Handbook*. Stephen D. Glazier (ed.). Westport, CT: Praeger, pp. 429–469.

Toynbee, Arnold. 1972. "The Religious Background of the Present Environmental Crisis." *International Journal of Environmental Studies* 3:141–146. (Reprinted in Spring and Spring 1974).

Trudge, Colin. 2005. *The Tree: A Natural History of What Trees Are, How They Live, and Why They Matter*. New York, NY: Three Rivers Press.

Tuan, Yi-Fu. 1968. "Discrepancies between Environmental Attitudes and Behaviour: Examples from Europe and China." *The Canadian Geographer* 12(3):176–191.

Tuan, Yi-Fu. 1990. *Topophilia: A Study of Environmental Perception, Attitudes, and Values*. New York, NY: Columbia University Press.

Tucker, Mary Evelyn. 1997 (April). "The Emerging Alliance of Religion and Ecology." *Worldviews: Environment, Culture, Religion* 1(1):3–24.

Tucker, Mary Evelyn. 2006. "Religion and Ecology: Survey of the Field." In *The Oxford Handbook of Religion and Ecology*. Roger S. Gottlieb (ed.). New York, NY: Oxford University Press, pp. 398–418.

Tucker, Mary Evelyn. 2007 (Spring). "The Ecological Spirituality of Pierre Teilhard de Chardin." *Spiritus: A Journal of Christian Spirituality* 7(1):1–19.

Tucker, Mary Evelyn. 2003. *Worldly Wonder: Religions Enter Their Ecological Phase*. Chicago, IL: Open Court Publishing Company.

Tucker, Mary Evelyn, and John Berthrong (eds). 1998. *Confucianism and Ecology: The Interrelation of Heaven, Earth, and Human*. Cambridge, MA: Harvard University Press/Harvard University Center for the Study of World Religions.

Tucker, Mary Evelyn, and John A. Grim (eds.). 1993. *Worldviews and Ecology*. Lewisburg, PA: Bucknell University Press.

Tucker, Mary Evelyn, and John A. Grim. 1997. "Series Foreword." In *Buddhism and Ecology: The Interconnection of Dharma and Deeds*. Mary Evelyn Tucker and Duncan Ryuken Williams (eds.). Cambridge, MA: Harvard University Press/Harvard Divinity School Center for the Study of World Religions, pp. xv–xxxiii.

Tucker, Mary Evelyn, and John A. Grim (eds.). 1998 (Fall). "Religions of the World and Ecology: Discovering the Common Ground." *EarthEthics* 10(1):1, 3–32.

Tucker, Mary Evelyn, and John A. Grim. 2001 (Fall). "Introduction: The Emerging Alliance of World Religions and Ecology." In "Religion and Ecology: Can Climate Change?" *Daedalus: Journal of the American Academy of Arts and Sciences* 130(4):1–22. http://www.amacad.org//publications/fall2001/tucker-grim.aspx.

Tucker, Mary Evelyn, and John A. Grim. 2007a (Spring). "Daring to Dream: Religion and the Future of the Earth." *Yale University Divinity School Reflections* 94(1):4–9. http://www.yale.edu/reflections/spring07_index.shtml.

Tucker, Mary Evelyn, and John A. Grim. 2007b. "Greening of the World's Religions." *Chronicle of Higher Education* 53(23):B9.

Tucker, Mary Evelyn, and John A. Grim. 2009a. *Living Cosmology: An Approach to the Study of Religion and Ecology*. New York, NY: Columbia University Press.

Tucker, Mary Evelyn, and John Grim. 2009b (January 13). *Religion and the New Environmental Ethic (Video, 13 minutes)*. New Haven, CT: Yale University. http://www.youtube.com/watch?v=BG0bQ3SwDI8.

Tucker, Mary Evelyn, and John A. Grim. 2012. *Living Cosmology: An Approach to the Study of Religion and Ecology*. Washington, DC: Island Press.

Tucker, Mary Evelyn, and Duncan Ryuken Williams. (eds.). 1997. *Buddhism and Ecology: The Interconnection of Dharma and Deeds*. Cambridge, MA: Harvard University Press/Harvard University Center for the Study of World Religions.

Tudge, Colin. 2005. *The Tree: A Natural History of What Trees Are, How They Live, and Why They Matter*. New York, NY: Three Rivers Press.

Turnbull, Colin M. 1961. *The Forest People*. Garden City, NY: Doubleday & Co.

Turner, Edith. 1992. "The Reality of Spirits: A Tabooed or Permitted Field of Study." *ReVision* 15(1):28–32.

Turner, Edith. 2006. *Heart of Lightness: The Life Story of an Anthropologist*. New York, NY: Berghahn Books.

Turner, Frederick. 1985. *Rediscovering America: John Muir in His Time and Ours*. New York, NY: Viking.

Turner, Nancy J. 2005. *The Earth's Blanket: Traditional Teachings for Sustainable Living*. Seattle, WA: University of Washington Press.

Turner, Terence. 1995. "An Indigenous People's Struggle for Socially Equitable and Ecologically Sustainable Production: The Kayapo Revolt Against Extractivism." *Journal of Latin American Anthropology* 1(1):98–121.

Turner, Terence. 2011. "From Ecological Disaster to Constitutional Crisis: Dams on Brazil's Xingu River." In *Life and Death Matters—Human Rights, Environment and Social Justice*. Lanham, MD: Left Coast Press, pp. 454–459.

Tylor, Edward B. 1871. *Primitive Culture*. London, UK: John Murray.

Udall, Stewart L. 1963/1988. *The Quiet Crisis and the Next Generation*. Salt Lake City, UT: Peregrine Smith Books, pp. 3–12.

United Nations Environment Programme (UNEP). 2005. *Millennium Ecosystem Assessment*. Geneva, Switzerland: United Nations Environmental Programme (UNEP). http://www.maweb.org.

United Nations Environmental Programme (UNEP). 2010. *Plant for the Planet: Billion Tree Campaign*. http://www.unep.org/billiontreecampaign/.

United Nations Environmental Programme (UNEP. 2011. *Interfaith Partnership for the Environment*. http://www.nyo.unep.org/ifp.htm.

United States Library of Congress. 2011. "Online Resources: Merwin," Washington, D.C.: U.S. Library of Congress. http://www.loc.gov/rr/program/bib/merwin/.

University of California Los Angeles (UCLA). 2003. *Higher Education Research Institute Survey of Spirituality in Higher Education*. Los Angeles, CA: University of California Los Angeles Higher Education Research Institute. http://www.spirituality.ucla.edu.

Upton, Charles. 2008. *Who Is the Earth? How to See God in the Natural World*. San Rafael, CA: Sophia Perennis.

Vaillant, George E. 2008. *Spiritual Evolution: A Scientific Defense of Faith*. New York, NY: Broadway Books.

Vajragupta. 2011. *We Live in a Beautiful World: Buddhism and Nature*. Manchester, UK: Manchester Buddhist Centre (43 minutes). http://www.videosangha.net/video/We-Live-in-a-Beautiful-World-Bu.

Valeri, Valerio. 2000. *The Forest of Taboos: Morality, Hunting, and Identity among the Huaulu of the Moluccas*. Madison, WI: University of Wisconsin Press.

Valliant, George E. 2008. *Spiritual Evolution: A Scientific Defense of Faith*. New York, Y: Broadway Books.

Van Boeckel, Jan van, Karen van der Molen, and Pat van Boeckel. 1997. *Arne Naess*. Rerunproductions (51 minutes). http://www.dailymotion.com/video/x8meah_arne-naess_creation.

Vaughan-Lee, Emmanuel, et al. 2011. Interview with Joanna Macy. Global Oneness Project. http://www.globalonenessproject.org/interviewee/joanna-macy.

Vecsey, Christopher, and Robert W. Venables (eds.). 1980. *American Indian Environments: Ecological Issues in Native American History*. New York, NY: Syracuse University Press.

Vendetti, Tom. 2006. *Sacred Tibet: The Path to Mount Kailas*. Maui, HI: Vendetti Productions, LLC (DVD, 102 min.).

Vendetti, Tom. 2007. *Bhutan: Taking the Middle Path to Happiness*. Kihei, Maui, HI: Vendetti Productions LLC (DVD 55 minutes).

Verschuuren, Bas, Robert Wild, Jeffrey A. McNeely, and Gonzalo Oviedo (eds.). 2010. *Sacred Sites Conserving Nature and Culture*. London, UK: Earthscan.

Vickers, William T. 1991. "Hunting Yields and Game Composition Over Ten Years in an Amazonian Indian Territory." In *Neotropical Wildlife Use and Conservation*. John G. Robinson and Kent H. Redford (eds.). Chicago, IL: University of Chicago Press, pp. 53–81.

Visalo, Phra Phaisan. 2011. "A Buddhist Perspective on Learning from Nature." Thailand: Phra Paisal's Temple School. http://www.visalo.org/english Articles/templeSchool.htm.

Vitale, Tom. 1991. *W. S. Merwin: The Rain in the Trees*" Silver Spring, MD:Atlas Video, Inc. (30 minutes).

Vitebsky, Piers.2005. *The Reindeer People: Living with Animals and Spirits in Siberia*. Boston, MA: Houghton Mifflin.

Viveiros de Castro, Eduardo. 1992. *From the Enemy's Point of View: Humanity and Divinity in an Amazonian Society*. Chicago, IL: University of Chicago Press.

von Essen, Carl. 2010. *Ecomysticism: The Profound Experience of Nature as Spiritual Guide*. Rochester, VT: Bear & Company.

Wade, Nicholas. 2009. *The Faith Instinct: How Religion Evolved and Why It Endures*. New York, NY: Penguin Group (USA) Inc.

Walden Pond State Reservation. 2011. http://www.mass.gov/dcr/parks/walden/.

Wallace, Mark I. 2005. *Finding God in the Singing River: Christianity, Spirit, Nature*. Minneapolis, MN: Fortress Press.

Waller, David. 1996. "Friendly Fire: When Environmentalists Dehumanize American Indians." *American Indian Culture and Research Journal* 20(2): 107–126.

Walls, Laura Dassow. 2001."Henry David Thoreau 1817–62." In *Fifty Key Thinkers on the Environment*. Joy A. Palmer (ed.). New York, NY: Routledge, pp. 106–113.

Wangari Maathai Institute for Peace and Environmental Studies. 2011. Nairobi, Kenya: University of Nairobi. http://www.uonbi.ac.ke/node/316.

Ward, Keith. 2008. *The Big Questions in Science and Religion*. West Conshohocken, PA: Templeton Foundation Press.

Ward, Tim. 1993. *What the Buddha Never Taught*. Berkeley, CA: Celestial Arts.

Warner, Brother Keith. 2010 (May 31). *Franciscan Care for Creation*. Santa Clara, CA.: Santa Clara University. [Parts 1–3, 17 minutes). http://www.youtube.com/watch?v=FUrAS1G1-9Y.

Warner, Faith, and Richard Hoskins. 2005. "African Religions and Nature Conservation." In *The Encyclopedia of Religion and Nature*. Bron R. Taylor (Editor-in-Chief). New York, NY: Thoemmes Continuum, 1, pp. 26–29.

Waskow, Arthur. 2000. *Torah of the Earth: Exploring 4,000 Years of Ecology in Jewish Thought*. Woodstock, VT: Jewish Lights Publishing Company.

Wat Lan Kuad. 2010. *Temple of Recycled Beer Bottles*. YouTube (April 19, 2010, 3 minutes). http://www.youtube.com/watch?v=fYAElPEz6MQ.

Watling, Tony. 2009. *Ecological Imaginations in the World Religions: An Ethnographic Analysis*. New York, NY: Continuum International Publishing Group.

Watts, Alan. 1968. *Buddhism: Man and Nature*. Westport, CT: Hartlely Film Foundation (14 minutes).

Wawrzonek, John. 2002. *The Illuminated Walden: In the Footsteps of Thoreau.* New York, NY: Barnes & Noble Books.

Weaver, Jack (ed.). 1996. *Defending Mother Earth: Native American Perspectives on Environmental Justice.* Maryknoll, NY: Orbis Books.

Webb, Caroline. 2007. *Thomas Berry and the Earth Community.* http://www .earth-community.org.

Webster, Richard. 2008. *Flower and Tree Magic: Discover the Natural Enchantment Around You.* Woodbury, MN: Llewellyn Publications.

Weintraub, Linda. 2006. *Ecocentric Topics: Pioneering Themes of Eco-Art.* San Reinbeck, NY: Artnow Publications.

Weintraub, Linda. 2007. *EnvironMentalities: Twenty-Two Approaches to Eco-Art.* Reinbeck, NY: Artnow Publications.

Weir, Bill. 1991. *A Guide to Buddhist Monasteries and Meditation Centres in Thailand.* Bangkok, Thailand: The World Fellowship of Buddhists.

Weisman, Alan. 2007. *The World Without Us.* New York, NY: St. Martin's Press.

Whaley, Rick, and Walter Bresette. 1994. *Walleye Warriors: An Effective Alliance against Racism and for the Earth,* Philadelphia, PA: New Society Publishers.

Whelan, Robert. 1999. *Wild in Woods: The Myth of the Noble-Savage.* London, UK: The Institute of Economic Affairs/The Environmental Unit/IEA Studies on the Environment No. 14.

Whelan, Robert, Joseph Kirwan, and Paul Haffner. 1996. *The Cross and the Rain Forest: A Critique of Radical Green Spirituality.* Grand Rapids, MI: William B. Eerdmans Publishing Company.

White, Lynn, Jr. 1962. *Medieval Technology and Social Change.* Oxford, UK: Clarendon Press.

White, Lynn, Jr. 1967 (March 10). "The Historic Roots of Our Ecologic Crisis," *Science* 155(3767):1203–1207.

White, Lynn, Jr. 1973. "Continuing the Conversation." In *Western Man and Environmental Ethics: Attitudes Toward Nature and Technology.* Ian G. Barbour (ed.). Reading, MA: Addison-Wesley Publishing Company, pp. 55–64.

White, Lynn, Jr. 1978. *Medieval Religion and Technology: Collected Essays.* Berkeley, CA: University of California Press.

Whitehead, Neil L., and Robin Wright. (eds.). 2004. In *Darknss and Secrecy: The Anthropology of Assault Sorcery and Witchcraft in Amazonia.* Durham, NC: Duke University Press.

Whitley, David. 2008. *The Idea of Nature in Disney Animation.* Aldershot, UK: Ashgate.

Whitner, Banta H., and Bruce R. Grob, 2009. *This Congruent Life: A Spiritual Ecology Practice.* Denver, CO: Outskirts Press, Inc.

Whitney, Elspeth, 1993, "Lynn White, Ecotheology, and History," *Environmental Ethics* 15:151–169.

Whol, Ellen E. 2010. *A World of Rivers: Environmental Changes on Ten of the World's Great Rivers*. Chicago, IL: University of Chicago Press.

Wieland, Carl. 2010 (January 5). *Avatar and the "new" evolutionary religion*. http://creation.com/avatar-movie-review.

Wiese, Michael. 2006. *The Sacred Sites of the Dalai Lamas*. Michael Wiese Productions. (DVD, 120 minutes).

Wilcox, Leslie. 2011 (February 24). *A Conversation with America's Poet Laureate: W. S. Merwin*. Honolulu, HI: Public Broadcasting Service Hawai'i Presents.

Wilhelm, Maria, and Dirk Mathison. 2009. *Avatar: A Confidential Report on the Biological and Social History of Pandora*. New York, NY: It Books.

Williams, Dennis C. 2002. *God's Wilds: John Muir's Vision of Nature*. College Station, TX: Texas A & M University Press.

Williams, Duncan Ryuken. 2011a. "Buddhism and Ecology Course Syllabus." New Haven, CT: Yale University Forum on Religion and Ecology. http://fore.research.yale.edu/education/resources/syllabi/williams1.html.

Williams, Duncan Ryuken. 2011b. "Buddhism and Ecology Bibliography." New Haven, CT: Yale University Forum on Religion and Ecology. http://fore.research.yale.edu/religion/buddhism/buddhism.pdf.

Williams, Terry Tempest. 1995. *Desert Quartet: An Erotic Land-scape*. New York, NY: Pantheon Books.

Williams, Terry Tempest, William Smart, and Gibbs Smith (eds.). 1998. *New Genesis: A Mormon Reader on Land and Community*. Layton, UT: Gibbs Smith.

Wilson, David Sloan. 2002. *Darwin's Cathedral: Evolution, Religion, and the Nature of Society*. Chicago, IL: University of Chicago Press.

Wilson, Edward O. 1984. *Biophilia: The Human Bond with Other Species*. Cambridge, MA: Harvard University Press.

Wilson, Edward O. 1999. *The Diversity of Life*. New York, NY: W. W. Norton and Company (2nd Edition).

Wilson, Edward O. 2003. *The Future of Life*. New York, NY: Alfred A. Knopf.

Wilson, Edward O. 2006. *The Creation: An Appeal to Save Life on Earth*. New York, NY: W. W. Norton and Company.

Wilson, Jeff. 2001 (Fall). "Moments in American Buddhism." *Tricycle: The Buddhist Review* 41:68–71.

Winkelman, Michael. 1999. "Altered States of Consciousness and Religious Behavior." In *Anthropology of Religion: A Handbook*. Stephen D. Glazier (ed.). Westport, CT: Praeger, pp. 393–428.

Winkelman, Michael, and John R. Baker. 2010. *Supernatural as Natural: A Biocultural Approach to Religion*. Upper Saddle Priver, NJ: Pearson/Prentice Hall.

Winter, Paul. 1982. *Missa Gaia Earth Mass*. Litchfield, CT: Earth Music Productions, LLC. (CD, 66 minutes).

Wirzba, Norman. 2003. *The Paradise of God: Renewing Religion in an Ecological Age*. New York, NY: Oxford University Press.

Wolens, Doug. 2000. *Butterfly*. Berkeley, CA: Doug Wolens (VHS, 80 minutes). http://www.butterflyfilm.net.

Wolf, Fred Alan. 1999. *The Spiritual Universe: One Physicist's Vision of Spirit, Soul, Matter, and Self*. Needham, MA: Moment Point Press, Inc.

Wolfe, Linnie Marsh (ed.). 1938. *John of the Mountains: The Unpublished Journals of John Muir*. Boston, MA: Houghton-Mifflin Company.

Wolfe, Linnie Marsh. 1945. *Son of the Wilderness*. New York, NY: Alfred A. Knopf, Inc.

Wolff, Robert. 2001. *Original Wisdom: Stories of an Ancient Way of Knowing*. Rochester, VT: Inner Traditions.

World Meteorological Organization. 2011. *Intergovernmental Panel on Climate Change*. Geneva, Switzerland: World Meteorological Organization. http://www.ipcc.ch/.

World Wildlife Fund. 1986. *The Assisi Declarations*. Gland, Switzerland: World Wildlife Fund International.

Worldviews: Global Religions, Culture and Ecology. 2011. http://www.brill.nl/worldviews-global-religions-culture-and-ecology.

Worldwatch Institute. 2011. http://www.worldwatch.org.

Worster, Donald. 1994. *Nature's Economy: A History of Ecological Ideas*. New York, NY: Cambridge University Press (2nd Edition).

Worster, Donald. 2005 (January). "John Muir and the Modern Passion for Nature." *Environmental History* 10(1):8–19.

Worster, Donald. 2008. *A Passion for Nature: the Life of John Muir*. New York, NY: Oxford University Press.

Yaffe, M. (ed.). 2001. *Judaism and Environmental Ethics*. Lanham, MD: Lexington Books.

Yale University Divinity School. 2011. *Initiative in Religion, Science, and Technology*. http://www.yale.edu/religionandscience.

Yamauchi, Jeffrey Scott. 1997. "The Greening of Zen Mountain Center: A Case Study." In *Buddhism and Ecology: The Interconnection of Dharma and Deeds*. Mary Evelyn Tucker and Duncan Ryuken Williams (eds.). Cambridge, MA: Harvard University Press, pp. 249–265.

York, Michael. 2003. *Pagan Theology: Paganism as a World Religion*. New York, NY: New York University Press.

Young, David E., and Jean-Guy Goulet (eds.). 1994. *Being Changed by Cross-Cultural Encounters: The Anthropology of Extraordinary Experience*. Orchard Park, NY: Broadview Press.

Young, Jon. 2011. Wilderness Awareness School. http://www.wildernessawareness .org.

Zeffirelli, Franco. 1972. *Brother Sun, Sister Moon*. Hollywood, CA: Paramount Pictures (DVD 121 minutes).

Zen Environmental Studies Institute. 2011. Mount Tremper, NY: Mountains and Rivers Order of Zen Buddhism. http://www.mro.org/zesi/.

Zerzan, John. 2008. *The Twilight of Machines*. Port Townsend, WA: Feral House.

Ziegler, Alan C. 2002. *Hawaiian Natural History, Evolution, and Ecology*. Honolulu, HI: University of Hawai'i Press.

Ziporyn, Brook. 2008. *Buddhist and Ecology* (61 minutes). http://video.google .com/videoplay?docid=-880945489573313589#.

Zsolnai, Laszlo, and Knut Johannessen Ims (eds.). 2006. *Business within Limits: Deep Ecology and Buddhist Economics*. New York, NY: Peter Lang.

Zuckerman, Seth. 2004. "Redwood Rabbis." In *This Sacred Earth: Religion, Nature, Environment*. Roger S. Gottlieb (ed.). New York, NY: Routledge (2nd Edition), pp. 644–646 (reprinted from *Sierra Magazine*, November/December 1998, pp. 62–63, 82–83). http://www.sierraclub.org/sierra/199811/rabbis.asp.

INDEX

Abbey, Edward, 55, 99
Across the Tibetan Plateau: Ecosystems, Wildlife, and Conservation (Flemming et al.), 162
Afterlife, belief in, 10, 144
Albanese, Catherine L., 51, 60
Alliance of Religions and Conservation (ARC), xiv, 80–81, 121
Altman, Nathaniel, 1
Amazonian peoples, 14–15, 25, 140, 144
American Association for the Advancement of Science, 75
Animism, 44, 77, 142, 162; indigenous peoples and, 7, 9–12, 13–14, 19; Paganism and, x, 7, 10, 11
Annan, Kofi, 115
Anthropocentrism, ix, 17, 42, 84; in Christianity, 76; nature and, 156, 171
Anthroposophical Society, 66, 67
ARC. *See* Alliance of Religions and Conservation
Asia, animism in, 11
The Assisi Declarations, 37, 79–80, 81. *See also* Francis of Assisi, Saint
Atheism, 147, 149–51, 156
Australian Aborigines, 10–11
Avatar (film), 23, 121, 137–46; ecological equilibrium in, 140–41; ecospirituality in, 142–44; indigenous rights in, 141–42; Na'vi

people in, 137–38, 139, 140, 141, 142–44
Avatar Home Tree Initiative, 144–45

Banyan tree (*Ficus bengalensis*), 2
Baobab tree (*Adamsonia digitata*), xix
Barrows, Anita, 113
Bartholomew I, Patriarch, 99, 115–19; interfaith dialogue and collaboration, 116–18; spiritual ecology symposia and, 115–16
Benedict XVI, Pope, 117–18
Bennett, John W., 140
Berry, Thomas, 69, 97, 149, 150
Bhagavad Gita, 1
Bhutan, Buddhism in, 5, 38
Bilimoria, Purushottama, 33
Biodiversity, 165, 170; conservation of, 3–5, 10, 35, 162
Biodynamic agriculture, 66
Biophilia, xi–xii, 47, 59, 143
Black Rock desert, Nevada, 131, 132. *See also* Burning Man festival
Bodhisattvas, 33–34, 41
Bodhi tree (*Ficus religiosa*), xx, 2, 31
Bodhi, Bhikkhu, 31
Boff, Leonardo, 46, 48
Bratton, Susan Power, 43–44, 45
Brockleman, Norbert C., 43
Buber, Martin, 69, 71, 73–74
Buddha (Siddhattha Gotama), 7, 31–34, 41
Buddhadasa Bhikkhu, 32, 35, 40

277

ABOUT THE AUTHOR

Leslie E. Sponsel earned the BA in Geology from Indiana University (1965), and the MA (1973) and PhD (1981) in Biological and Cultural Anthropology from Cornell University. Over the last four decades he has taught at seven universities in four countries, two as a Fulbright Fellow. In 1981 he joined the Anthropology faculty at the University of Hawai'i to develop and direct the Ecological Anthropology Program. His courses include Ecological Anthropology, Environmental Anthropology, Anthropology of Religion, Spiritual Ecology, Sacred Places, Anthropology of Buddhism, Ethics in Anthropology, and Anthropology of War and Peace. Although retired since August 2010, he teaches one or two courses annually and devotes the rest of his time to research and publications.

From 1974 to 1981 Sponsel conducted several trips to the Venezuelan Amazon to study human ecology with the Yanomami and other indigenous societies. Almost yearly since 1986 Sponsel has made research trips to Thailand to study various aspects of Buddhist ecology and environmentalism together with his wife, Dr. Poranee Natadecha-Sponsel of Chaminade University of Honolulu. In recent years their work in northern Thailand has focused on exploring sacred caves.

Among Sponsel's extensive publications are more than two dozen journal articles, three dozen book chapters, 29 entries in eight different scientific encyclopedias, and two edited and two co-edited books. Henceforth he will focus on publishing other books integrating his previous articles and chapters on several different subjects as well as on developing the Research Institute for Spiritual Ecology (RISE) and its website.

The website for this book is http://spiritualecology.info. Comments on this book are welcome and most appreciated at les.sponsel@gmail.com. Please specify subject as SE Comments.